# "P" POINT MANAGEMENT

GET BIG RESULTS BY DOING LITTLE THINGS

# "P" POINT MANAGEMENT

## GET BIG RESULTS BY DOING LITTLE THINGS

William Cottringer

ATLANTIC
PUBLISHERS & DISTRIBUTORS (P) LTD

Published by

**ATLANTIC**

**PUBLISHERS & DISTRIBUTORS (P) LTD**

B-2, Vishal Enclave, Opp. Rajouri Garden,
New Delhi-110027
Phones : +91-11-25413460, 25429987, 25466842

Sales Office
7/22, Ansari Road, Darya Ganj,
New Delhi-110002
Phones : +91-11-23273880, 23275880, 23280451
Fax : +91-11-23285873
web : www.atlanticbooks.com
e-mail : info@atlanticbooks.com

Branch Office
5, Nallathambi Street, Wallajah Road,
Chennai-600002
Phones : +91-44-64611085, 32413319
e-mail : chennai@atlanticbooks.com



Printed in India
at Nice Printing Press, Delhi

# What is "P" Point Management?

*The ability to simplify means to eliminate the unnecessary so that the necessary may speak.*
Hans Hofmann

- "P" Point Management is a simple system that uses ten core activities from supervision, management, leadership and stewardship, to produce optimal organizational success.
- "P" Point Management is based on **Psychological Power Points**, which are simple but powerful activities that get big results. "P" points are ordinary practical applications of bigger governing principles, profound insights and creative solutions. They are small keyholes that lead to big doors.
- The goal of "P" Point Management is to simplify and clarify unnecessary chaos and confusion in the organization to allow for productivity, success and satisfaction.
- "P" Point Management is not a gimmick. It is simply doing the most important things in the best ways at the right times to get the desired results with the least cost and side effects. If it seems too simple it is because it is. All the difficult work has already been done in discovering the magic of "P" points through much effort in simplifying and clarifying mountains of chaos and confusion.
- What makes "P" Point Management easy is that all the core activities are interrelated and reinforce each other for the best possible results. This way you actually get more done by doing less.

# Preface

*"P" Point Management* is a book of the few most important ideas that rose to the surface in my mind after wading through about forty years of complex and complicated management, education, training, professional work experience and information overload. I plowed through more management books, graduate classes, research projects and seminars than I wish to remember, and somehow they all seemed to be saying many similar things in different ways but included too many new unproven gimmicks.

That experience was a bit much for someone like me who prefers to keep things simple. So this was my inspiration to make things simpler by boiling all these and the other hundreds of things I have learned throughout my own management career, into a more manageable list of ten simple "P" Point Management activities. These "P" points represent the few most important things managers can do to get the best results with employees and their organizations, in being truly effective. They are often the smaller, but well-timed and strategically placed interventions, that return maximum gains on the investment.

I have three purposes of writing this book:

- To reach closure in clarifying some of my own chaos, particularly in regard to the mountain of management information.
- To plant some thinking seeds for those who are still in the process of wading through their own complexity,

confusion and chaos in trying to get a handle on what is most important in management.

- To share the amusement of my particular landing spot through this wild sea of complexity with others who also made it to the other side.

We seem to have two primary sets of opposing drives in life that carry over into the management role: (1) To create possibilities and the confusion, complexity and chaos they bring; and (2) To discover what is most important in remembering simplicity and restoring sensible order. These opposing drives create a gap between where we are and where we want to be. We try every possible brand of solution to bridge this gap but that process only adds more chaos and confusion. After much frustration we finally wake up to the inevitable conclusion that there are only two ways to get where we want to be: Run faster or shorten the distance to where we are running. The above insight is a good example of a "P" point. "P" points are the simplest of all solutions. The simplest "P" point is the awareness that as we are voluntarily engaging in this process of creating chaos, just so we can simplify it.

In engineering terms "P" point concept means the strategic stress points of a building, which can facilitate easy, quick demolition by imploding. I played with this "P" point concept for years, not really knowing the gold mine I had discovered. It is one of those things you use successfully several times before you really begin to understand it. I unknowingly applied the "P" point concept in a variety of settings and situations. These experiences started when I began taking advantage of "teachable moments" first as a student and later as an instructor in university settings, and then experimenting with strategic therapeutic interventions with clients at a community mental health center.

The applications then widened with my efforts to influence inmates indirectly on desired democratic values in prisons through recreational activities and later trying to build valuable sales relationships in business through power communication connections. These successes were all based on different applications of this simple, but powerful perturbation point principle.

Later I finally named this simple but powerful notion **Psychological Power Points**, or just "P" points for short. "P" points are any small but intensified, well-timed and well-placed intervention that produces major results. Or put more simply, they are small keyholes to big doors.

"P" point management is a simple way I can package the few most important things I know that have true value and throw away most of the other unimportant information. It is also a way to reverse the so-called 80-20 rule, where most people spend 80 per cent of their time getting 20 per cent of their results. "P" point management is a simple system to help you use 20 per cent of your time to get 80 per cent of your results. What you do with the other 80 per cent of your time is your business!

Professional success in management is really based on personal development. In turn personal development is based on the answers you give yourself to two compelling "P" point questions. These are: Who are you and where are you going? These two burning questions affect everything you do, and are the very foundation of personal and professional development and well-being.

The other part of the problem involves our inability to see something staring us right in front of our faces. In our attempts to be so logical, we allow illogical thinking to contaminate some of the most important things we should be thinking about, with nothing but logic. We want quick results without going through the required "who", "what", "why" and "how" sequence. I call this universal mental mistake we all fall prey to, "priority reversal".

Let's stop and reflect upon a few illogical priorities we have all helped to perpetuate. We pay sports stars and entertainers huge sums of money for amusing us, while neglecting farmers, truckers, prison guards and many other people who are working hard to give us the most essential things we need to survive. We make marriage easy and divorce hard. We look for legality in morality and our personal development in our professional development. The list goes on, and yet nobody seems to be disturbed enough to challenge the sequence of how we do things. We just do them that way and suffer the consequences.

The plain and simple truth is we are going about our personal development in the wrong sequence. We are busy rushing out and practicing the "how" of achieving and living out our potential, *before* we have bothered to study the "who," "what" and "why" of it. We cannot achieve "wholeness" and live out our full potential, *before* we stop to ask and answer the two basic questions, which we often spend most of our lives avoiding. Again, these two questions are:

- Who are we?
- Where are we going?

Most of us could come up with plenty of clever answers to these questions, but we know we are not fooling ourselves because the answers are really very unsatisfying. The more we try, the wider the gaps become between who we pretend to be and who we really are, and where we think we want to go and where we actually need to go. These gaps are undeniable and very annoying.

I think there is general agreement that the goal of professional development is growth into "wholeness," and becoming better at what we are doing, whether it be teaching, managing a manufacturing crew, taking over as CEO of a new merger, writing books or magazine articles, starting up a dot.com company in a garage, learning, or communicating. Only the correct answers to these critical two questions of who we are and where are we going, can prepare us for genuine professional development. We live our lives doing things which we *think* answer these questions. But no matter how meaningful, honorable or interesting all these activities are, we can't escape the nagging doubt that they don't satisfy our void. Our cart is before our horse and the tail is wagging the dog. We haven't taken the time to really study these questions *before* we started looking for and applying somebody else's answers.

Nobody has the right to declare the answers to these two questions for anyone else. The asking and answering of these two basic questions is a very private matter. We were all born with a piece of a map which gave clear directions as to our real identity and our real destination, but somewhere along the line, we forgot to study it. It is time to get out our piece of the map and study it.

The present book will guide you idealistically in this direction. It is a one-stop shopping, easy-to-read management book that covers all bases. If you learn and practice (or in some cases re-learn and re-practice) these ten simple "P" points of "P" Point Management, you will become successful in your leadership skills and help your organization reach peak performance. It will be a win-win outcome for all, and well worth your investment.

In the real test of the importance, value and truth of all the information and knowledge in this book—the onerous and daunting task of the final manuscript editing—I realized something important. Key points are often repeated in subsequent, related sections and frequently presented in different formats. But, these are the things that deserve the most airtime. They are the ultimate "P" points that I hope you will be underlining.

If the simple presentation of these ten basic management "P" points leaves you craving more information or a desire for more descriptive details, by all means feel free to aggressively "attack" the comprehensive suggested reading list at the end, for that very purpose. And be sure to look over the several value-added Appendices and take the "P" Point Manager evaluation questionnaire to see where you are at in practicing all the points of the book.

The Total Quality Communication Appendix is rather lengthy, but it summarizes the best communication techniques from several other books and articles I have written over the past 40 years. Communication is a very important "P" point that we never really perfect. Communication is a road always under construction.

I also have a self-help, personal development book out called *Do What Matters Most: Simplify Your Overload,* which is being released by this same publisher. This other book, which outlines the ten toughest tests life challenges us with, is a good companion for *"P" Point Management*. It is a much longer and deeper book, and so *"P" Point Management* will probably be the best start, because work is one of the most important parts of life. Success at work helps improve enjoyment at home all that much more.

I hope you enjoy reading *"P" Point Management* as much as I did improving and writing about it.

**WILLIAM COTTRINGER**

# Contents

# Introduction to "P" Point Management

1

*"The shortest way to do many things is to do only one thing at a time"* (Sydney Smiles).

The primary roles of management are to establish the organization's mission and goals, help employees achieve maximum productivity and to guide the organization to success. These roles start by clarifying chaos. "P" Point Management emphasizes the use of *psychological power points* to simplify unnecessary complexity in uncovering what is most important. "P" points are the small, intensified and well-timed, well-placed efforts that produce major results. They are ordinary but powerful activities that are reflective of bigger governing principles, profound insights and creative solutions. "P" Point Management helps you get more accomplished with less effort.

## "P" POINT MANAGEMENT ACTIVITIES

"P" Point Management simply involves carrying out critical "P" point activities. Below are ten critical management activities, which will assure your success as a manager.

### ☛ ACT LIKE A CHAMPION

Sooner or later we all realize the wisdom that it is who we are that outspeaks what we are trying to say or do. To be successful, you have to first imagine it. Then you have to manage yourself and display the attitude and conduct of a champion as a standard for others to follow. How you are as a person is what other people see most and hear loudest.

The championship attitude includes being positive during adversity, being committed to continuous self-growth and improvement, and being open to possibilities. Championship conduct makes up an excellent role model that demonstrates important virtues that are known to produce success, such as balance, integrity, fairness, tenacity, flexibility, reverence, humility and kindness. Being a champion takes hard work, but anyone who has ever achieved success knows that it doesn't come free.

Being a good role model for others to follow is the most important activity on which any leader can focus. You have to live up to ideal standards that survive microscopic observation. That takes much self-awareness and self-control. A critical "P" point activity is to know how others perceive you and then work on closing the gap between that person and the one who you intend to be. Another advantageous "P" point is being aware of the image you project in your wardrobe, car, house, office décor, leisure activities and other revealing reflections of your personality.

A big part of being a champion has to do with attitude. Attitudes are what drive behavior, and if you want others to perform well, you have to demonstrate the right attitude, consistently and clearly. Wrong attitudes can undermine the best efforts and are difficult to correct. The right leadership attitude to model is one which includes virtues such as temperance, harmony, positivism, patience, integrity and tenacity. One of the most important attitudes to display is one of being positive and confident during adversity.

Being a champion requires you to discover transformational attitudes. These are powerful, pivotal attitudes that bridge the gap between unproductive thinking to more productive thinking. Key transformational attitudes are uncovering your real power, focusing on yourself, realizing your true freedom, and being creative, responsible and realistic.

An effective leader must remain balanced. This is so he or she can have the best vantage point to see in all directions and make the smartest decisions. There are many "P" point balancing acts that challenge leaders. A few of these include talking vs. listening, thinking vs. acting, change vs. stability, autonomy vs. control, giving vs. taking and ideal vs. real. One of the biggest challenges for today's leaders of a diverse workplaces is to consistently enforce sanctions to promote employee equality for the good of the organization while still allowing for the individual employee's freedom and concerns.

Saying "thank you" with valuable acts of stewardship is the last responsibility of a good leader. "P" point stewardship activities include building employees' self-esteem, mentoring potential leaders, teaching skills to others, cultivating virtues, enforcing and reinforcing sanctions fairly and consistently and again, being a good role model for others to follow.

### ☛ BE A LIKABLE SALESPERSON

What you aren't lucky enough to be born with in the way of brains, good looks or other genetic luxuries, you can more than make up for by being likable and practicing effective salesmanship. Being likable is merely a matter of being consistently positive, friendly, helpful, energetic, interested in others and honest. The quickest way to be perceived as likable is to control any negative reactions to other people.

Being a successful salesperson is simply a matter of finding common ground with people, making people feel good about themselves, being honest, showing resilience, focusing on intermediate goals, being persistence in following up, and getting accurate feedback about your approach. Being a likable salesperson is one of the simplest things a leader can do to bridge the gap with followers. It is a small effort that pays major dividends.

Being likable is the silent secret behind much success. Being friendly, positive and approachable helps bring about success with the more difficult and unpleasant aspects of the job. "P" points for improving likability include having a pleasant appearance, displaying a positive attitude, showing high energy and demonstrating control over your reactions. Other strategic "P" points to build likability are making a commitment to continuously improve, learning to live more in the now moment to enjoy what you have, and slowing down to see what is really most important.

It is too bad that the sales profession has such a negative reputation. Successful leadership is the ultimate salesmanship and you can learn much from successful sales people. You have to put the negative connotations aside and look at ways you can incorporate successful sales techniques. A few valuable sales skills are knowing your audience well, making people feel good about themselves, getting them to say "yes" repeatedly, knowing and believing in your "product," setting intermediate goals, being persistent but not obnoxious and following through with details.

There are certain rules that govern who we like and who likes us. These rules are proximity, reciprocity and utility. We are more attracted to people who are nearby, physically and psychologically, than those who are farther away. This includes people who have similar attitudes, values and beliefs. We also tend to like people who already like us and who demonstrate their attraction by doing us favors and saying nice things about us. And finally we tend to like people who satisfy our needs and have needs that we can also satisfy.

For over 35 years, I have asked psychology students what characteristics they thought made up the ideal personality to strive toward, and also what personal things they had learned which helped them get along with others better. This is important information that sets a standard of what to do to become likable. A summary of this "prescription" is at the end of this section in the book.

## ☛ LISTEN TWICE, TALK ONCE

Just like the delay in understanding that what you do has more impact than what you say, it takes a while to wake up to our natural anatomy and the good reasons for it being that way. Once you start practicing power communication by listening with both ears and talking with one mouth, your words and actions convey the same thing that has double the impact.

This subtle sequencing change from talking to listening has another small side benefit. By listening more carefully, you get better hints about what you need to be saying and how you can best say it. By talking only once, you can ask questions that tell people what you want them to hear. Power communicators get heard and understood with their written headlines and spoken sound bytes.

Successful leadership today requires power communication skills. You can only command small bits of people's attention so what you say and how you say it has to be clear, concise and powerful. "P" point communication skills include using two-eared listening to hear everything that is said and not said; playing with word psychology to take advantage of connotations and value dimensions of words; asking good questions; and audience-connecting to knowing how your listener processes information. Power communication avoids communication termites such as over-interpreting non-verbal communication, distracting mannerisms, assumptions, pre-judgments and pre-occupations.

Much of the information on which a leader has to act comes from the questions he or she asks. It is imperative to ask the right questions in the right way to get accurate, clear, concise and complete information. "P" point activities to improve the quality of answers you get are avoiding offensive or accusatory questions, stopping to think what you are trying to ask and why, and phrasing the question to achieve a balance between setting artificial limits and being too open-ended. Another important "P" point is to not ask questions to which you already have your own answer. The object of asking a question is to learn information you don't know.

Communication termites can ruin the foundation of any relationship. You must avoid making assumptions and judgments, being hurried or pre-occupied, imposing or arguing about beliefs, or letting your moods get in the way. You should also be sensitive to distracting or incongruent non-verbal behavior, the needs of your particular audience and your natural tendency toward self-centered thinking. Furthermore, it is smart to get past one-eared listening where you miss *what* was being said because of *how* it was said.

### ☛ THINK WITH A BIG IQ

Fortunately you can boost your thinking IQ without having a brain transplant. Having a big IQ involves regaining common sense, verifying assumptions, disengaging from unproductive thinking and avoiding fatal thinking errors. You can do this easily by asking more questions, looking below the surface, checking out details closer, challenging sacred assumptions, thinking about your thinking and learning from your mistakes.

The biggest boost in your thinking IQ can come when you realize that what you see depends mostly at what you are looking at. When you can un-morph your thinking from your viewpoint you can see how much more there is to learn and know. The field of view is really infinite and small views are the way of efficient but small brains. Stop thinking on auto pilot and reclaim the controls.

One important critical thinking "P" point is slowing down to think about your own thinking and becoming more aware of your lack of present mental productivity. This opens the door to realizing how to improve the quality of your thinking (without a brain transplant) by avoiding critical mental mistakes such as over-simplification, dualistic thinking, mirroring, fatal thinking errors and making unverified assumptions. Critical thinking further helps you become aware of other unproductive mental habits such as perceptual biases, over-generalizing, obsessing with certainty, being held hostage by impossible paradoxes and paradigm-morphing.

Since time is the manager's most important resource, excellent time management skills is a "P" point worth practicing. Good time management is simply developing a system to turn time wasters into time savers. Practicing all these other management "P" points *is* working smart by using less effort to get more results. Working smart involves one other "P" point. That is saving enough time to laugh. Things are rarely as tragic as we often imagine.

Common sense is important in critical thinking. The process of gaining common sense involves careful thinking, forming sound judgment from experience and learning to take effective action based on your thinking and judgment. You can increase common sense by not making assumptions, checking details for accuracy, asking lots of questions and learning from mistakes.

The process of making assumptions results in much incorrect information that frequently gets acted on incorrectly.

Assumptions are especially dangerous in communication and in your expectations of other people. Examples of things to not assume are what you see and hear is true, that your starting point is correct and how much or how little someone else knows.

Fatal thinking can derail you quickly. A few examples of fatal thinking errors to avoid are being convinced you have to choose between two opposing alternatives, believing you can outrun a lie, or any thinking that is over-flavored with negativism, pessimism, worry, blame, guilt or any unproductive emotions.

### REMEMBER CREATUITIVITY

The seemingly unsolvable problems we face today require massive doses of intuition and creativity. Fortunately we are born with these resources and just have to let go to seeing, hearing and feeling them again. The main block is judgment and the main judgment is our hesitation in believing we can affect and change reality. Of course you can create amazing new realities! But only if you believe so and work hard to do.

Actually all we have to do is get inside it and understand a small portion of reality a little better. When you make an effort to fit in first and then make what you are fitting into better, you learn two things: (1) at least half the stuff you thought needed changing doesn't and (2) there are many more ways to change the things that do need changing, than you had previously thought.

The problems that confront today's leaders are complex and unique. Many solutions require tools that haven't even been invented yet. Leaders have to join their creatuitivity skills to uncover valuable intuitive insights and to encourage divergent, wiggly 3-D thinking in their organizations. The major "P" point to tapping into creatuitivity is to remember how much of it you had as a child. It was suppressed because it wasn't viewed as a priority value. Other "P" point activities to increase this valuable leadership skill are verifying hunches more, suspending judgment about things, looking at ordinary things differently and engaging in creative projects without worrying about your finished product.

Leaders have to learn how to create new realities. A starting point is to realize that life is driven more by thought than physical realities. What you see really depends more upon what you are looking at and the location from which you are doing the looking. When you stop taking your viewpoint so seriously, you start realizing how little you actually know and begin to open up to bigger possibilities. Each new door ahead widens your field of vision so you can spot all the most important things in life, valuable insights, the enduring principles that govern it, and creative solutions to problems, which are all "P" Points.

### KNOW WHAT MAKES PEOPLE TICK

Good leaders have to become master psychologists in reading and dealing with people effectively. Fortunately you don't need to re-enroll in a graduate psychology program to succeed at this. You already know all the things that make you tick. All you have to do is apply this knowledge.

We are all just trying to get where we think we want to be by using whatever means are available. To be a successful leader all you have to do is help people get what they want. Don't we all want to be respected, productive, liked, successful, independent, happy, understood, responsible and useful? When in doubt, treat others the way you wanted to be treated yourself. That is the short-cut of all short-cuts.

Successful leadership requires an intimate understanding of how to deal with people effectively. Although people seem to think and act in all different ways, there are important commonalties to understand. In their own unique way, people are just doing what they perceive they need to do to be where they want to be. You will be a successful leader when you start giving other people what they want and need. A few simple things we all need are understanding, acceptance, encouragement, recognition, appreciation and freedom to be responsible and productive.

Human behavior is paradoxical. We are often driven in opposite directions by our thinking, motives and behavior. Leaders must learn to accommodate these paradoxes. A few of these important human paradoxes are needing autonomy vs. independence, wanting freedom vs. equality, being creative vs. being logical, wanting to be told what to do vs. choosing how to do it, and listening to our heads vs. our hearts.

There is so much to know and do and so little time that leaders must learn and apply valuable psychological principles that generalize to many similar situations. Leaders can improve his or her arsenal of "P" point psychology principles by reviewing important information about human beings' motivations, individual differences, learning, group processes, and general behavior. A good source for learning principles is to observe nature where important life principles are abundant. Taking the time to understand the details of how something works is also an excellent way to learn principles that explain other things.

Perceptions are what people act on and therefore they are important to understand. The object is to create right perceptions and correct wrong ones. Wrong initial perceptions can be lasting and resistive to change, despite their accuracy or evidence to the contrary. Therefore it is extremely important to project the right character, personality and thinking that set the stage for trust, cooperation and employees' commitment and enthusiasm to follow you. Once you have done everything you can do to assure the creation of a right perception, you need to set up a reliable way to make sure the gap doesn't widen between how you want to be perceived and how you are perceived. Changing wrong perceptions requires an understanding of how they got started and consistent demonstration of compelling behavior toward the desired perception.

**LIGHT THEIR FIRES**

I think that in our efforts to simplify things to the lowest common denominator, we inadvertently make some of them much more complex and complicated than they may need to be. Such is the case of human motivation. It is so complex and mysterious that it has become an entire industry of gurus. The last time I counted there are over 200 theories of motivation. An Internet search of "motivation" will get you overwhelmed.

There is only one easy, straightforward way to motivate employees effectively. That is to take the time and effort to get to know each employee well enough to understand what best motivates him or her. Then you can help them all get what they want by creating quality work places, providing job enrichment, removing barriers to performance, introducing beneficial change, offering helpful feedback, and arranging the right rewards. Doing these simple activities gets big results with small efforts. It only takes time and you will have more of that when you start practicing all these other "P" points.

Motivation is one of the most complicated and complex of all human behaviors. It is not something that is tangible or easily defined. Motivation can only be inferred from the presence or absence of certain desired attitudes and performance. It is important to separate personality issues from performance ones and to remove all barriers to performance, which might be wrongly perceived to be low motivation.

There is no doubt that being a good motivator is an important activity in management. Although human motivation is a complex phenomenon, there are commonsense motivational principles that can help make the job easier. It is important to start out knowing the good news and the bad news, demonstrating your own enthusiasm and taking the time to know what best motivates each employee. From there you can concentrate on removing barriers to good performance, creating a quality work environment, improving job enrichment and many other things that can stoke the fire.

Leaders must become masters of managing change productively by overcoming resistance of employees, minimizing disruption to the organization and reducing discomfort to all. "P" points in this process are establishing a work culture that is supportive of change, understanding the change process itself, learning how to sell the change by dispelling doubt and assuring success, staying ahead of external trends that affect the organization and keeping personal changes from spilling over to the workplace. A critical "P" point for leaders is to be able to spot unproductive, undesirable changes that violate known principles essential to the organization's productivity and welfare of employees.

## ☛ ATTACK DIFFICULT THINGS ASSERTIVELY

Problems, conflicts and mistakes are all opportunities to learn valuable information and to grow people and the organization exponentially. Cure problems instead of treating symptoms by breaking bigger problems down into more manageable parts and being systematic in diagnosing causes and choosing treatments. Approach conflicts by separating thinking from feeling, and identifying issues, investments and costs of alternatives.

Rectify mistakes gracefully by openly taking blame, implementing a quick fix, developing a long-range preventative cure and offering some form of penitence. Don't worry about failures either. As Henry Ford said, "Failures are an opportunity to start over again with better information".

A critical management "P" point is teaching problem-solving skills to employees by demonstrating this important skill firsthand in an actual problem situation. This requires trust and patience with the results. Learning useful problem-solving strategies is an important "P" point too. Some of these are identifying the real core problem apart from symptoms, separating solvable problems from unsolvable ones and breaking complex problems down into more manageable parts. Unusual "P" point problem-solving strategies include working backwards, changing languages and reapplying older solutions in newer and more unusual ways.

Conflicts are necessary for employees and organizations to grow. They are not problems to avoid but opportunities of which to take advantage. "P" point conflict resolution activities include determining the importance of the issues, uncovering the investments that have already been made with certain outcomes, anticipating the impact different outcomes will have on everyone and learning the difficulties in implementing the various resolution strategies. The values of all these aspects dictate the appropriate application of either acting, adjusting, accommodating or avoiding the conflict. A major "P" point for leaders to practice is to resist the natural tendency to try and resolve conflicts too quickly before all the issues have been explored in sufficient depth.

Leaders are bound to make mistakes but are not bound to those mistakes they make. A "P" point regarding mistakes is to develop a good recovery strategy. A simple one that works well is to own the problem non-defensively, offer a sincere apology, implement a temporary quick fix, plan a long-term cure to keep the problem from re-occurring and offer a token of penitence for absolution. A good "P" point attitude to have about making a mistake is that it is an opportunity to start over again with the correct information.

## USE A TELESCOPE AND A MICROSCOPE

Knowing what to do is useless information if you don't stay focused and avoid all the tempting distractions that can lure you away from seeing what you need to see and do what you need to do. You need to keep your focus balanced between seeing the big picture out there and the details that make it up in here, so you can do the right thing in the best way to get the desired results with the least effort and side effects. Nothing gets done without steady, clear and accommodating focus. Start by focusing on your ability to focus.

With today's fast pace and all that is going on it is a real challenge for the leader to stay focused. "P" point areas of focus that have the biggest payoffs include the organization's mission, goals and values; employees' productivity and welfare; knowing the details of how important things work and getting useful feedback to assure continuous improvement. Perhaps one of the most important "P" points to keep in focus is your own self-care. Excellent leadership requires a physically, mentally, emotionally and spiritually healthy leader.

There is always a gap between where you are and where you want to be. There are usually many smaller "P" point gaps making up this bigger gap that needs closing first. These gaps are what you focus on. Such gaps are the ones between how you see yourself and how others see you, what you say and what employees hear, what you know and can do and what others know and can do, what you think you want and what you actually need, and what you expect and what employees expect. Effective gap-closing requires a good understanding of the inter-relationships between these smaller gaps. Sometimes you have to get in the gap to see what it is all about.

A benefit of good focus is the ability to be able to seize the moment and take advantage of opportunities. To do this you must be present in the now. You can get to the now by paying attention to what is going on around you, asking more questions, challenging assumptions, listening, shedding your stress and focusing on now.

### ☛ LIVE A SUCCESS FORMULA

> As a leader, you have one mission and that is to go for the gold. You start out with a big dream and then you translate that big dream into concrete intermediate goals. You come up with a clever approach to use your main talent in a new and unusual way that others just talk about doing. Then you apply an unlimited reserve of pure determination and self-discipline to work hard in using this talent to achieve your goals, with the understanding that you have to make big sacrifices and difficult exchanges. You never quit, knowing that success is probably just around the next corner that you are most inclined to give up getting to. Once you achieve success, you realize it was a gift and you share your success secrets with others.

At the heart of any success is a game plan. This is your private success formula which you must live fully. Fortunately there is a good success model which you can adapt and implement. The key steps in this simple success formula are: (1) *Dream big*. You are only limited by the smallness of your beliefs and dreams, but you have to translate your dreams into concrete goals. Dreams will evaporate if they don't move from your head to your hands; (2) *Work hard*. Commit to using your main talent gracefully to be the best you can be in doing something in a new and unusual way that others only talk about doing. Stay focused and resist all the tempting distractions between you and your goals; (3) *Never quit*. Success is often just around the next corner that you are most likely to give up getting to.

Management positions offer an excellent opportunity for a leader to fulfill all his or her potential. It is imperative for you to have a deep desire to grow and improve and become the best you can be in whatever you are doing, no matter how far you have already gotten. There is always much more ahead. The art of becoming self-actualized is in seeing what you can do right now to get to where you need to be to facilitate your next move forward. As a leader, you can never stop learning and improving. Everything you are doing now is preparation for a more important responsibility.

Managers can achieve much success in their personal and professional development by identifying and managing major "P" points in their lives. The most important of these include principles, polarization's, paradigms, priorities, paradoxes, perfection points, pre-judgments and problems.

Success requires a down payment. The dues you should be prepared to pay include the struggle to identify your main mission, the effort to uncover important governing principles, the difficulty of reconciling opposites, and the battle to get your two halves working together.

Every success requires you to abandon your comfort zone. Actually all you are doing is expanding your comfort zone. You can begin doing this by letting go and giving in, eating dessert first, re-arranging your furniture, reaching out and jumping in, resetting your thermostat and including more possibilities into your present realties.

There are five questions that can stimulate tremendous personal growth. These questions are: What can I really control? How do I sabotage my own self? Why don't I apply all the good things I learn? For whom am I doing it for? What is the best I am capable of doing? The right answers to these questions will result in a major growth spurt in personal excellence.

By practicing these ten management "P" point activities, the leader will be improving the productivity of the organization for all stakeholders. This results in big success. The "P" point manager gets better results by doing less, smarter.

Each of these "P" point activities is explained in more detail in the following pages. There is nothing complicated about "P" Point Management. It is as straightforward as anything can be. You get big results by doing little things.

One thing you will notice throughout this book is that many of these skills are very much inter-related and almost inseparable at times. For instance power communication and effective problem-solving will both help you get the information you need to resolve conflicts or manage change better. When you resolve conflicts or implement valuable change, you remove an important barrier to employees' motivation and job performance. Certain critical thinking skills are useful in problem-solving, motivating others, rectifying mistakes and managing change. This is the main benefit of "P" Point Management. By using these simple skills together you are actually doing less but getting more results.

"P" point activities are the best way to make progress in closing critical gaps between where you are and where you want to be. They are genuine, intelligent short cuts. They help you get more done by doing less, smarter. You have more time to focus on what is really important by saving the time you have been wasting on unproductive activities.

# Management "P" Point # 1: Act Like a Champion

2

*"If you are going to build something in the air it is always better to build castles than houses of cards"* (George C. Lichtenberg).

**Management Problem # 1:** It usually takes many failures and much frustration before you can finally wake up to the obvious fact that you can't begin to manage others until you learn how to manage yourself first. Realizing the value of changing focus away from others and toward your self is the first and most important management "P" point. Unfortunately this shift is hampered by a larger bad habit we all have of reversing important priorities in putting the cart before the horse. We need to question why we do that.

## BE A GREAT ROLE-MODEL

Management of others starts with self-management. In fact if you can't manage yourself effectively, then the chance of being able to manage others is nil. The first step in self-management is to see the gap between where you want to be and where you actually are. The second step is doing something positive to close that gap. Another important gap to work on is the one between how you see yourself and how others see you. Sometimes these two gaps are the same.

The main "P" point management gap that needs closing is the one between your actual everyday behavior and the high standard of being an ideal role model for others to emulate. As a manager, your character and performance standards are up on a pedestal. Since you are constantly being viewed under a microscope, it only makes good sense to avoid doing *anything* that shouldn't be seen. This means always being the best possible role model you can be. Here is a warning that can never be overstated: There is no room for error in management role modeling. The slightest mistake in being less than a perfect role model can take away your reason for reading this book.

So, what all is involved in being a good role model? Three things:

1. Manage yourself.
2. Walk your talk.
3. Make improvements.

### Manage Yourself

We try to manage everything except the one thing that can manage everything else for us—our brains. Our brains engage in three primary functions which mirror those of the rest of the universe: Creating, destroying, and maintaining. Until we stop putting our brains on autopilot, these functions occur haphazardly and progress is uncertain. The worst case scenario is where we destroy balance and strength, create weakness and problems, and maintain the wrong attitude.

The object is to create, destroy and maintain the right things. "P" point management requires you to take more control of yourself: Creating strength, insights, and principles to live by; destroying weakness, problems and rationalizations, and maintaining the right attitude, healthy balance and good timing, all to get you to where you want to be.

Our lack of self-management is ironic, given the widespread activities of our egocentric conceit. You would think our self would focus more on itself than it really does. We have to learn to manage ourselves more so that we can become more in touch with who we really are and be more inner-directed.

The problem is that we are not focusing enough on the process of getting smarter or regaining control of what can control the things most needing to be controlled. The consciousness that we think comes from our brains, may be more of a force, which drives them. Such a force is a good thing to get to know better.

This entire book has many suggestions about important self-areas to manage, but here is a priority list to consider:

1. Take a personal inventory and make sure you are presently living your life in a way that allows you to enjoy your most important needs and values. If you don't know what these are, find out.
2. Identify your most destructive problem behaviors to be eliminated and then develop and carry out a concrete action plan with definite goals that get results. Separate behaviors that need to be eliminated altogether from those that need to be cut back. Identify behaviors you can redo smarter to help carry all this out. Start by realizing anything that is keeping you from number one above.
3. Practice controlling your own wrong reactions so that you can become freer to act in the ways you really want to.
4. Force yourself to slow down so you can begin to see how things are interacting with each other below the surface and learn how to use better timing to influence more productive outcomes in your favor. Make sure you want to do the right thing for the right reason.
5. Challenge and replace the unproductive beliefs, which interfere most with you getting to where you want to be. But first, make sure it is the right place.
6. Start hanging around other people who are honest, positive, loving, motivated, creative, responsible, intelligent and kind.
7. Put yourself under a microscope and practice being who you pretend to be.
8. Fine-tune your sensitivity to those critical moments when you can make a contribution to your own natural growth process.
9. Set up a reliable system to get useful and accurate feedback about how you are doing in your efforts at personal self-development.
10. Look for the things you may have to exchange to get there.

How well do you know the force that drives you and how well are you using it to manage yourself? What parts of yourself do you need to manage most? Are you in control? What do you need to do to get more control of yourself?

### Walk Your Talk

When you walk your talk you have personal congruence and it shows big time. You appear to be all together, because you are. There isn't any noticeable disparity between what you say and what you do. There is a gapless, total integrity. Having this personal congruence is the main requirement of being a good role model for other's to emulate and that talent alone is the most powerful influence you can ever have on other people. This behavior demonstrates certain answers to our important questions of "Who am I? Where am I going? Why? And how do I get there?" This is when you are using your intelligence fully by doing the least to get the most. You have found your success code and are applying it.

Achieving personal congruence is a simple recipe of mixing self-confidence and humility with the values of honesty, respect for everyone, perseverance and adaptability to change. The main focus here is entirely on managing ourselves. It may be that personal congruence is a product of improvements in many of these other areas. Obviously the process involves some work in making sure others are perceiving us the way we want to be perceived because that is the way we are. The point is that we have to actually be that way first. This is one area where you can't just act a certain way to be that way. When your behavior doesn't follow your attitude, the incongruence is too obvious. This is when you have to practice a desired habit so well, it actually becomes one.

Many times we make the wrong assumption that we have to be perceived a certain way to be accepted. We think our momentary fears, stupidity, inability or other weaknesses will cause outright rejection. Even the most integrated person has these lapses and they are okay to have. Admitting them appropriately can even build acceptance and credibility.

Walking your talk is the perfect opportunity to prove that you are the person you pretend to be. Back in the days when I worked as a prison administrator I learned much from prison inmates about pretending. Oddly, inmates are experts at seeing past phony pretenders and any other kind of pretending even in the slightest way. There is no hiding yourself from prison inmates. Being continuously confronted about my earlier pretending was good motivation for me to start learning how to walk my talk as a person and a manager. This experience is why I always recommended inmates who were getting released to consider getting a job where they could use their keen "interviewing" skills at seeing the real person behind the façade, position, resume or application. Not all prison experience is wasted.

Do you feel as though you are walking your talk? Do other people see you as walking your talk? What do you need to do to bridge this gap? Do you disclose the real you enough?

### Make Improvements

Making improvements is a two-part process: (1) looking back at the past and correcting critical mistakes; and (2) looking ahead and doing things differently. There are some behaviors we need to avoid altogether, some we need to cut back and others we need to do smarter. The first thing we need to do is get unstuck from our invisible prisons. This involves digging to understand some of the unhealthy scripts we wrote for ourselves early on in our lives, and realizing the impossible injunctions others shackled us with.

Scripts are little games kids play, which can have far-reaching affect on the adult games and roles. They hide some potent self-understanding, such as the origins of our darker sides and the reasons for our ignorance. When I was a little boy, one of my favorite games was being the jailer of the neighborhood's "gangsters." I was able to control other kids. Later, when I became a prison warden, I was in-charge of controlling inmates. For me, control was power. I even carried this power thing over to the field of mental health where I did a stint as a psychologist at a community mental health center. That is a book in itself.

Injunctions are the verbal commands significant people give us, which limit our choices. These are types of paradoxical statements, such as "Try to please me, but you probably can't," which really can't be obeyed or disobeyed. The more we try, the more frustrated we get. A close friend of mine stayed in an extremely unsatisfying and unhealthy marriage for over 25 years, mostly because of the Catholic injunction against divorce. Now that church is sending out, "A Catholic is always welcome home" messages as part of their recruiting plan. What are they saying here?

Another friend may have suppressed her artistic abilities and passions because teachers told her to "calm down". I pursued much more education than I really needed just to try and impress my father, which wasn't possible, at least in that respect. My investment of time and money in higher education lead me to expect to get somewhere better, which didn't happen. In turn that unmet expectation led to frustration and unintelligent behavior.

Between these early scripts and injunctions, we are not really living our own lives now. We are still trying to please others or rebel against them, neither of which contributes to success. Once we understand such origins of this particular gap, we have to gradually start making some serious personal changes.

To become smart and successful we have to be at our best physically, emotionally, intellectually, socially and spiritually. We have to be fully self-actualized. This effort involves remembering and re-practicing all the personal and professional "P" points we can tune into. Starting at the beginning, with the right attitude and good communication, will most likely produce the quickest improvements. At the same time this will make the changes that follow much easier.

One special area to improve, which can help trigger other improvements is in the area of our friendships. The quality of our friendships has a great deal of influence over our personal growth and well-being and so it only makes sense for us to make an effort to develop quality friendships. Between moving around geographically, changing careers and getting divorced, which just about covers us all, we can lose good friendships that need to be replaced. Actively look for quality friendships that are intellectually stimulating, emotionally supportive, vocationally mentoring, spiritually comforting and recreationally fun. We all need good friends, and sometimes just starting a simple conversation with someone else can evolve into a lifetime friendship.

Make a list of other improvements you need to make, which will increase your intelligence. Try to have a positive attitude and don't think of excuses. Here are 15 inexpensive hints on improving external attractiveness:

| | | |
|---|---|---|
| Smell good. | Show good manners. | Achieve humbly. |
| Practice eye care. | Listen more, talk less. | Cultivate an asset. |
| Show high energy. | Speak & write well. | Stop swearing. |
| Smile often. | Walk with style. | Drive a clean car. |
| Dress in style. | Develop your voice. | Be spontaneous. |

If you are not successful now it is likely that you are not smart enough. Make the needed improvements and become smarter. It is not that you aren't good enough. You can be better, so be better. My suggestion is to focus more on developing positive behaviors and less on avoiding negative ones. Try developing your assets while accepting your liabilities. This is a healthy adult version of compensation.

What assets of yours need upgrading? What liabilities could you easily avoid altogether or at least cut back? What thoughts interfere with doing these things you know need to be done?

## DEMONSTRATE THE RIGHT ATTITUDE

Attitudes are complicated things. At the same time they often drive behavior, can be made up of those same behaviors and even bring about consequences, which may reinforce those behaviors and the attitude itself. Formation of a 'wrong' attitude is a negative vicious circle that is hard to break.

Having the *right attitude* is critical in just about everything you do. It is especially important for the leader to demonstrate the right attitude consistently. The wrong attitude can quickly spell doom for the best effort. What exactly is the right attitude? It is something we can easily spot if it is there or not, but it is not so easy to define. Below are ten critical behaviors, which I think all work together to define the right attitude.

### Temperance

The wiser course eventually leads us to the value of moderation and avoiding extremes. This even includes having excessive optimism or an overly positive attitude, which can actually get on other people's nerves. It is unfortunate that this wiser course of temperance takes so long to learn. In the process of learning the right attitude of temperance we can alienate too many other people with extremes in either negative or positive behavior when all we are really trying to do is get accepted and be liked. We just don't go about it in the right way the first time around and need this hindsight lesson.

### Harmony

Success requires us to be in sync with others, be cooperative and work together as a synergistic team. This does not mean you have to be overly conventional, uncreative and put your own uniqueness and personal needs aside for the sake of the group. It just means you have to figure out how to get along with other people the best you can. Having the right attitude with all these other behaviors can go a long way toward that end. Harmonious songs are the most pleasing to the ear and there is always a symphony in the making when it comes to interpersonal relations.

### Maturity

Maturity doesn't have to mean being dull and over-serious or confining yourself to an "act your age" syndrome (you are never too old to be silly and have fun). It simply means that you take responsibility for the connection between your behaviors and their consequences, especially how they affect other people. Another definition of maturity I like comes from Stephen

Covey. According to him the mark of a mature person is when he or she fulfills all promises made and only makes promises that can be delivered.

### Positivism

The trick is not to set up a showdown between positives and negatives, but to adopt a wait and see, neutral attitude. Allowing things to happen without pre-judgments will reduce your disappointments, which will in turn increase the likelihood of positive outcomes. This reversal makes having a positive attitude much easier. When you are more able to have a positive attitude when things are going well, then having one when things are just average becomes easier. That in turn prepares you for being able to have a more positive attitude when things start going sideways or downhill, when it is the hardest and most noticeable by others. That is when having the right attitude counts most. It is a matter of practice.

### Patience

The world is going at such a fast pace that it is easy to get caught up in a compulsive desire for immediate need gratification. However, the person who exercises a little patience and willingness to wait for something will never go unnoticed these days. The attitude to have is that *anticipation* is still half of the enjoyment. Also, being patient with others is a sure way to make a friend. Very few things will cancel the world if not done immediately. Besides, when you take a little time to think about something you can often discover a better way to do it. At the least you will avoid having to do it over again to correct mistakes because things were too rushed the first time.

### Integrity

Integrity is not made up of honesty and morality. These are the things that show when you are integrated. You are integrated when: (a) you achieve internal consistency with self-management; and (b) there is congruence between this internal consistency and what people see on the outside. Then you are able to walk your talk naturally and be the kind of role model other people respect and want to follow. There is nothing more annoying than a person who says one thing and does another. Inconsistent moods, unpredictable reactions and relative morality are a sure path to failure. It is your integrated wholeness that sets up success between right behaviors and right results.

### Reverence

When you treat other people with respect, politeness and gentleness something happens. You get it back in return. I think this pleasant consequence generalizes to everything else in life. We have been designated as the keeper of this planet and have an obligation to do an excellent job in this regard. The best way to do this is to treat *everything* the way we would like to be treated ourselves. That guideline is the ultimate moral compass and is guaranteed to work correctly all the time without any maintenance whatsoever. Reverence towards all things is a cornerstone of the right attitude that forms a very strong foundation below the surface. It shines brightly.

### Acceptance

I think life reacts the same way that people do when they are over-controlled, judged and misunderstood—not very well. When you invest heavily in trying to control things and people, most of the time you are just setting yourself up for failure and disappointment. *Nothing* wants to be controlled, just accepted and understood. By focusing more on the few controllables that are actually under your influence, you can do a much better job on those things. You will not be wasting valuable time doing so much and getting so little in the way of results. Acceptance and understanding determine if something needs changing and if it does, they offer valuable clues how to do that more effectively.

### Tenacity

Life isn't always kind and easy. If we want to survive the most difficult, trying situations, we must develop fortitude and learn to hang in there when things start getting tough. This prepares us for the strength that is required to win life's best prizes. Weakness and quitting are not behaviors that are looked up to and people who display them are not in favor with others. Anybody can give up, but the tenacious person will have both success and respect and admiration from others. Besides all this, it is perseverance that builds the most important thing a human being can have, which is self-confidence. There is no such thing as the right attitude *without* self-confidence.

### Tentativeness

When all is said and done, what is left that you really know for sure? "Very little," is the only honest answer. So why profess to know certainty? Why do battle over a belief that you can't prove to be true? Taking a more tentative approach allows you to relax, open up and learn much more. Personally, I have never felt more energy, wellness and excitement than the moment in the second half of my life when I discovered I was still a student and not the teacher. This was the right attitude that improved both my likability and smartness. It didn't hurt my credibility and success either.

By striving to develop these ten virtuous behaviors, you will be showing the right attitude. The right attitude will bring about the right consequences, which will increase your success rate in anything. The real winner will be your self-confidence, which may be what really drives the right attitude in a positive vicious circle.

## DISCOVER TRANSFORMATIONAL ATTITUDES

Attitudes are amazing. They can result in anything from a Super Bowl victory to mediocre job performance to suicide. Many people can be dealt with a lousy hand of cards and somehow come up with a royal flush. Others can have five aces and still lose the poker game. The development and effects of our attitudes are indeed strange and unpredictable.

Self-improvement requires us to tap into this powerful force we call attitudes. First we have to understand how attitudes are developed. Then we have to figure out how to change them when they are not helping us get where we want to be.

For the sake of simplicity, let's say that there are three main directions of attitude development. Generally, if you are originally dealing a strong hand of cards and experiencing repeated success in the things you do, then you start developing a positive, happy, and optimistic attitude. You feel good about life, yourself and the future. You smile a lot.

If you are given an average hand of cards and get a mixture of results in what you do, then you start developing more of a neutral attitude. You have good and bad feelings about life, yourself and the future. You smile or frown, depending on the situation.

And if on the other hand, you have dealt five weak cards and experienced repeated failures, then you are likely to develop a negative, unhappy and pessimistic attitude. You feel badly about life, yourself and the future. You mostly frown.

Of course most of us go down all three of these paths, depending on what actually happens to us at the time and how we interpret and react to those things. Some successes and failures mean more than others and have more impact on shaping our overall attitude. And individual perceptions are so different that no two people react to the same situation in a similar way.

For instance, in a failed relationship one person might get depressed, feel inadequate and think things are hopeless, whereas another might see the situation as an opportunity to start over again with the information needed for success. Still another person might just move on without giving it much thought. The next time this happens to these same three people, there might be three different reactions.

Sometime during the process of developing our attitudes something interesting happens. The tail starts wagging the dog so to speak. The type of attitude that we have formed as a result of our hand of cards and subsequent experiences actually starts attracting more of the same outcomes all by itself.

For example, the person who gets the poor card hand and has many early failure experiences, starts forming a negative attitude, which leads that person to anticipate, expect and experience more negative consequences. The more negative the consequences, the more negative the attitude gets and the more powerful it becomes.

These mega-attitudes then start driving behavior behind the scenes. They become a major ingredient in the recipe that happens to us. The cart is now before the horse.

We are not entirely aware of this attitude development process or how powerful our attitudes can become. Some people can become victims of their own attitudes before they even realize what is going on. They can become prejudiced, angry, dishonest, quitting or hopeless without knowing why or how. These people become a passenger in their own car instead of being the driver. Sadly, sometimes the car even stays parked in the driveway or gets wrecked on the highway.

Most if not all of us would probably agree that a positive attitude is the way to go. This is taking the steering wheel of your car and driving where you want to go. At the very least, a positive attitude can help soften the worst of unpleasant adversities. We can't often control or prevent such things as a marriage failure, job lay off, death of a loved one or physical illness. But, a positive attitude can lesson the negative impact these things can have on us and decrease the likelihood of a negative attitude sneaking up on us unnoticed.

Obviously it is not that easy to have a positive attitude all the time or everyone would have one. This is because when we are not where we want to be, we tend to blame everyone and everything else other than the real culprit, which is the wrong attitude. Without attacking the core problem, nothing changes. Having the wrong attitude is what generally keeps us from getting to where we want to be. It is this attitude that needs changing but this is difficult to see when you are knee deep in unhappiness and disappointment.

Let's take a common work example. If you don't get a promotion or job you want, you can either think that you did something wrong again and will never get a break, or you can see that there might be an even better opportunity waiting for you just around the bend. You may even ask some questions to determine exactly why you didn't get the promotion or job and then make some changes to improve your chances the next time around. Then again, you may dismiss it all as luck of the draw.

The biggest difficulty in all this is that it takes the *right* attitude to even see the consequences and folly of a *wrong* one. You can have a predominately negative attitude and not even see how that attitude is affecting the quality of your life. Or, you can have an overly optimistic, positive attitude and not see that such an attitude alone cannot prevent all the negative things from happening that are frustrating you.

Another problem is that each person has to discover this subtle connection between attitudes and consequences by him or herself because instruction from others usually isn't as meaningful or effective. Still another problem is that much of the problem itself is on an unconscious level of thinking that isn't easy to access, let alone talk about. Even when you sense what is going on, it is difficult to put it into words.

Changing an unproductive attitude into a more productive one takes some deep thinking, a sudden realization of what is going on and some creative thoughts to get you ready for change. First, you have to think about all the things that have happened to you, what attitude you reacted with and what the consequences were. This may require digging into thoughts of which you are not even aware. Next you have to start seeing the role that your own attitude plays in bringing about undesirable outcomes. Then you have to gradually have some new thoughts about what you might do to change things for the better.

These new thoughts are what I call *transformational attitudes*. These are powerful, pivotal attitudes that bridge the gap between unproductive thinking to more productive behavior. These potent mini-attitudes have to appeal to your mind, feel right in your heart and be comfortable enough in your hands to apply them.

Here are a few transformational attitudes I have discovered that might stimulate you to have your own, in taking your attitude development to the next higher level:

1. **Uncovering your real power.** I may need to slow down and pay more attention to the connection between my attitudes and the quality of my life. When

I do this I will probably notice many opportunities right now to make different choices that will get better results than I have been getting. I might find out that I actually have more power over what happens in my life than I now think I have. I have the power to change every moment with each new opportunity to react differently.

2. **Focusing on your self.** There is nothing really so wrong with me that needs fixing compared to some people I know. However, I realize I could be a lot better if I tried a little harder. And I might get further if I would stop comparing myself to others and start competing against myself. After all, the only person I can really control is myself.
3. **Realizing your true freedom.** Maybe the most precious gift in this life is having the complete freedom to choose how to interpret and react to the things that happen to me, rather than being able to control or prevent those things from happening in the first place.
4. **Being creative.** If I want to close the gap between where I am and where I want to be, there are really only two ways to do that. These are to either run faster (increase my effort) or shorten the distance to where I am going (change my attitude). I can even do both of these at the same time. These are the types of win-win choices of which I need more.
5. **Being responsible.** I know I didn't dig this hole and create this mess all by myself, but no one else is going to help me get out of the hole and clean up the mess. I only have myself to do this, but then again I will be the one who will benefit the most.
6. **Being realistic.** Having a positive attitude won't guarantee that everything in my life will turn out positive, but it will help me to react better to the negative things that are bound to occur.

## GET BALANCED

The first and most important rule of good management is *fundamental fairness*. This is the foundation behind good motivation and is the management *Golden Rule*. Simply treat employees the same way you want to be treated yourself. This requires an attitude of openness and a keen sensitivity to know when you are approaching the point of no return in crossing over the line of fundamental fairness into unfairness. Fundamental fairness involves achieving a workable balance between valid opposing behaviors that keep all of us going back and forth. Without establishing a sense of fundamental fairness in your own mind and then transferring it into workplace reality, "P" Point Management is not possible. Below are ten such pairs of divergent issues for managers to work toward achieving a workable balance.

### Giving vs. Taking

Managers who constantly take in the way of mandating new rules and procedures and making isolated management decisions, *without* considering employee input and concerns, will eventually lose support from employees when they may need it most. The manager, who gives a little to employees, especially when the issue is important to both management and employees, will gain tremendous respect and support from them. For instance, suppose a ten week window for a critical task accomplishment is a cost-effective method, felt doable by management, but not by employees. Adding two weeks, could buy a lot of productivity and good morale, without jeopardizing effectiveness. Arriving at a fair balance in this area requires checking pride and ego at the door, and just answering the question of, what will I lose by giving in on this one and what will I gain?

### Autocracy vs. Democracy

Every good manager knows when it is time to lead and act, and when it is may be more appropriate to listen from employees to get a consensus, *before* taking action. A general rule is that management gets to choose the "what" of the organizational direction, leaving the "how" do we get there to the employees. Management has the better foresight and vision to establish the mission, primary goals and values of the organization, but allowing employees to use their own creativity and abilities to figure out how to actually get things done, is really what empowerment is all about. And of course, during emergencies, management has both the obligation and right to take over and dictate which way the cow eats the cabbage, without consulting employees. Furthermore, when any important policy changes will be unanimously unpopular, it will pay to be firm, with some explanation and good propaganda proceeding the fiat to come.

## Autonomy vs. Supervision

Arriving at a smart balance between under- and over-supervising employees is a not any easy task. The effective manager will take the time to know the competency and motivational level of each new employee and even the cycles of older employees, in order to apply just the right amount of instruction and motivation to get maximum productivity. Of course, taking the time to be very clear on both spoken and unspoken expectations for performance and outcomes, will always have big payoffs. Another fundamental fairness rule here is to never delegate responsibility without assigning authority with it. "Letting go" of the reins and delegating responsibility with authority to employees, is an area managers, and especially *effective* ones, need to make efforts to improve. Trust is usually the main issue, and that only comes when you have taken the time to know your employees and the time to fully explain your expectations. Also, don't bother delegating only the things you can't do well yourself, that is very unfair.

## Change vs. Stability

Most employees fear and resist change, preferring familiar routine and stability. Change can be very scary and disruptive to productivity. But, sometimes change is absolutely necessary to help an organization get unstuck and make real progress. Often, change gets dictated externally by society and consumer trends and all these changes aren't necessarily good. An effective manager will learn how to orchestrate and facilitate the specific types of changes that can help the organization and get support from employees. The tricks are in knowing what routines and stability to preserve, which won't inhibit productive change and to manage change so that it isn't counterproductive. The urgency of good and frequent communication during changes, is too often overlooked, even by the best of managers. Usually, a good technique to employee in facilitating needed changes, is to encourage the open dialogue of imagined fears by the employees and to dispel needless myths. This catharsis can smooth the way for more productive, un-resisted change.

### Aloofness vs. Approachability

Management positions tend to foster aloofness as a self-preservation defense. This is very normal, because it can be very lonely at the top, and nobody really understands the unique pressures of management, so you tend to rely on yourself as your own best counselor. Self-sharing may even be seen as a weakness. But, when this aloofness keeps employees from approaching mangers with genuine concerns and issues, this self-defense mechanism has crossed the line of fundamental fairness. A good rule of thumb is to preserve aloofness for private and social matters, while presenting an approachable personality when it comes to professional and business matters. Approachability in the workplace can result in learning things you need to know to be an effective manager. The critical informal communication and power networks of the organization can only be accessed by this approachability, and without correct information from that source, there can be no real leadership.

### Idealism vs. Realism

An effective manager has to choose "wars" of pushing ideal standards of employee conduct and performance carefully. A sensitive manager will learn when ideal standards are just not achievable or when more "realistic" results are just a cop-out. Most employees want to achieve the best results in what they are doing and even want to be held accountable for getting those results. However, as they approach the threshold of doubting their ability to achieve what may be expected, they tend to get very resistive and very un-idealistic. They will fight tooth and nail over resisting doing something they claim can't possibly be done, when they don't really feel that way. The wise manager has to be brave and err on the other side of realism, constantly guiding and gently pushing employees to achieve more than they think they can. This idealistic flavor, tempered by *real* realism, is the way the universe operates, and being in sync with that process, can never be wrong.

## Talking vs. Listening

The natural tendency is for the manager is to do most of the talking and have employees do most of the listening. After all, all those years of schooling and management training had to teach something worth talking about. But, in terms of how many employees there usually are, as compared to managers, a reverse sequence of listening more and talking less, might be fairer. Not only that, but careful listening always gives you an edge on saying the right thing. Careful listening can alert the manager to important *communication "P" Points*, where small, but well-placed and well-timed comments can have a major impact on what employees hear and do. Moreover, when you don't say much, people tend to listen very carefully to what you say, when you do talk. The constant talker doesn't really get listened to. More time spent listening can lead to "two-eared listening," where you pick up on both *what* is being said or not being said, and *how* it is being said and what that means. There are a lot of important clues there, which will help determine what really needs to be said in response.

## Simplicity vs. Complexity

Every effective manager has evolved through the cycle of starting out doing things the most simple way possible and then getting things so complex nobody understands anything, only to realize the necessity of simplifying them again. Unfortunately education tends to teach us to make things more complex then they really need to be, by dividing everything and over-analyzing it all. It is probably the time to start putting things back together again. There will always be some tension here between management and employees. Simple things scare managers, who "know" there are no real shortcuts and that there is always a bigger picture to attend to; things can never be simple enough for employees. The object is to identify and sell simplicity just on the other side of complexity. That point is difficult to get to, but once there, it is one of those things everyone can agree upon. A good balance between thinking and acting (see # 10) can be a good way to get to this place.

### The Organization vs. Individuals

Traditionally, the good of the group and organization is always more important than the welfare of individuals. This is a very difficult position because it interrupts two fundamental but exclusive human drives: To be treated fairly in line with the rest of the group, but to be seen as unique and different from all others. Pure numbers dictate that general rule of organizational morality. While this rule is not likely to change, the way it is carried out may need some attention. Listening to and trying to understand individual employee's issues and concerns, is a good practice, even if you know beforehand you cannot honor them because of bigger and more important priorities. So is explaining *why* you are unable to bend and accommodate them.

### Thinking vs. Acting

Nothing is more unfair to employees than a manager who will not take action on reasonable requests. That conveys a lot of potential messages, which can be very counterproductive, like not being important enough to get concerns acted on. There is a built-in fear that once a decision is made and precedence has been set, nothing can ever be changed and negative results will be forever haunting. This fatalistic thinking is only true for those who believe it to be so.

The other side of this problem is that we have all been brainwashed into believing the ultimate rightness of *consistency*.

Reality, however, is rarely consistent. In fact, inconsistency may be the only thing that is really consistent. A smart manager will soon sort out what needs to be consistent for fundamental fairness within the organization, vs. what just needs to be consistent for the sake of convenience. Consistency should probably just be reserved for carrying out the most important consequences effecting employees.

## GIVE BACK STEWARDSHIP SERVICE

The wise leader not only applies the right principles of good leadership and practices the best management techniques and smartest activities, but he or she also displays important "P" point acts of stewardship service. Such small acts, when well-timed and well-placed can have major impact on leadership success and subsequent organizational productivity. Below are ten acts of stewardship that are worthy of becoming a permanent part of a leader's daily agenda:

### Lead by Example

Being an excellent role model is a valuable service, which takes continuous attention and effort. Such excellence requires your attention to what employees are and are not learning from you. It also requires you to consistently walk your talk by living the core values on which the organization is built. Another subtle but powerful act of service is to always follow-through and follow-up promises made to employees. Offering this valuable service to employees requires a conscious effort to remember to do it.

Carrying out a leadership role in the organization not only involves modeling basic behaviors and values but also learning new things that can stimulate employee's interest and productivity. This requires continuous learning on your part. That is also modeling behavior itself that attracts employee's attention.

### Build Self-esteem

The leader has to establish and maintain an overall climate that encourages and nurtures positive self-esteem. Care has to be taken to integrate this service into the goals and values of the organization, rather than allowing it to dangle as a secondary consideration. The climate most conducive to building positive self-esteem is one that has tolerance for mistakes, encourages reasonable risk-taking and offers frequent recognition. It is also one that follows helpful criticism with a demonstration of a better behavior. Here are ten pledges you can make to the employees in your organization that just happen to spell *self-esteem*:

- Spread trust by making sure you walk your talk and that you are completely trustworthy. A high level of trust is the basic building block of positive **S-E-L-F-E-S-T-E-E-M.**
- Encourage open and frank communication by being approachable and keeping employees well informed. People can't do what they don't know and performance failure is not particularly conducive to building confidence.
- Look for talent in everyone. Fashion jobs around this talent as opposed to trying to stuff square employees into round holes. When employees are confined by rigid job descriptions they don't have the opportunity to display the valuable talents they have.
- Focus on a passionate mission that gives employees clear direction, meaning and hope. People's confidence is always raised when they can become part of tangible, doable goals.
- Eliminate fear by separating reasonable motivational anxiety from debilitating job insecurity. First, take the time to learn what hidden fears are prevalent in your organization.
- Speak the truth honestly to build the foundation of trust. There is no other way to do this.
- Teach responsibility by clearly presenting expectations, providing appropriate training, removing obstacles and holding employees accountable for activities that help achieve the organization's mission.

- Establish a sense of future where employees know where they will be tomorrow.
- Express recognition frequently and in a variety of ways by getting to know what rewards each employee.
- Make time for play so that work can be fun.

### Be a Resource

Leaders must remain approachable, show resourcefulness openly and be aware of when employees need this expertise the most. Employees depend upon leaders to solve the more complex problems and to make sure they have all the necessary resources to do their jobs efficiently and comfortably. Employees need to know there is someone to go to when they need help. These two functions alone can prevent many performance problems in the making.

For instance, an employee may seem resistive to your instructions, but the real concern is not knowing what the expected level of performance is or what will happen when he or she fails to meet those unknown expectations. Sometimes being a valuable resource may just involve listening, answering questions, offering support and giving soft advice. Other times you must keep up in learning new resources for doing the job better.

### Teach

Employee learning is a continuous process and leaders should always be on the lookout for teachable moments where they can make a difference. Taking the time and effort to teach problem solving, offering useful self-disclosures, emphasizing the advantage of assertiveness and modeling the right attitude, are all investments that will have big payoffs. Leaders may have much knowledge and many talents they themselves take for granted. Teaching this information to employees is a valuable service. A good starting point is to learn how wide the gap is between yourself and employees.

### Demonstrate Kindness

Sometimes kindness is not exactly a priority, given all the other more important functions of a leader. However, being a kind leader enhances your ability as a salesperson, adds much to the influence of your role modeling and encourages more open communication. Being kind simply means making an effort to convey sincerity, putting your own needs aside now and then, holding back unnecessary criticisms, being helpful and showing sensitivity. It also means avoiding cynicism, vindictiveness, self-righteous superiority, self-importance and moodiness.

### Cultivate Virtues

An added responsibility of good role modeling is demonstrating important virtues. The leader must take advantage of critical moments to display acts of patience, fairness, trustworthiness and perseverance. Other virtues employees need to see include forgiveness, thriftiness, decency, courage and kindness. Things employees don't need to see are dishonesty, unreliability, sloppiness, unfairness and meanness. The organization's core values should be virtues that all employees should embrace, see and practice consistently. This process starts at the top.

### Enforce and Reinforce the Right Things

An important service a leader can provide employees is the diplomatic correction of undesirable behavior, demonstration of desirable behavior and the rewarding of desirable behavior, frequently and consistently. This is not a function the leader can delegate altogether. And leaders cannot assume that this is being done enough by others.

This valuable service requires the leader to get unstuck from his or her desk and do some walking around the plant or campus. It is important to know where, when and how to do this to have the most impact. For example, some employees actually respond better to public criticism whereas others prefer private sessions. All employees are different. There is one caution concerning the need for vigilant consistency and that is leaving a little wiggling room for employee's past records, present attitude and any mitigating or aggravating circumstances that warrant variation.

## Maintain Equilibrium

Maintaining a healthy balance within the organization is an important service that only the leader can deliver. There will always be a constant need to mediate between individual concerns and those of the overall organization, and to go back and forth between orchestrating productive change and maintaining stability. There will also always be occasions to switch between keeping employees productive and accountable and doing things to increase personal contentment and job satisfaction. Being in a balanced position, the leader offers a valuable view to share with employees.

## Mentor Someone

Leaders should hand pick employees who have good potential for leadership and take a few on as their students. This service involves leaders showing genuine interest in these employees, making leadership training available, giving career advice and offering a helping hand in career ladder-climbing. Such a service also requires leaders to stimulate these students to be their best. Too often there are lost opportunities to mentor greatness. Such mentoring is going on naturally, but without the mentor knowing it.

This mentoring role is important enough to take a side trip here. I am fortunate to have five good mentors who have come from unexpected places. Unfortunately, only one knows of his or her mentoring role in my professional development so maybe this is a good time to recognize their efforts. First there is Joyce, a secretary of long ago who still demonstrates the value of likability and reminds me that some problems just aren't solvable.

At about that same time there was Karen, the prison warden who was my first female boss. She had a knack for being able to demonstrate critical management skills such as problem-solving, conflict management and managing change, in such a way that it couldn't help but have lasting impact. She also encouraged my creativity in an environment where conservation was the rule, and asked difficult questions that always made me dig deeper for needed information.

Next came an older and wiser colleague Herb, the retired MIT professor who figured out how to reach prison inmates through the power and intrigue of mathematics instruction. He continues to be a valuable colleague who reminds me of the importance of humor. He also has a magical way of stimulating my creative thinking with his own subtle, indirect approach to ordinary things.

I also had a domestic partner who I affectionately called "Toots." She amazed me by the way she gently shared her intelligence instead of being superior or imposing. Her brilliant learning insights, practical applications of abstract principles and clear expression of difficult spiritual truths that all made their mark on me.

During all this time I have been lucky enough to have a lifelong friend Bob. He gives me the gifts of just listening, acknowledging my creativity and building my self-esteem. Thank you mentors!

### Keep a Scrapbook

A practical and fun service a leader can provide employees is to keep a company scrapbook. Pictures, news articles, important events, funny memos, organizational charts and social celebrations can all provide a valuable and interesting documented journal of where you've been and where you are going. Whenever I begin wondering if I am making any progress, I get out my old scrapbooks and remember all that I have done. The answer always erases self-doubt and the process always helps me to remember something from the past that is valuable.

### Be Active in Your Community

A final stewardship service for the leader is to play an active role in community groups such as churches, schools, welfare organizations and other civic groups. Here you can volunteer your time and donate your leadership talents for worthwhile goals to make life worthwhile for large numbers of deserving people. Sometimes your participation in these groups will encourage mutual benefits such as promoting your organization, offering the community groups unused spaces for meetings and employment opportunities.

Leadership excellence demands attention to many responsibilities including stewardship service. Often these "P" point acts of stewardship service can make the other responsibilities easier and help increase their impact. Stewardship service should not be seen as an obligation but rather as a worthwhile investment. It is the best way to say "thank you" to employees, your organization and the bigger community in which you live.

**Critical role-modeling "P" point question:** Are you who you pretend to be?

**➤ Three role-modeling "P" point actions:**

1. Pay closer attention to the image you project with the car you drive, the clothes you wear and the things you have in your office.
2. Find out the most important thing you say to others but don't do yourself.
3. Learn how people perceive you.

*"If you want to manage somebody, manage yourself. Do that well and you'll be ready to stop managing and start leading"* (Source Unknown).

# Management "P" Point # 2: Be a Likable Salesperson

# 3

"*You can catch more flies with a teaspoon of sugar than you can with a gallon of vinegar*" (Benjamin Franklin).

**Management Problem # 2:** Just like the tendency to forget to focus on your self in being a good role model, you may be inclined to over-attend to everyone else's unlikability. Often likability is not even seen as a management concern. Understanding that your likability can make everything else much easier is an attitude worth having. First you have to understand why that is so difficult to do. A big part of the problem is that you may be waiting to get certain things like success and contentment before you do the one thing that could easily get you those things-being likable.

## BE IRRESISTIBLY LIKABLE

A secret ingredient of most success is *likability*. What you may lack in talent can easily be made up with likability. The degree of your likability is based on ten important behaviors that are under your control. Here are ten simple suggestions, which will improve your likability and increase your success in all personal and professional areas.

### Look Your Best

Like it or not, we are all judged on how well we look. It is not a secret that our appearance plays a major part in the degree of success we have in anything from getting a job to finding a marriage partner. Unfortunately, we *do* judge books by their covers. It only makes sense for us to try and look our best and make a favorable first and lasting impression. It is one of those little things you can easily do to get big results.

Most of us aren't lucky enough to be born with drop-dead gorgeous or handsome movie star good looks, but that doesn't mean we can't do certain things to look our best. A few ordinary things that can improve your appearance include a friendly smile, warm and alert eyes, high energy, fashionable clothes, an easy-going nature, sensitivity and a pleasant voice.

Other appearance-improving behaviors are good grooming and hygiene, proper posture, adequate rest, regular exercise and all of these other suggestions below. It pays to cultivate all these things to help present yourself in the best possible light. Getting off on the right foot in looking your best is the quickest and surest way to get where you want to be.

### Demonstrate a Positive Attitude

We all know that it makes much more sense to have a positive attitude rather than a negative one. Negative attitudes don't get anybody anywhere. The thing we need to practice is having a positive attitude when things aren't going well or when we just don't feel like it. Other people respond to us much better when we are positive.

Being positive is highly contagious but so is being negative. Negativity of any sort decreases likability. This is especially relevant when it comes to something as important as your basic attitude toward life, which drives all the rest of your behavior. Do you express a positive attitude toward life consistently?

When others see you maintain a consistently positive attitude, even when things are going miserably, your stock value goes up considerably. We all like a good role model to follow and when you concentrate on being positive during adversity, you are being the best possible role model for others to like and follow.

Besides all this, there is a more concrete, practical reason for maintaining a steady positive attitude. A positive attitude improves the smile lines on your face, whereas a negative, pessimistic one only helps you develop an unattractive frown or scowl. Warm smiles open doors and cold frowns close them.

## Treat others with Reverence

There has never been a more practical, effective rule guiding our interpersonal behavior than the *Golden Rule.* There is never a situation in which this rule doesn't produce positive results. As children, we learned the value of treating others the way we wanted to be treated ourselves and it always worked well. Somewhere along the process of growing up, many of us have forgotten this simple but valuable rule.

We all want to be treated with polite respect, listened to, given reasonable freedom, be considered equal and be seen as worthwhile. When we give these things to others, we always get them in return. When we are controlling, judging, dishonest, uncaring, disrespectful, impatient and intolerant of others, that is what we get back in return too.

What is so hard about understanding the likely consequences of the way we treat others? The choice is really a no-brainer. A big part of increasing our own likability is treating others as if they were already being that way.

## Focus Mainly on Yourself

It usually takes awhile to finally figure out that focusing on others and trying to change them is a complete waste of time and effort. People make changes for themselves, not us. And we can't ever make others happy, only unhappy, so why try? If you are trying to change another person, the smart thing is to change something about yourself or your approach to that person which forces them to change in reaction to your change. Doing nothing and wishing for the other person to change first is not smart.

When you finally learn this lesson and begin to stop wasting so much of your time and energy worrying about other people, you have freed up much more of these valuable resources to use making yourself more likable. The idea has always been to control what you can control and let go of the rest. The only thing you can come close to controlling is yourself. Many of us have much to improve when it comes to likability and so time and energy are too precious to waste worrying about what other people are or aren't doing.

Probably the most important thing to focus on within yourself is the gap between where you are and where you want to be. How big is this gap? What are the main barriers that are keeping you from getting to where you really want to be? Can increasing your likability be a helpful shortcut?

### Practice Humility

Our world today makes it easy to be an egomaniac with the lure of personalized license plates, Web Pages, monogrammed clothing and all the other ways we have invented to draw attention to ourselves. But other people like humility, not big egos. If you have to tell people about yourself to get them to show interest, it will not do anything to improve your likability. On the contrary, there is nothing more other people like than a "quiet achiever" who has plenty to brag about, but doesn't.

Even if you are lucky enough to become famous and achieve much success, being humble is a small but powerful way to stay as likable as the way that got you famous and successful in the first place. Sometimes we forget how we got to where we are and it is good to have that humbling realization. I try to humble myself by realizing just how little I know compared to all that is knowable. I also like to lay down on the ground at night and look up at the stars to remember how insignificant I am compared to all that is.

Although most of us aren't famous celebrities, we all still have plenty of things about which we can still practice being humble in order to improve our likability ratings. We all have valuable knowledge, skills and abilities that we can use to help and serve others. When we learn to use our talents humbly, our help is much more likely to be accepted. It will also be more effective. The act of helping others unselfishly is a good way to boost likability. Do you do enough for others without wanting credit or expecting to get something in return?

### Control Negative Behaviors

Just like negative attitudes, negative behaviors such as worrying, blaming, complaining, arguing, moodiness, lying and gossiping, make us appear more unattractive both physically and socially. The smart way to control these behaviors is to slow down enough to catch each moment of opportunity that you have to react to each new situation in a positive way rather than in a negative way. Then it gradually becomes a positive habit that you don't have to control.

Understanding our own motivations behind negative behaviors can help too. Most negative behaviors are just a lazy way of not doing what we can to change something we don't like. Take complaining as an example. By complaining, we really just want someone else to solve a problem for us, instead of doing something about it ourselves. With worrying, if we take the time to do what we can to prevent the thing about which we are worrying come true, then we no longer have anything to worry about.

When you engage in negative behaviors such as reacting with anger or telling yourself how hopeless a situation is, you start feeling bad and that attracts more negative behavior. Then of course you start feeling worse. When you engage in positive behavior such as being assertive or solving problems, you start feeling better and start acting better. Then it becomes easier to keep going in that direction.

## Act Smart

Being smart is not necessarily imposing your high IQ on the rest of the world. Even people of average intelligence can act smart to improve likability and increase happiness and success. Acting smart involves plenty of ordinary things like asking good questions, taking the time to look below the surface of something in order to spot relationships, listening to your intuition, paying attention to the details of how something works and expressing your creativity.

The best way to define being smart is "doing whatever it takes to close the gap between where you are and where you want to be." That way smartness can mean more than just pure intelligence, which is not necessarily a likable sort of thing. In some situations high intelligence might even be intimidating. On the other hand, other people like smart people who get results by working hard, being clever and ingenious, thinking critically to sort through difficult problems, applying common sense and practicing all these other useful suggestions.

One of the best ways to start acting smart is to realize even small slips of your unlikable habits may be keeping you from being where you want to be. Sometimes all your past good behavior gets forgotten with one slip at the wrong time and place. That is a smart insight to allow yourself to have.

**Be Balanced**

By being balanced you can sometimes literally double both your likability and success. One of the most important areas that affects likability is the way you respond to others who are being unlikable. If you are *passive* and let them roll over you, that doesn't do much for your likability at all. If you go the opposite way and react *aggressively* and roll over them, you are sure to become unlikable. The balanced approach is being *assertive*, or standing up for your self without stepping on toes. When someone hurts your reputation with malicious gossip, the assertive approach is to confront the person with your hurt feelings.

Another way to double likability is to try and look at both sides of something. If you automatically exclude somebody else's point of view that is different from yours without trying to understand it first, you are excluding the person and he or she certainly won't like you. Taking the time to understand the other side of the coin can also give you something more to enjoy. The more you have to enjoy, the happier you are and the more you will be perceived as likable.

Being in balance in all the major areas of your life is a healthy position that can't help but result in much likability. Such balance involves learning how to work and play, pay equal attention to yourself and others, talking and listening, thinking and acting and giving and taking. The main benefit of being in the middle is that you can see in all directions and that increases your alternatives and helps you make the best choices.

Are you getting out of balance in certain areas of your life? Do you try to see both sides of an issue without judging and being critical?

## Enjoy Things

If there is one thing I have always tried to keep in mind it is my appreciation for all the opportunities there are in this life to enjoy things. In fact, there are very few things you can't enjoy if you simply suspend your tendency to judge things before you try them. When you can relax and enjoy the simpler things in life, you become happier and more content on the inside and that improves your external likability. Enjoying people is an excellent way to start doing this. Everyone has an interesting story that is worth listening to.

One lesson that seems to take some of us a little longer to learn is the one that helps us realize "you never get to have what you want until you learn to want what you have." This makes perfect sense from a gift-giver's perspective. Why give something more to someone who can't even appreciate what he already has? Learning to enjoy things that are right in front of you is a good way to increase your enjoyment and that should be enough reason in itself to do that. The fact that such an attitude will probably bring you more things to enjoy is icing on the cake. Why would you even hesitate a moment?

If the things you usually like to do seem to be getting too expensive for you to enjoy these days, it is time to make a list of items that represent "real wealth." These are the simple, inexpensive pleasures you can get from taking a walk in the forest, watching a sunset, reading a good book by the fireplace, making an imaginary gourmet meal out of left-overs, or listening to some great music on a comfortable sofa. Do you enjoy things enough? Can you appreciate simple pleasures?

## Grow and Improve

An important attitude to have is that growing and improving are a natural part of life for everyone and everything. We are all in the process of getting better at what we are doing. This is not to mean we aren't okay as we are. It simply means that we can all get much better and by not doing so, we are just loitering.

By putting all the above ten suggestions into practice, you are already improving and getting better. For instance, when you start paying more attention to your appearance, act smarter, be more reverent with others, show a positive attitude during adversity and control your negative behaviors, you improve your overall likability and increase your chances for success. This in turn builds self-confidence and that subsequently improves likability even more.

Likability is a simple but powerful way to close the gap between where you are and where you want to be. It is an extremely easy and effective tool to help you get more by actually doing less. Being more likable has big payoffs. Are you sure you are likable enough? Which of these suggestions will be most helpful to you in improving your likability? What needs to happen before you decide to get busy becoming more likable?

## BE A GREAT SALESPERSON

Successful management involves acquiring sales skills. Below are some selling "P" Points to help you master this new "career."

### Establish a Common Ground

Successful selling requires building rapport and trust with prospects in order to increase their comfort and familiarity with you and your product. The quickest way to do this is to find something you have in common with the other person. Do your homework ahead of time or do a quick study of the person's office to get the right clues. Fortunately, we all have much in common and the more commonalities you look for, the more you will find. Gradually you become an expert conversationalist who people respect, feel comfortable being around and like to listen to.

### Make People Feel Good about Themselves

Although people are often hesitant to talk about themselves, they do like the opportunity. Once you have established something you have in common with the other person, the best way you can get their ear is to give them both of yours first. Ask the person a few door-opening questions to determine what he or she is most interested in. Be sincere in complimenting people on their offices, positions, accomplishments, family or something they are obviously proud of. Also, never miss the opportunity to acknowledge another person's individual uniqueness. This is something we all need, in opposition to our drive to be connected.

### Be an Expert Communicator

To be successful in sales, you have to be an expert communicator. You have to know enough about your audience to say all the right things and avoid pushing any of the wrong buttons. You also have to listen aggressively to hear everything that is important. You may have to separate what is being said from how it is being said, along with what is said from what is not said. Time is always precious so careful planning of what you want to say and how to best say it, is a must. Learn to write headlines and speak sound bytes. Use symbols, statistics and metaphors strategically. Always meet people on their levels.

### Be Honest

Nothing is more disarming than honesty spoken clearly, directly and quietly. Honesty is also the quickest way to build trust and comfort. You, your product and your company all have weaknesses and shortcomings and there is no harm in admitting to a few of them. The fact is that nothing and nobody is perfect and none of us ever really expects that. People are not dumb and they always see right through smoke screens. All people really want is for you to be concerned enough to try and fix a problem when it does occur, which it will. You know that and they do too. Honesty is the safest common ground we all have.

### Follow Your Gut Instincts

We all had good survival instincts before we invented language. The fact is, language may confuse us and lead us away from trusting our gut feelings. This can be a big mistake and huge loss. Policemen, professional athletes, business executives and many other highly successful people depend upon their intuitive feelings everyday. There is no reason sales people shouldn't take advantage of this skill too. When your gut tells you to change the topic, follow up at a particular moment or that you have lost, then do what is most appropriate in a timely manner. Gradually, you become more comfortable in trusting these vague intuitive whispers that can help you avoid disasters and be more successful.

### Study the "Gap"

There is always a gap between you and the person to whom you are trying to sell something. The more you know about what makes up this gap, the quicker you will close it and the smaller the gap, the easier the sale. There can be a gap between what you think the person wants and what he or she actually wants or between what is wanted and what is needed. There can also be a gap in understanding between what you know and what the other person knows. One especially important gap is the one between how we all process information. Some of us need to see things in pictures, some of us need to hear their details in words, and some of us need to pick up and feel the thing we are trying to look and talk about. Successful sales involve a full arsenal of presentation types.

### Display a Sense of Humor

People enjoy and have fun laughing. It is good to take time out from the serious, difficult and complex world we live in today. We all need a welcome break in the stress and tension of modern-day living. Besides, humor is an effective gap-closer to get to common, safe ground where selling and buying are most comfortable. Collect good stories, colorful metaphors, catchy one-liners and funny jokes that you can use strategically in your conversation to break the ice, emphasize an important point or melt an iceberg. Be careful to delete anything that may be interpreted as offensive, though.

### Focus on the Positive

Over 75 per cent of what we see, hear or read today has negative content. Negativity is the strongest force that inhibits selling and you must eliminate it entirely. Always start out the discussion on a positive note, get the person to say "yes" frequently, and finish with an optimistic, upbeat phrase. Look for ways to turn negative comments and objections into positive outcomes. Control all unconscious negative body language and avoid being artificially positive, which can be a real turn-off. Sometimes you have to psyche yourself up with practicing positive mental imagery, which can be recalled when things start going south.

### Set Intermediate Goals

One of the most common mistakes in sports, counseling or business is to focus too much on the end outcome that is expected, like a Super Bowl championship, complete self-actualization or a record-breaking bottom line. All desired outcomes are made up of intermediate goals that must be achieved first. Selling is the same way, especially when it involves long-term relationship building. Always set and focus on a short-range goal for each phone call, piece of correspondence, meeting or follow-up. Try to avoid getting ahead of yourself and put all your attention and energy into the particular task of the moment. The object is to keep positioning yourself better to get to the next place you need to be, one step at a time.

### Seek Feedback Every Time

You can't improve and get better at what you do, if you don't ask what you are doing right and what you are doing wrong. Although it may feel uncomfortable asking for feedback, it is the only predictable way to achieve success. Oddly, we don't learn much from our successes, but it is from our failure experiences we can learn and grow the most. It is important to get accurate and useful criticism about our failures. A practical technique is to send follow-up notes asking for such feedback on a "report card" that is user-friendly and easy to return. Of course, colleagues can be especially helpful in giving you some useful hints for needed changes. All you have to do is ask.

Applying these ten practical *"P" Points* will improve your confidence and increase positive "sales" performance. Discover your own psychological power points to achieve excellence.

## KNOW THE ABC's OF LIKING

The reasons why and how people come to like each other can be explained by three primary rules. These rules are proximity, reciprocity and utility. Each of these is briefly discussed below.

### Proximity

People tend to be more attracted to other people who are "nearby," physically and psychologically, than those who are farther away. We are more likely to like another person if he or she has similar attitudes, values and beliefs. This is because dissimilarities are likely to result in unpleasant encounters, which would not be rewarding. We also tend to seek out people who we feel mutuality and equality with, regarding various aspects such as physical attraction, competencies, intellectual level, knowledge and interests.

### Reciprocity

People like others who already like them and who demonstrate their attraction by doing them favors and saying nice things about them. These rewards arouse positive feelings that reinforce the liking behavior. The point here is to make a conscious effort to initiate the liking in order to be liked. In this case, being likable may not be enough.

### Utility

People like others who satisfy their needs and who have needs that they can satisfy. This is the so-called *Exchange Theory* of social liking. The mutual liking continues so long as the utility of the relationship does. The rewards and costs of the interactions result in a psychological profit. However, when the rewards start decreasing and the costs increasing, there gets a point where the psychological profit gets in the red and produces a deficit. That is when the utility of such a relationship ceases and unlikability starts.

Obviously, liking behavior that is based on all three of these rules simultaneously will be much stronger.

## STRIVE TO HAVE THE IDEAL PERSONALITY

Over the past thirty-five years, I have asked the psychology students I taught to brainstorm all the traits they considered to make up the "ideal personality." This is their collective consensus of a comprehensive standard to strive toward in becoming a likable salesperson.

| | | | |
|---|---|---|---|
| Friendly | Positive attitude | Tolerant | Varied interests |
| Energetic/zestful | Confident | Happy | Peaceful |
| Dependable | Unselfish | Balanced | Empathetic |
| Competent | Outgoing | Honest | Morally upright |
| Trustworthy | Socially poised | Warm | Approachable |
| Non-judgmental | Agreeable | Thoughtful | Assertive |
| Open-minded | Humble | Articulate | Creative |
| Mature | Even-tempered | Funny | Attractive |
| Fair-minded | Good listener | Steady | Intelligent |
| Sensitive | Willing to grow | Intriguing | Diligent |
| Practical | Easy going | Team player | Stable |
| Helpful | Compassionate | Understanding | Polite |
| Realistic | Courageous | Forgiving | Predictable |
| Kind | Responsible | Patient | Supportive |
| Organized | Blends in | Goal-oriented | Adaptable |
| Loyal | Strong-willed | Loving | Interdependent |
| Generous | Wise | Centered | Respectable |

## GET ALONG WITH OTHERS

Here are some common sense tips from all the same students for getting along with others, which are guaranteed to improve your likability.

1. Treat others the way you want to be treated yourself.
2. Ask other people about themselves; take interest in them.
3. Listen to them and acknowledge what they are saying.
4. If you criticize the way somebody is doing something, take a little extra time and show him or her how to do it better.

5. Tell the other person when he or she is saying or doing something that offends you or hurts your feelings.
6. Avoid unnecessary defensiveness by not conveying arrogance, over-controlling behavior, dogmatic certainty, and accusatory or judgmental attitudes.
7. Don't make promises you can't deliver and deliver the ones you make.
8. Take the time to understand why a person thinks and acts the way he does (there are usually very good reasons, even for the most bizarre behavior).
9. Don't ask questions you already have your own answers to and don't force dishonest, artificial or incomplete ones.
10. Be fundamentally fair in giving and taking.
11. Be tolerant of things another person doesn't have any control over.
12. Don't take your stress out on others.
13. Do more listening as you do talking.
14. Be sensitive to the other person's needs.
15. Always take time to think about what you want to say and try to say it as clearly and simply as you can. Always clear up any potential misunderstanding.
16. Be able to give in when something is more important to the other person.
17. Don't impose unsolicited advice or criticism on another person; wait until he or she asks for it.
18. Don't waste your time trying to change the way another person thinks or acts, you won't ever be successful and you will only frustrate yourself.
19. Always try to smile and be friendly, especially when you don't feel like it.
20. Be more patient than you think you can be.
21. Practice good manners and be polite. Be nice and kind to people who need it.

22. Don't tell another person something he or she is not ready to hear, just to get it off your chest.
23. Don't lose your temper unless it is advantageous.
24. Don't waste your time hanging around negative people who can't do you any good. They just drain you and keep you from being your best with others who deserve your attention more. Hang around people who have similar values to yours.
25. If you have to do something unpleasant or unpopular, take some time to explain your reasons ahead of time.
26. Learn how to walk away from destructive, emotional situations where you can't win from losing.
27. Learn the art of getting through difficult conflicts with others instead of avoiding them; conflicts offer opportunities to learn much about your self.
28. Look for the things you have in common with others and focus less on the differences that may irritate you.
29. Give people compliments.
30. Respect other's private space and don't crowd them.

**Critical likability "P" point question:** What makes you most unlikable?

➤ **Three Likability "P" point actions:**

1. Take some time out from a hectic schedule to be sociable with employees.
2. Demonstrate admirable patience during the next crisis situation.
3. Gain more control over your most unlikable habit.

*"If you're not using your smile, you're like a man with a million dollars in the bank and no checkbook"* (Les Giblin).

# Management "P" Point # 3: Listen Twice, Talk Once

4

"*Nothing is so simple that it cannot be misunderstood*" (Jr. Teague).

**Management Problem # 3:** Communication is the main tool by which managers give direction, share important ideas, get input and provide feedback. The trouble is that all the spoken and written words can easily get lost in the present information overload that has us all overwhelmed, without a concerted effort to make them stand out with maximum clarity and impact. We also disregard basic anatomy which tries to tell us to talk with one mouth and listen with both ears.

## PRACTICE KEY ELEMENTS OF POWER COMMUNICATION

Today being a good communicator is not enough. Professional success requires superior *power communication* skills. Here are six steps to help you take your good communication skills to the next higher level:

### Develop a Signature Style

Study your best personality traits and build a unique style of communication based on those traits. Match the way you talk or write with all that makes you a unique, dynamic, successful individual. Make sure your communication style is versatile enough to include a full array of characteristics that will cover a wide range of situations and audiences. At times you will need charm and emotional charisma, other times serious rationality and detail and other times generalizations and light levity.

Develop an effective cool-headed, problem-solving style of communication to use in tight, tense situations. Nurture the likability aspects of your personality and communication style in normal situations. Let your communication style convey who you are in a distinct, positive way, while saying what you mean to say with maximum clarity and explosive impact. Leave a speaking and writing signature for people to remember.

### Accommodate Audience Differences

Every audience and each individual member of an audience has a unique communication style. These unique differences play an important role in communicating with an audience. You have to understand and adjust to important audience differences to remove potential obstacles and make the best connection. The more time you spend getting to know the audience and planning your communication, the better.

Audience differences include varieties of information processing styles such as seeing, hearing, reasoning and feeling. Other differences are listening skills, intellectual levels, degrees of open-mindedness and thinking vs. feeling orientation. The power *communicator* will get to know the specific differences of the audience and customize communication content and style to maximize connection and impact.

Stop and think about the particular audience with who you are trying to communicate, *before* you start talking or writing. What motivates these people? Does the person see pictures or hear words? What range is the group's understanding or interest? What deadly hot buttons need to be avoided? What has gone on before or what may happen afterwards, that will effect what I am trying to communicate? Taking the time to answer these and other difficult questions will help bridge the gap between you and your audience.

### Practice Two-eared Listening

We probably wouldn't get much dissent if we made the claim that poor listening is the biggest obstacle to good communication. However, it depends on what is meant by good listening. Good listening goes beyond just paying close attention, clarifying potential misunderstanding, putting aside personal biases and avoiding distractions. Those are obvious obstacles we should all be able to avoid easily.

Power listening requires aggressive "two-eared" listening, which hears *everything*. This is when you learn to use both ears to hear *what* is being said over the clamor of *how* it is being said. It also involves tuning into what *isn't* being said which may be more important that what *is* actually being said. Power listening begins with the realization that there is a good reason why we have two ears and only one mouth.

### Play With Word Psychology

Rarely will your communication only convey denotative, or strict dictionary definitions of your words. This is even true when your message is straight and to the point. Most of the time it is the other things that your words *imply,* which will be heard loudest and remembered longest. These other things can include the non-verbal gestures you use to emphasize your words, the common connotations of the words you use, or the images or values that may be connected to your words. Even voice tone, word ambiguity, or silence can modify what you are trying to say. Unfortunately, much of *what* you say is lost to *how* you say it. If your message is not received the way you meant it, then some adjustments have to be made.

*Power communication* involves choosing words wisely that clearly convey powerful images or meanings, such as lightening bolt, crucifixion, or a ten foot chartreuse hairy alien. These image words can be delivered in unusual formats such as metaphors, alliterations, aphorisms, or panache. The object is to always use your communication style to flatter and enhance the content of your message, rather than confuse or take away from it.

### Write Headlines, Speak Audiobytes

There is a plethora of information already available for consumption that is overloading us all. This requires you to show that what you are saying or writing is more valuable than what is already out there. To be successful at doing this, you must communicate with utmost clarity and high impact. Also, never underestimate the importance of the packaging which is wholly responsible for the initial draw.

Plan clear, concise and high impact “headlines” to lead the charge of your message with good propaganda. Follow this with a clever emotional hook to connect with your audience and then outline three supporting rational points to which there can be no objections. Reinforce these points with unforgettable audiobytes and summarize everything in one sentence. For best results, use unusual words or invent them yourself, such as cooptetition, creatuitivity or extrapreneur. Write and speak as though every word costs money and you are working from an extremely tight budget.

### Measure Success

You must set up a reliable and accurate way to measure the success of your communication. Begin to ask yourself and others tough questions. Are you talking too loudly or too softly? Are you over-intellectualizing with too much jargon? Do you let annoying, distracting mannerisms get in the way? Are you into style or content too much or too little? Are you making real contact with your audience? Are you believable? Are you saying anything worth listening to? Moving from good to excellent communication requires answers to these and many other difficult self-deprecating questions.

*Power communication* requires practice and continual self-analysis, but the payoffs yield high dividends both personally and professionally. Practice *power communication* daily in all your interactions with others. Let your best personality characteristics speak for you, use words that people can *see* or *feel*, and customize your communication to the unique characteristics of your audience. Practice aggressive two-eared listening, be economical, and seek useful feedback on needed improvements.

## ASK GOOD QUESTIONS

Most of what we do or say is based on what we know. Much of what we know comes from the answers we get to the questions we ask. If we want to be successful in doing anything, it would seem that the best starting point is learning how to ask the right questions in the right way. A departed lawyer friend of mine left me with this valuable advice: "The quality of the answer is related to the quality of the question."

The main purpose of asking a question should be to get accurate, clear, concise and complete information. To improve chances of getting this type of information, you need to stop asking the wrong questions in the wrong ways. Below are some suggestions to improve the quality of answers you get by upgrading the quality of questions you ask.

### Accuracy

To improve accuracy of answers, it only stands to reason that you have to eliminate the content and style of questions that can generate deceit, defensiveness, over-control or wrong assumptions. Questions that are leading, accusing, tricking, probing, assuming or baiting do this too well. Examples are: "Why did you make such a stupid, irresponsible mistake?" "You made a mistake before, so how do I know if you aren't doing the same thing again?" "At least two other people heard you yell at her, are you calling them liars?" "You really don't trust me, do you?"

If you think someone doesn't trust you and you want to know something that can actually help you understand, try asking, "What have I done in the past that would indicate that I am not trustworthy?" Or ask, "What can I do now to regain your trust?" Sometimes a simple exchanging of the words "You" and "I" can set a more supportive tone to open the way for more accurate communication.

When you have to ask emotional questions, make a special effort to eliminate all chances of creating a defensive climate. Defensiveness almost always produces distorted information. Avoid sounding too controlling, authoritative, superior, certain or accusatory. If you want to find out whether or not someone said something wrong, ask, "Now tell me in your own words, what exactly did you say?" If there is a dispute, you might try prefacing your question with, "We seem to have some different perceptions as to what went on." Then ask, "Can you help me understand what you saw happening?"

One of the worst habits you can get into is the one of asking someone a question when you already have the answer. Just like throwing a pass in football, there are only three things that can happen and two of them are bad. You will either get the lie you expected which really doesn't answer anything, or you will hear something that you may not be prepared to hear. Avoid the tendency to want to paint someone into a corner with his or her back against the wall just so you can prove your point. If you have your facts, you can present them in a statement and then invite the other person to prove you wrong.

## Clarity

To increase understanding of information, it is important to avoid awkward phrasing, confusing language, abstract ideas or just plain nonsense. You must ask straightforward, simple, concrete and sensible questions. Think about what you want to ask and then ask it directly, in the most simple, easy to understand words in a short sentence. Avoid sarcasm, long-winded statements, jargon, ambiguous words and abstract concepts. Give specific, tangible examples to help avoid any chance of misunderstanding. Sometimes the best question to ask is, "Do you completely understand what I am asking?" You may even try asking yourself if you understand what you are asking. If your question isn't understood, don't just repeat it. Reword it.

If someone is late and you want to know why, ask him, "Why were you late?" If you want to know if someone loves you, you may want to first invest some time establishing a mutual understanding of what exactly that means. If you have trouble figuring out how to ask a question, that should be a clue that you need to get clearer yourself as to what you want to know and why you want to know it. Sometimes we make a question more difficult than it needs to be by beating around the bush. When someone smells badly, you may just have to ask, "Have you taken a bath today?"

You've heard the statement that there aren't any dumb questions. Unfortunately there *are* plenty of dumb questions to avoid asking. However, when you have a gut feeling about this question you would like to ask but usually don't out of fear of ridicule—that is probably the one you *should* ask. My favorite such question is, "What is the main purpose of this meeting?"

### Completeness

Although there has to be some limit as to the length of an answer, critical blank spots from a hasty question can be worse than too much information. Sometimes rigorous follow-up is necessary to avoid the loss of important information you need to know. If the first question gets a shallow answer, then a second one should start by acknowledging that deficiency and then be reworded to dig deeper.

To improve the chances of getting more complete information, don't flavor the question with artificial limits. Avoid asking questions such as, "Give me one good reason why you think that?" You may be wrongly assuming there is only one good reason and that the reason is actually a "good" one. When you want to get useful, well-rounded feedback about how you are doing, you may have to encourage frankness and completeness by giving permission. You can do this by saying, "I respect your opinion, so feel free to tell me all the good and bad things I am doing." At times, a simple follow-up opens the door for more complete information, such as "Is there anything more you might like to add?"

### Conciseness

We are already overloaded with too much information and so global, completely open-ended questions that only encourage more rambling should be avoided. Careful thought has to be given to phrase a reasonably open-ended question with some direction and structure. The object is to get complete, but manageable information.

Unless you have all day and night to listen to the answer, don't ask, "Tell me all about yourself?" or "How do you feel?" Think about what you really want to learn about the other person and how much you are willing to listen to and ask just that.

The quality of answers to broad sweeping questions in job interviews can be improved with a brief explanation ahead of the question with some limitations added. For example, phrase such a question like this: "We want to know how organized you are. Please tell us some of the more important ways you typically organize a new job?"

Think about questions you are asking and the answers you are getting. If the information you are getting seems to be wrong, unclear, too abundant or incomplete, think about what you may be doing that is bringing about those results. First think about what it is you want to know. Then plan a question that will allow honesty, insure accuracy, be easily understood, and result in complete but concise information. Good questions can't help by inspire good answers. Ask the right question in the right way and you will get useful information, which you can act on correctly to assure success.

## AVOID COMMUNICATION TERMITES

The foundation of any group or individual relationship is built with good communication. Without being detected, *communication termites* can be working behind the scenes, crumbling that foundation. Conduct an inspection to see if any of the following communication termites are eating away the foundations of your important work relationships.

### Assumptions

Assumptions are your brain's lazy way of answering questions your mouth needs to be asking. There is no room for making assumptions in the communication process. It is often those very assumptions, which are the focus of your communicating, so why short-circuit the process? Instead of assuming something, ask a question to find out the real answer. You may even be able to use it to answer another employee's question.

### Preoccupations

Your own preoccupations as a manager will dominate and interfere with any interaction, so it is best to make the conscious effort to put them aside when you are trying to communicate. One way to do this is to realize you may not be managing your time or priorities well enough, or you wouldn't have these things occupying so much space in your mind. Use your spare time productively to find solutions to those things about which you are preoccupied so you can communicate with an open mind.

### Hurriedness

Good communication requires patience. First of all, there is not much chance of getting it right the first time. The second go around offers the opportunity of clarifying any misunderstanding, and that is what usually translates the confusion back into clarity. Good communication takes time. Conveying a sense of hurriedness during communication is neither smart nor respectful of the other person.

### Judgments

You are bound to make judgments, but when the other person perceives these judgments you will be judged back, which gets neither one of you anywhere. Such mutual judgments create a climate of defensiveness, which most always shuts down communication. You can't do much about the human habit of judging, but you *can* choose neutral words and ways of communicating those words that do not emphasize the judgments.

### Beliefs

It doesn't make much sense to try and communicate beliefs. These things are highly personal, usually unverifiable, often wrong, and extremely resistive to change. Most of the time, the attempted exchange of beliefs doesn't have a happy ending. Time can be better used to developing good communication techniques such as practicing active listening or improving clarity, completeness and conciseness in your speech.

### Routines

Saying the same thing in the same way over and over again is the best way to get tuned out and risk losing all impact. Changing both the content and style of delivering your messages requires a significant amount of effort, but the payoff is worth it in producing better communication. You can easily get caught up in a boring communication routine if you don't take the time to see yourself doing so. Experiment with new words, word psychology and animated presentations. Try paraphrasing, asking more questions and using silence strategically. Avoid depending on familiar "fillers."

## Moods

Just like our human habit of judging, moodiness is normal but it must be controlled during the communication process. The only way you can do this is to realize it simply isn't fair to impose your bad moods on someone who wants to tell you something important or get a constructive answer to a compelling question. Fundamental fairness dictates that you set your mood aside when you are communicating. Isn't that what you expect?

## One-Eared Listening

One-eared listening occurs when you allow yourself to get caught up in the trap of over-attending to the noise of *how* something is being said while missing *what* is actually being said. It also happens when you only hear what *is* being said while failing to listen closely to what *isn't* being said which may be more important. Good communication requires aggressive two-eared listening, which hears *everything*.

## Non-Verbal Behavior

Wrongly interpreted non-verbal cues can hinder good communication and even destroy relationships. This is unfortunate, because all it takes to prevent such a disaster is to take the time and verify the interpretation. There is a further difficulty to consider here too. We think we can accurately interpret non-verbal behavior verbally, but we really can't. They are two entirely different things. Verbal communication is definitive, concrete and tangible, while non-verbal communication is ambiguous, abstract and intangible.

## Bad Timing

Good communication is always a proper mixture of what to say, how to say it and *when* to say it. Often, it is the right timing, which produces the best results. Bad timing can be responsible for poor communication that may never get straightened out, so it pays to plan when the best time may be to say something or ask a particular question. When someone asks you a question that might be the best time to work something in you have been trying to say all along. That is when you have 100 per cent of the person's attention. Saying it at the wrong time may preclude that opportunity.

## Misconnections

Just about everytime you communicate, you are dealing with a different audience with different characteristics, abilities and interests. Failure to tune into these differences and adapt your communication content and style accordingly, is a sure way to lose impact or miscommunicate altogether. When a person needs to see a concrete picture and you lecture with irrelevant details, you are wasting your time because nothing is getting communicated.

## Myopia

It is extremely difficult to avoid self-centered thinking, but that unchecked habit can interfere significantly with the communication process. When you over-screen all new incoming information through your own viewpoint and other perceptual biases, you are really not participating in communication. You are just reinforcing your own viewpoint, distorting reality, and missing valuable new information. Doing more listening than talking is the best way to cure this fault.

**Critical power communication "P" point question:** When was the last time you stopped to ask a colleague how effective a communicator you are?

> **Three power communication "P" point actions:**
>
> 1. Look through a dictionary or Thesaurus and identify some powerful words that produce dynamic images, for later use.
> 2. Catch and correct yourself the next time you are just listening so you can fire back a good response, rather than listening to understand better.
> 3. Update your resume to speak simply, clearly and have unbeatable impact, all on one page.

"*Quality questions create a quality life. Successful people ask better questions and as a result they get better answers*" (Anthony Robins).

# Management "P" Point # 4: Think with a Big IQ

5

*"A thought that does not result in action is nothing much, but an action which does not proceed from thought is nothing at all"* (Georges Beranos).

> **Management Problem # 4:** Many of us put forth a great effort to act smarter than we really are. The energy we use to maintain this façade depletes the mental strength we need to think critically, which *is* being smart. Like a few of these other problems, you have to reach the point of being able to admit what you don't know before you can start learning what you need to know. Critical thinking starts with thinking about your thinking, which you have to think about first.

## BOOST YOUR THINKING IQ

One of the most important skills we can have is the one of *critical thinking*. The ability to think critically is essential to success in any activity. Critical thinking will help us get more complete and correct information to make better choices and wiser decisions, use our time smarter, use more sound judgment, and develop more effective strategies for getting what we want and getting to where we want to be. There is probably no better way to make the best use of what intelligence with which we were lucky enough to be born, than to learn how to think more critically. Critical thinking can make an average person smart and a smart person brilliant.

I recently came across what I think is one of the most valuable documents about critical thinking I've ever seen and it came from a very unlikely source—The CIA website on the Internet! This book, entitled, "The Psychology of Intelligence Analysis," was written by; Richards, J. Heuer, Jr., a 47-year veteran administrator of the Central Intelligence Agency. This book explains our mental machinery behind the actual processes of human cognition—how we perceive, gather information, think, form beliefs, make judgments and decisions, remember and get creative. The book was designed to help CIA analysts improve critical thinking skills and the subsequent quality of American intelligence information they could give government policy makers. However, the author's ideas have wide applicability to help us all improve our ability to think more critically about *anything*, and increase chances of being more successful in what ever we are doing.

I have taken some ideas from this book and joined them with my own ideas, along with important research in cognitive psychology, to form this section. Below are some of the more important realities as to how human beings typically operate mentally—the mental machinery behind the actual processes of human cognition—how we perceive, gather information, think, form beliefs, make judgments and decisions, remember and get creative. Becoming more aware of these cognitive processes and how they actually operate will enable you to make the changes you need to make in order to start thinking more critically and get better results in what you are trying to do.

### Thinking About Thinking

Our greatest challenge is to slow our minds down long enough to start thinking *about* thinking. This is the point at which we finally find out the quality of our thinking isn't all that it could be. Then we can begin to uncover all the typical obstacles to being able to think critically, which are discussed below. Just like the problems caused by poor communication, thinking problems can't be sorted out until we start talking *about* them. A relevant bit of advice comes from former UCLA basketball coach John Wooden, who once said, "When you finally open up to admitting all that you don't know, you start learning much."

### Most Thinking is Unconscious

The actual process of *thinking* is mostly unconscious, meaning that we aren't aware of what is going on inside our heads. What we *think* we are thinking is only the resulting thoughts of that unconscious process. We are usually a day late and a dollar short. Critical thinking is the attempt at understanding this unconscious thinking better so that it becomes more conscious. The object is to rearrange the horse *before* the cart so we can stop *reacting* to our thoughts and start *acting* with them. Much of the information we have inside our heads may be wrong, but being unconscious, we can't correct it until we know about it.

### Over-Simplification

Our brains are designed to simplify reality greatly so we can deal with it easier. Otherwise, we would get too overwhelmed by all the volume and complexity of what is really going on around us. (Here I am reducing libraries of 400+ page books and thousands of research projects down into a couple of pages!) In essence, we may be missing most of what is going on in any given situation because of our brain's natural tendency toward tunnel vision.

When you fail to look below the surface, you are failing to see many of the more important core problems and real causes of the less important, simpler symptoms you see above the surface. Critical thinking makes you become more aware of your basic need to over-simplify things, realize the benefit of opening up to all the possibilities you are missing and then start looking harder. Some good advice comes from former Chief Justice Oliver Wendell Holmes: "I wouldn't give a plug nickel for simplicity this side of complexity, but for the simplicity just on the other side of complexity I would give my life."

### Mirroring

One particular over-simplification habit you can get easily get caught up in is assuming that the way *you* think is common for everyone. You project your thinking style onto other people and interpret their behavior in terms of your own thinking manner. Critical thinking helps you to understand how different people actually are when it comes to their thinking. Peoples' "brainprints" are as different as their fingerprints. Not only is the content of peoples' minds different, but so is the manner in which they get and use all that content.

### Certainty Obsession

The mind is poorly wired to deal effectively with uncertainty. We need to reach closure in arriving at certainty, no matter what it takes. We are driven to explain and understand everything logically and rationally. This often includes filling in the empty gaps with incorrect or incomplete information and arriving at totally artificial interpretations. Like it or not, some events are random and accidental and defy reasonable explanation. Critical thinking can help you build tolerance for ambiguity and tentativeness. It also cautions you from rushing into completing things wrongly just to get them done or explain things incorrectly just to be able to move onto something else.

### The Conservative Mind

The human mind is basically conservative and resists change, especially anything that causes unsettling disruption. We tend to keep on using older solutions that have worked well in the past long after they have become obsolete, solely because they are comfortable and familiar. Critical thinking allows you to learn new and valuable information from surprise. Critical thinking evaluates change fairly instead of automatically rejecting it.

### The Lazy Mind

Along with this conservative nature, the mind is also lazy. There is much "half-thinking" that goes on. Examples are: "Satisficing," or the tendency to select the first identified alternative that appears good enough, the failure to generate a full range of potential answers, the failure to look for disconfirming evidence, and the failure to consider the different values of different evidence. Critical thinking takes you from just sitting down and thinking about a problem to really analyzing a problem.

### Biased Perception

We take in new information through the act of *perception.* This process is dominated by many influential biases, which *distort* this incoming information. Information can be over-flavored by cultural values, education, expectations, personal needs, upbringing, past experiences, etc. Critical thinking helps you separate yourself from these biases so that you can begin to see things more the way they are rather than how you want, need or expect them to be. This is extremely difficult to do, but in order to ever arrive at an objective opinion or make a fair judgment, you have to be able to put aside perceptual biases.

### Reality-limiting Viewpoints

One of the most important outcomes of our perception process is the formation of a *viewpoint*. This is our perspective of reality. Something to be aware of though, is that this viewpoint is more a function of the location from where we are looking, rather than what we are seeing. People kept thinking the world was flat until they kept moving locations without ever finding the edge. Critical thinking helps you become more aware of the influence of the *perspective* from which you are looking at a situation, so that you don't become the dog being wagged by the tail. When you become able to question your own major viewpoints, you open yourself up to whole new worlds. This is how most great inventions and discoveries occur.

### Unsubstantiated Beliefs

Some of the most important information we have is in the form of *beliefs*. It normally takes very little information or facts to form a belief, but it takes tons of proof to undo one. We actually search out new information that confirms what we already know or believe, and we reject any new information that disputes what we think to be true. Critical thinking helps us realize how we may just be perpetuating wrong information this way and helps us to gradually unlock our close-mindedness to evaluate new information more fairly. Critical thinking also guides us to the principle of *inclusion*, or trying to discover what points of agreement contained in a different viewpoint can be included in our own perspective.

### Unverified Assumptions

Much of what we believe to be true or decide to act on is based on underlying assumptions that we either don't see or see and don't verify. These assumptions are just the brain's lazy way of answering questions our mouths should be asking. Critical thinking helps us spot these assumptions and ask more questions, before we act on wrong information. This simple maneuver can double our chances of being successful.

### Over-generalizing

We can be quick to over-generalize results from a very small sample of "proof." A brief personal experience quickly becomes a universal law, unless it gets questioned by critical thinking. Critical thinking seeks reasonable proof.

### Quantity over Quality

Getting more information may not always help improve the correctness of your judgment though. It may just serve to increase your confidence in that judgment. You usually have enough information way before you think you do, but just haven't analyzed it in the right way. Or, there may just be one assumption you need to check out. Critical thinking helps improve the quality of your thinking about the information you already have and then be able make the right decisions and predictions without requiring you to waste time trying to gather more information. Critical thinking is smarter thinking, not just more thinking. Shifting from quantity to quality makes more room for both.

### Concrete over Abstract

Information that is vivid, concrete and personal has greater impact on our thinking than second-hand, more abstract information that may actually have substantially greater value as evidence. Critical thinking makes us aware of the value of this distinction and frees us to see the right evidence for its true value.

### Linear Cause & Effects

We have an especially hard time with evaluating causes and effects accurately and completely. We overestimate the importance of the internal personal characteristics, attitudes and personality of individuals and underestimate the importance of external or situational determinants of a person's behavior such as incentives and constraints, role requirements, social pressures and other forces outside an individual's control. We overestimate our own importance of being a cause or a target of others' behavior and we often perceive relationships that do not in fact exist. Critical thinking expands our viewing area to catch all these biases and even lets us see that some effects are actually causes in disguise. Things are not always the way they first appear.

## Uncreativity

Developing creativity is the best way to undo the many mental ruts we unknowingly engage in that lead to incorrect or incomplete information, poor judgment, wrong decisions and costly mistakes. Developing creativity is more of an attitude than a skill and it can certainly be acquired. Creative thinking is enabled by deferring our tendency to be prematurely judgmental, lifting any self-imposed constraints, and realizing that quantity of ideas will eventually lead to quality. Creativity can also be developed by experimenting with using old information in new and unusual ways, thinking backwards, analogizing to other fields and perspectives different from our own, questioning basic assumptions and working in environments that value creativity.

## Thinking and Feeling Confusion

Thinking and feeling are constantly interactive and sometimes we have a difficult time separating one from the other or knowing which is driving the other. Sometimes we feel a certain way and then have disturbing thoughts about that feeling and other times we think a certain thing and then end up feeling a certain way about that thought. Separating our thinking from our emotions is a challenge but what we usually find out from doing this is that many beliefs and things we think are true are based more on emotions than cold hard facts.

Furthermore, responding to another person's emotionality with your own emotions can only result in uproar. This is when you *must* separate your thoughts and feelings. Critical thinking can help you uncover all these tendencies, especially when they are working against you or otherwise keeping you from seeing the truth or getting desired results.

### Not Acknowledging Being Part of the Cause

Probably the most important thing critical thinking can help us realize is the fact that we are always an active player in any situation of which we are part. There is no such thing as an impartial, objective, passive observer and there is rarely a single cause, which produces a single effect. Things are always already going on. You will always have some influence in changing any situation you are in.

You are often already part of an ongoing situation before you know it. When you interview employees, your style of asking questions will influence their answers and when you are conducting an investigation, your approach to the evidence will help determine the outcome of the investigation. You really can't do much to change this reality, but just being aware of your active role in any given situation, is a big step in critical thinking to limit any causal effects you don't want to bring about.

### Dualistic Thinking Trap

The greatest challenge of critical thinking is to rise above the trap of *dualistic thinking* where we are convinced of the rightness or wrongness of something without allowing any varying shades of gray in the middle. This dualistic thinking is a major way that the brain simplifies reality for us. Everything is either yes or no, up or down, in or out. It can't get any simpler than that. But is that really the way it is?

Interestingly, an extended quantity of this either-or thinking finally takes us to seemingly unsolvable problems in the form of *paradoxes*. This is where we get stuck and frustrated and make no progress until we get uncomfortable enough to do something about the situation. These paradoxes, however, are not problems but rather *symptoms* of the real problem of dualistic thinking. Paradoxes cannot be solved with the same kind of thinking which created them in the beginning. Critical thinking helps us to separate the surface meaning of the words that define the paradox from those of its implied meaning. Then we can decide what to *include* from both, rather than *excluding* one or the other in a continued dualistic fashion. In other words, the only way out of this dilemma is to figure out how you can "eat your cake and have it too."

## WORK SMART

Whether you are an office manager, a construction site manager, a corporate executive, or The President of the United States, you have one important resource in common. This important resource is *time.* Oddly, time is probably the only natural resource that is equally distributed. Unfortunately time is not equally valued or used appropriately, much of the time.

There are twenty-four hours in each day. Subtracting eight for sleeping, two for eating, hygiene and other bodily functions and two more for odds and ends such as going and coming, that leaves is a total of twelve hours each day to be productive. If you have a normal schedule, you will be working 8-10 hours, with 2-4 hours left over for recreating. Sometime we may want to question that remarkable imbalance, but that is another issue in itself.

So how can we save 12 hours a day to be more productive? Here are 12 common sense suggestions to turn time wasters into time savers.

### Stop Reacting to Other People's Emergencies and Non-Priorities

To be a good time manager you must be ruthless in setting and keeping your own urgent priorities. You must also avoid getting caught up in responding to other people's semi-emergencies and non-priorities. Learning to say no and demonstrating the importance and value of what you are doing are two good skills to learn. By taking the time to react to other people's poor planning and unimportant requests, you teach them to continue such inefficient use of their own time and waste your time to boot. That can be *two* lost hours.

### Stop Making Bad Choices

When you make a wrong choice that gets undesirable results, you usually have to start all over again and make several right choices to get back to the starting block to be in the right place to be able to achieve the desirable results you were trying for the first time. You are then spending double the time you need to be spending on what you are trying to do. Do it right from the beginning and you don't have to do it over again. And learning how to do it right the first time can save valuable learning time with your approach to the next similar situation that comes along.

### Think More Critically

Simplistic or superficial thinking wastes a significant amount of time. Our brains are designed for maximum efficiency by labeling and categorizing things for easy retrieval, but that process can boomerang if you are not at least aware of it. Very few things are black and white, cut and dry or this or that. There are always many complicated interactions going on below the surface that need to be understood if you are going to be successful in doing something. An ounce of thoughtful understanding can result in a ton of results.

### Make Insignificant Decisions Hastily and Deliberate on the Difficult Ones

Paralysis can set in when you start tabling little, insignificant decisions, worrying you might select the wrong choice of actions. In doing that, you rush the important decisions that come along and then risk having to go back and do some damage control or repair work when these hastily made wrong decisions don't get the desired outcome for which you had hoped. Learn to separate simple decisions that can be easily rectified when wrong, from the difficult ones that need to be made correctly. This is a skill that can save much time in the future.

## Separate Core Problems from Surface Symptoms

Surface symptoms are usually so luring that they distract you from what is actually *causing* them. Problems such as poor performance and negative attitudes can be time-consuming in trying to cure. Curing symptoms just suppresses the real problem and makes it even more difficult to access. The problem just re-occurs requiring more time to deal with later.

In regards to poor performance and negative attitudes, the core problem might be a poor employee selection process, inconsistent sanctions, unclear expectations or an underground informal power structure—all of which can show up with enough symptoms to occupy your attention for a year or so. That is a lot of lost hours.

## Invest 59¢ in a Do-List Tablet

Sometimes a little cash investment can have big payoffs. This is the case of a pre-printed Do-List, which will help you avoid forgetting what your priorities are for the day. Actually, the main benefit is to plan and think about what your priorities *should be*. Writing them down takes them from your head to your hands. Your priorities are more likely to get accomplished when you have to look at them all day. They won't go away until they get done. Getting them done can result in satisfaction and pride, which will reinforce the motivation to increase productivity and get more done.

## Claim Some Private Time

You are making a serious mistake if you don't close your door and claim an hour for yourself each day, even if it is only during your lunch hour. Free, uninterrupted time frees your mind to identify the activities that can have the biggest payoffs. A busy mind has a funny way of focusing on itself and getting caught up in more business, which gets no results. An open mind sees what it needs to see, clearly so you can do it easily.

## Plan Some Spontaneity

You would be surprised about how many useful and important activities surface, when you plan some free time to react to whatever might be going on. This time the reaction is your choice. Lots of people won’t tell you something you may need to know or think about, when you appear too busy trying to appear that way. Structure some free time each day to just walk around and do the three L’s—looking, listening and learning. You may discover useful and valuable information that you have already wasted much time trying to discover on your own.

### Slow Down

When you run around 1000 mph in a panic to get everything done, you are just speeding up time and making it pass much quicker. A smart trick is to slow yourself down so that time slows down too. It may be hard to fathom, but the consistent, mechanical passage of time is more of an illusion than a reality. Besides that, it is the psychological perception of time that counts most. If you *think* you don’t have enough time to do something, you won’t, but if you do you will.

### Organize Your Physical Environment

An hour spent organizing your physical environments at home and work will save a week’s time in the next year. Looking for the right clothes to wear, pens or pencil sharpeners, certain papers or bills, phone numbers and addresses, files, books, tools, coffee filters, watches, glasses, cooking utensils, printer cartridges, batteries or other trivial things can occupy whole days in the big scheme of things. You should make a list of all the things you need and use most and find the most convenient place and order in which to put them for efficient retrieval and usage.

### Unplug Your Phone

What time isn’t wasted on looking for something in a disorganized physical environment, is wasted on phone interruptions. Whenever you get a phone call, you are always working on something else, which may be a more important and urgent priority. Structuring a time each day when you take phone calls and return them, can save much time to carry out the things the phone calls may generate. Also, when the phone calls are on your own time, you are not inclined to rush or project impatience, both of which may require more time to correct later.

### Apply "P" Points

The smartest way to manage time so that you get the most results with the least effort, cost or side effects, is to focus on *"P" Points*. "P" Points are the small but strategic interventions that get the biggest results. These other time saving suggestions are good examples. Others examples are planning your communication to get maximum clarity and impact with the least amount of words, delegating duties to the person who can best get them done, and listening aggressively to people to make sure you hear what they meant.

Now you have saved 12 hours a day to be more productive. How can you save some more hours to allow more time to have fun and take care of yourself?

## REGAIN COMMON SENSE

Much can be said about common sense, but let me say the most important thing. It is not so common. Common sense is simply the knack of seeing something the way it is and doing something the way it should be done. What is so difficult about this?

Unfortunately much common sense has been washed out of the gene pool and much intelligence with it. Maybe it will help to understand what makes up common sense and how we get it. Even though common sense is not that common, it is available to us all. Common sense has three main elements: Critical thinking, sound judgment, and effective action. Critical thinking most always results in sound judgment and likewise, sound judgment usually results in effective action.

Common sense involves: (a) not assuming anything; (b) always checking details for accuracy; and (c) asking a lot of questions. Sound judgment requires us to have a reliable internal "thermometer" with which to make good comparisons. This thermometer is developed by: (a) the common sense acquisition process above; and (b) evaluating consequences of possible choices. Effective action is a result of: (a) picking actions that have more positive than negative consequences; and (b) learning quickly from mistakes.

The good thing about knowing this process is that we can start developing common sense now, by thinking about each new situation and asking ourselves important questions before we exercise judgment or take action. Common sense is a powerful tool for increasing smartness and getting you closer to where you want to be. All these other "P" points are just plain common sense that has been hanging around for us to see and use. Common sense is definitely a way to get more by doing less, smarter.

Here is a top ten list of common sense items submitted by grade school kids who haven't lost it yet:

1. Never trust a dog to watch your food.
2. Wear a hat when you are feeding seagulls.
3. Don't flush the toilet when your Dad's taking a shower.
4. Never bug a pregnant lady.
5. Don't be too full for dessert.
6. Never dare your younger brother to paint the family car.
7. Don't answer someone who asks you, "Do I look stupid?"
8. Don't pick on your sister when she is holding a baseball bat.
9. Stay away from prunes.
10. Listen to your brain. It has lots of information.

Are you seeing and using enough common sense? In what ways can you increase your store of common sense? Do you ask enough questions? Do you make too many assumptions? Do you learn from mistakes?

## STOP ASSUMING

Assuming is one of those things you probably do too much of without giving it much thought. You can assume too much about what the other person says, the way it is said, and even what is not said. The result is a head full of questionable information. Unfortunately, you usually act on this information as if it were always correct. When it is not, the consequences can be disastrous. For instance, you may give up on implementing a valuable work process change in your organization because you wrongly assume there will be too much resistance.

An assumption without any form of verification has a 50-50 chance of being right or wrong. Depending on how many assumptions you are making, you could be storing a great deal of incorrect information with a high potential for wrong actions. You might want to start being more careful in checking out your assumptions.

Take the example of communication. You assume you are expressing yourself clearly, that *how* you say something matches *what* you are trying to say, that the other person is hearing what you are saying. You also assume that he or she is interpreting your words the same way they were meant and that there isn't any misunderstanding. In addition to this, you assume the other person is doing the same thing the same way. This is a lot of assuming!

Another example is in the area of our expectations. You often assume what is okay or not okay without asking first. Wrong assumptions can backfire. Sometimes they can result in bad feelings and other times they can keep you from being able to take advantage of something good. One employee, who goes to school at night may not want a schedule change. Just because a few employees in a work group understand the need and value of an important change, doesn't mean the others do. Don't assume a subordinate understands what it is you are delegating to him or her without asking. Besides being the quickest way of knowing something, the simple act of asking is a nice show of intelligence and courtesy.

Granted, you do have to make certain assumptions. It isn't practical to verify everything and always check details. But you should probably stop automatically assuming things and start asking a few more questions. This is especially important in situations where potentially wrong assumptions can be hurtful such as wrong interpretations of a person's non-verbal communication. When the other person appears to be preoccupied with something else, you may assume he or she isn't respecting you. Then you react to your feelings of irritation. At that time the dialogue starts going sideways. By asking questions you improve the quality of information, which you can act on. That will increase the chances of acting correctly.

Here are a few assumptions that are worth your efforts to avoid:

1. Never assume how much or little someone else knows. It is usually much more or much less.
2. Never assume another person understands you. Actually there is not much chance of that ever happening.
3. Never assume it is okay to borrow something from someone without asking. People are peculiar about ownership of some things.
4. Never assume you will have enough time to do something. And, the more you plan for, the less you will need.
5. Never assume your starting point is correct. It only has a 50-50 chance at best.
6. Never assume the best or worst in somebody. People will continually amaze you.
7. Never assume something won't work before you try to do it the right way. Sometimes neither way works.
8. Never assume what you see and hear is true. Your eyes and ears can have a mind of their own.
9. Never assume desired outcomes are related to your efforts. Your efforts could be directed at the wrong objects and there is such a thing as luck.

10. Never assume somebody else's "inability" to do something is lack of ability, understanding or desire. He may just be waiting for the right challenge.

What assumptions are you making right now that might need checking out? Are you asking enough questions? Are other people making assumptions about you that aren't correct? How can you go about correcting that situation? Do you have a significant amount of potentially wrong information hanging from one particular assumption?

## AVOID FATAL THINKING

We all make our share of thinking mistakes, but a few can prove to be particularly fatal in regards to our attempts to get where we want to be. A few such fatal thinking errors to avoid are: Thinking you have to accept the situation you are in, thinking that changes have to come at the expense of others and thinking you always have to do something. Others include thinking you are completely free to make any choices you want and thinking something good has to happen if you make the right choice.

All of us have our own particular fatal thinking errors, which keep us from our goals. You have to learn to recognize these errors and think smarter. Fatal thinking is a behavior to avoid because it paralyzes you from being able to cut back many other behaviors and redo others smarter.

Any thinking which doesn't get you where you want to be is faulty, and you should give serious thought to correct it. Any thinking which gets you going in the opposite direction is fatal, and you should not have to think twice about avoiding those thoughts altogether. As with all critical thinking, "healthy thinking" opens more doors than it closes. Fatal thinking locks doors. In fact it even makes them disappear.

Here are ten other faulty and potentially fatal thinking errors to avoid:

1. Thinking the wrong thing is responsible for the way you feel.
2. Being convinced you have to choose between two opposing alternatives.

3. Thinking the other person has to be wrong if you are right.
4. Believing you can outrun a lie.
5. Being right for the wrong reason or wrong for the right reason.
6. Thinking which leads to a narrow trail of options.
7. Missing the most important point in trying to include too much.
8. Thinking that jumps from the beginning to the end without any appreciation for the middle.
9. Failing to think through a situation systematically and missing important relationships between things along the way.
10. Any thinking which is overly flavored with chronic negativity, pessimism, worry, blaming, anticipation, guilt or other such unproductive motivations.

Do you have your own list of such fatal thinking errors? Are you aware of any faulty thinking you need to give up? How is your thinking keeping you from being where you want to be? What is the main thought you have which limits you most? Would it help to ask someone else about this?

**Critical thinking "P" point question:** Are you beginning to become aware of how much you don't know?

➤ **Three critical thinking "P" point actions:**

1. Make a list of the top three "truths" you haven't bothered verifying.
2. Catch yourself in the act of artificially simplifying the reality of a complex situation just to make it easier to deal with.
3. Think about a reality you don't believe possible and then think about how your life might be different if that reality were true.

"*We generally over-estimate what we can get done today and underestimate what we can finish in a year*" (Unknown author).

# Management "P" Point # 5: Remember Creatuitivity

6

*"Creativity, as has been said, consists largely of rearranging what we know in order to find out what we do not know. Hence, to think creatively, we must be able to look afresh at what we normally take for granted"* (George Kneller).

> **Management Problem # 5:** You were born with all the creativity and intuition you ever needed along with the whole brain to be able to translate these software programs into tangible products. Somewhere along the line you bought into the suppression campaign against these wiggly, uncertain things. Now you have to figure out how to relearn what you forgot. The problem is that takes both creativity and intuition.

## INCREASE CREATIVITY AND INTUITION

Success in any type of organization requires managers to tap into their intuitive and creative powers. Using yesterday's prescriptions today does not solve problems. Things are moving so fast that we have already arrived at uncharted territories without any maps. Unfamiliar organizational problems now require intuitive and creative problem-solving skills. Below are some practical guidelines to increase the intuitive and creative energy flow in yourself and your organization.

1. First, distinguish between these two inter-related processes: *Intuition* is listening to important, hidden clues as to how life really works, and *creativity* is dreaming ahead as to how we might use these insights to do things differently and better than you do now. Applying *creatuitivity,* or effectively translating all this information into action, is a whole brain activity. Both hemispheres of your brain have to work

cooperatively to turn vague notions into tangible products. Creatuitive problem-solving is both an art and science.

2. The habit of judging may be the single most important thing that works against creatuitivity. Creativity and intuition can be judged wrongly by three levels—ourselves, others and society. These things can then be kept hopelessly locked into a vicious circle of judging the judgment of the judgments. This extended judging habit uses much energy that could be better spent creating and intuiting. Give serious consideration to stop making judgments whenever you can. You can start by paying closer attention to your judging thoughts and then attack the judgments and see how ridiculous they really are.
3. Begin to force yourself to change in little insignificant ways. This paves the way for shedding restrictive and rigid thinking. Vary your daily routine. Change the words with which you write and speak. Learn something new so it challenges something you only thought you knew for sure. Work on weekends and take weekdays off. Re-arrange your household or office furniture. The object is to shock your brain a little. Loosen up!
4. Continue this "brain shock" by striving to learn something new and important each day. Expanding your limited views of reality can quickly change the way your brain thinks and processes information. This in turn can generate valuable intuitive and creative energy. And remember: As a leader in your organization your actions speak louder than anyone else's, so *live* these changes.
5. Study larger, dynamic processes rather than smaller static details. Watch a basketball game and see how teamwork gets results, rather than focusing on individual players and shots. Notice how things work together, rather than just noticing the things

themselves. Look for things you normally don't notice and try to look at the things you always notice differently. Experiment with using ordinary objects in different and unusual ways.

6. Avoid thinking in terms of cause and effect and beginnings and endings. Look carefully at things and see how they are inter-related to the point where there is no clear cause and effect or clear beginning and ending. Think in terms of inter-looping, multi-dimensional *wobbly circles* instead of a single straight *line*. Invent new dimensions in thinking. Stop and think about how you change something by just perceiving it or how you alter a situation just by being in it.
7. At least express your intuitive gut feelings about something, even if you don't follow up on those feelings. Start following hunches. Keep a scorecard of wins and losses, when you do follow them. This can build confidence. Learn to *hear* and *trust* your intuitive feelings through practice. These feelings are just semi-conscious brain whispers.
8. Watch children at play at least once a day for several weeks. We can remember a lot about the intuition and creativity we all started with, simply by watching kids being spontaneous in their play. They always let their imagination run freely, seeing things as they *could* be, not just as they *are*. They are in awe of everything and that is the way it should be for adults too.
9. Encourage others in the organization to express themselves intuitively and creatively without fear of ridicule. These things can be contagious; but, the atmosphere has to be relaxed enough to undo all the powerful constraints placed on us throughout our lives. We have been taught to *suppress* these important skills. It is time to pull the plug on this priority reversal.

10. Stop allowing employees to cure *symptoms* and start encouraging them to dig for root *causes* in organizational problems. This means digging much deeper than they think they have time for, and just when they think they have uncovered the real problem and core cause, encourage them to go a little further until there is no further place to go. You will be surprised at the results.
11. Collect "perturbation points," or situations where you have noticed a well-placed and well-timed small intervention produced a major beneficial outcome. Such "P" points have much general application value to make progress solving difficult problems. "P" points are often the most cleverest of all the hiding places where we can relocate intuitive insights and bursts of creative energy.
12. Expand the spirit of *inquiry*, while maintaining the rule of *advocacy*. Ask more questions to which you don't know the answers, and impose your own answers less. "Why not?" should be a frequent question which is asked, and "No, because..." is a usual cop-out, which should be discontinued. A spirit of inquiry has no room for judgment until alternatives have been evaluated and it is decision-making time.
13. Try to reverse your typical approach to looking at something. If you look for details first and then put the whole picture together afterwards, then start looking at the whole scene first and then look at the individual "snapshots" which make it up. If you usually speak first, try listening first. Re-arrange your sequencing.
14. Study your own main failures closely and thoroughly to see how you turned them around into successes. That critical information is a "P" point that has a lot of valuable information about the intuition and creativity you already use without being aware of it. Creatuitivity is not something you have to invent but

rather just re-discover. You already have it. You just aren't using it.

15. Experiment with suspending traditional boundaries in such things as schedules, organizational structure and communication. Growth knows no boundaries and boundaries typically inhibit intuition and creativity. Do what you can do to make the organization seem *fluid* and flowing, rather than solid or fixed.
16. Form small management teams for special projects, which can allow for intuitive and creative thinking without judgment. Teams are more likely to be innovative than individuals, especially when there is synergy.
17. Hire good talent and experiment with making positions for the person's skills rather than just following the status quo practice of filling vacancies that already have set job duties and responsibilities. Develop the job descriptions for the new talent as you go.
18. Start taking reasonable risks for the sake of taking risks. This will build trust in your intuition to take bigger ones when you may need to. This also encourages you to loosen up a little and become more open and sensitive to your own and others' intuitive and creative energy. It also counteracts over-conservatism in anticipating failure or other undesirable outcomes.
19. Do not allow cynicism or pessimism and enforce a can-do attitude throughout the organization. Intuition and creativity are positive forces, which get stifled by negativity. Negativity is too draining.
20. Maintain an active spiritual life. Intuition and creativity are closely tied to spiritual integration and wholeness. You are putting creatuitivity into action when you start searching for genuine answers to questions such as, Who are You? Where are you going? Why?
21. Resurrect older ideas and obsolete solutions and use them in new and unusual ways. Just because an idea

or solution didn't work before, it doesn't mean it won't work now. The timing could have been off before. Besides, all situations and everything that is part of them changes once time passes.

22. Practice some form of creative therapy—listen to music, write or read poetry, paint or do something creative. Don't worry about the results, just let go to the urges.
23. Study the *principles* of something, whether it is car racing, firing weapons, doing mathematics or building a house. The basic principles of doing something can generate all kinds of wider applications and solutions to problems in even unrelated fields. This is taking advantage of *rational creativity.*
24. Open up to meaningful feedback. This requires courage to hear the faults you try to ignore. The things that need changing most that go unchanged, can eat up a lot of energy which could be used more intuitively and creatively. Applying such feedback can also energize some of these other solutions. Growth can't occur without getting and using feedback.
25. Separate interesting information from the critical information, which you really need to know. Information overload pushes intuition and creativity way down in the conscious process. A more "relaxed" brain is required to allow these two other forces to energize. Set aside some dreaming time to plan how you can better use the important information that keeps coming back even after a major mind purge.
26. Accept the fact that nothing is ever really "finished." Our minds fool us into premature closure and certainty. It is all a journey, not a destination and there is no rush to get there. Understanding this insight expands time, which opens portals to intuition and creativity.
27. There is usually one place where you are more able to be creative than usual. Find that place and use it!

28. Don't worry too much about being confronted with situations about which you don't have a clue. These are the situations that can teach you much. Besides, this is where you are going anyway and by the time you get there you will have acquired all these creatuitivity skills in your virtual toolbox.
29. Become more trusting in life and its natural processes. Take a deep breath and let go. The small things you work so hard to control are just a small drop in a very large bucket. You go to sleep every night and completely trust that tomorrow will come and it does. Surrendering just means you are giving up trying so hard to control the particular outcomes to which you are emotionally attached.
30. Devalue consistency, which stifles creatuitivity. Look for ways to be legitimately inconsistent. The only inconvenience will be that you have to explain the reasons behind such inconsistencies. I remember empowering a security company owner to break the mold and pay people different rates by just helping him understand the value of explaining the specifics of why he was paying one employee more than the other. Once he started doing that nothing disastrous happened.

Practicing the above suggestions will greatly increase a manager's confidence and competence in using the important skills of intuition and creativity. A good starting point is the attitude of realizing the importance of these two valuable skills. Then you can release them from their hiding place.

## CREATE AMAZING NEW REALITIES

Our personal and professional development journeys can reach warp speed once we start letting go of older obsolete realities and begin exploring new ones. Below are ten new realities you can't live without—if you are serious about personal and professional development.

### Reality can be Invented

Life is driven by thoughts more than physical realities. Once you understand a small portion of reality intimately and completely, and your intentions are right, you can change it into something entirely new. Such a new reality worth considering is this: You are really only limited by the smallness of your beliefs and what you are looking at. What you see actually depends mostly on where you are standing and what you are looking at. Changing locations opens up a whole new field of vision. One new viewpoint can help you see even bigger ones and the benefits start becoming endless.

### There is Plenty of Time

We waste too much time rushing around like maniacs trying to control everything, always ending up short on time, which just furthers the panic. Time is one of our most precious resources. Ironically it is equally distributed but not equally valued. When we slow down and get more in touch with the now moment, we start to fathom the true meaning of eternity. When we start focusing on making the right choices in each new opportunity that comes along, we have merged the past, present and future. The mechanical illusion of time disappears and there seems to be enough time to get everything done.

### You are a Team

You do not really have a split personality and you are not separate from anything including God. When you start reconciling your own two halves and become a whole person, you can start putting the rest of the world back together again. When you do this, you will discover amazing governing principles. A good one to take advantage of is the *Gestalt* principle. This is the notion that the whole is much greater than the mere sum of its parts. Individual hemp fibers are fragile but when woven carefully into a rope, they become extremely strong. The collective synergy of a team made up of all your halves can achieve unlimited success. Your team can join others and become stronger and more successful.

## Down is Really Up

Many things in life are not as they seem and some are really bass awkwards. Why do we make less money in the beginning of our lives when we need it most? Why do we invest so heavily in housing recalcitrant inmates and do so little for innocent victims? Why do we have to lose ourselves to find ourselves? Why do we have to experience failure before we reach success? These are more than just intriguing questions. They hide valuable clues. You can make significant progress in your self-actualization journey by resolving these paradoxical illusions and re-arranging some awkward priority reversals. You can start by answering these two questions: (1) are you concentrating more trying to change things outside you or inside you? (2) are you living your own priorities or those imposed upon you?

## It is not Really that Serious

Life is mostly a comedy that we too often mistake for a drama, tragedy, epic, action flick, foreign film or documentary. Seeing the humor in serious events dissolves their distaste and removes a very large barrier between where you are and where you want to be. Granted, there may be a few real tragedies in life, but you tend to miss their importance and urgency when you are being held hostage by an over-serious philosophy of life. Laughing at some of the insanity you are guilty of opens a wide portal to self-growth. Besides that, laughing is physically healthy for you.

## You have to Pay to Play

There is definitely a down payment required to enter onto the highway of success. This dues includes finding out your main talent, deciding what to do with it and then figuring how to do it. You are entirely on your own in figuring out this personal mission, but there are plenty of proven success formulas from which to draw. My personal favorite is this one (because I invented it): (1) dream huge; (2) translate your dreams into goals by making them go from your head to your hands; (3) work hard and smart to achieve those goals; (4) be creatively clever and do something in a new way that others only talk about doing; (5) keep focused on your goals and avoid the entertaining distractions everywhere else; (6) never quit, knowing that success is probably just around the one corner you are most inclined to give up getting to; and (7) share your success secrets with others.

### You are Not Alone

People have more in common with one another regarding what they are thinking, what they fear and what they are trying to do, than most of us realize. The fact is that everyone else has an important piece of the big puzzle that can fit with yours to make your piece bigger. The more people with whom you share your suspicions and secrets, the bigger your piece of the puzzle becomes. This is the beginning of a team of teams all helping each other get to where we are all going.

### There are No Wrong Turns

The *Law of Karma* is just a friendly reminder to help you evaluate your choices so that you can eventually make the right ones that are effective in getting you where you really want to be. When you make wrong choices, you are not being "bad," but rather just loitering. All that you have done in the past is what got you to where you are now. A funny thing is that even the disasters always seem to work out for the best in the long run. If you don't like a particular ending, it is likely that you still have a work in progress. Be patient.

### There is Wisdom in Insecurity

Oddly, when you abandon your comfort zone, it just gets bigger. Letting go of the illusion of external control and giving in to the natural flow of life results in a more real sense of security, peace and comfort. Change is one of the few certainties there are and once you start embracing that reality everything becomes less changeable and more stable. That way you can spot the things that really do need changing and be more effective in making those changes. Part of the wisdom of insecurity is giving up the silly notion that external things offer real security because they don't.

## There is no Tenth New Reality

Surprise! Every time you convince yourself you have finally figured it out by including everything, something else shows up later or the rules get changed. Life is incompressible in its entirety and realities are only limited by our artificial need to have ten or so things. Our brains are only tiny peepholes to infinity and these ten new realities are just scratching the surface. What new realities can you explore and benefit from? What obsolete reality is keeping you from doing this?

**Critical creatuitivity "P" point question:** Do you always trust your instincts?

➤ **Three creatuitivity "P" point actions:**

1. Verify your next few hunches.
2. Implement a creative group at your office to meet once a month to brainstorm innovations for your organization.
3. Re-arrange your office.

"*The uncreative mind can spot wrong answers, but it takes a very creative mind to spot wrong questions*" (Anthony Jay).

# Management "P" Point # 6: Know What Makes People Tick

# 7

*"The deepest principle in human nature is the craving to be appreciated"* (William James).

> **Management Problem # 6:** One of the most valuable skills in management is being able to deal with people effectively. The knowledge behind this skill generally comes from many years of personal experience, which is often trial and error. However, a quick review of basic psychology can put the necessary knowledge and skill development on the fast track.

To a large extent, excellence in leadership is dependent upon the knowledge and ability to deal with people effectively. An effective leader must learn important governing principles in this area by critical and thorough self-understanding. Here are some important principles about people.

## PRACTICE PEOPLE PRINCIPLES

One of our most important challenges in life is getting along with other people. This basic skill is an integral part of everything we do in life and so it can't ever be emphasized enough. Here are twenty-five tips about getting along with others that I learned along the way between trial, error and success.

1. Trying to change another person is mostly frustrating and futile. When you figure a way to change something about your approach to the other person, he often has to change something in his response to you. Then you have some changes going on. One small change may lead to a bigger one.

2. We all want to feel accepted and be assured that we are quite okay as we are with all our shortcomings, *before* we are reminded of these faults and told that there are other things we could be doing better. If you want to challenge someone to change or become better at something, you have to invest some time building rapport by conveying understanding and acceptance, *first.*
3. Most interpersonal conflicts have to do with competing individual needs. Resolution of such common conflicts has to do with choosing the right response in three possible situations. The first thing you have to do is to determine whose needs are most important. Are the other person's needs more important and urgent than yours? If so, you need to sacrifice and give into the other person. Are your needs more important? If they are, you need to speak up and make a case to convince the other person, and are both your needs more or less equal? If that is the case, what is a compromise or a viable alternative? Relationships in which you are giving, taking or compromising too much are ones you need to walk away from.
4. We all secretly want to have our "cheese" and eat it too, but some of us are a little more adept at figuring out how to do that. For instance, we all want to be recognized as unique individuals and have the freedom to be the way we want to be. Yet at the same time we all demand to be treated fairly and equally (especially when the consequences aren't so pleasant). Another example is that we all want the challenge of a new adventure *and* the comfort of familiar stability. Figuring out these and other paradoxes in life leads to much happiness and success, and our solutions make exceptional gifts to other people. Life often works in paradoxes and knowing how things work is real power.
5. We all have a small piece of the puzzle and when we make contact with others and share our pieces, we all

get a bigger and clearer picture of the reality we are trying to fit into and make better. A balanced interdependence gets us all where we want to be quicker and easier.

6. Probably the most fundamental difference between people is the degree to which they believe they can influence reality and achieve their dreams. Some people are proactive optimists who are willing to do whatever it takes to make things happen to be where they want to be. Others are powerless pessimists who wait and react to the things than happen to them. Everyone wants to have control of his life, but it takes a positive belief to do that, despite the many negative failures and obstacles we all face. Sharing your own positive attitude in a gentle, non-threatening way can have a big impact with people who don't have it but want it.
7. Being likable is a big part of getting along with others. All this requires is for you to show interest in others, have a positive attitude, focus on your own shortcomings, be balanced, enjoy things, act smart, and learn and improve.
8. Although people are slightly hesitant to talk about themselves, but they would rather do that than listen to you talk about yourself. The best way to start a conversation is to ask people about themselves. They'll get around to you soon enough.
9. When somebody says or does something to offend you or hurt your feelings, you need to be assertive and stand up for yourself and let the person know the consequences of what she did. Being passive and letting such behavior go or being aggressive and fighting back never has a good outcome. Those approaches just build resentments or collect enemies.
10. Be tolerant of things another person doesn't have any control over. It is not fair to remind someone of

impervious conditions. And never impose any feedback on someone before he asks for it.

11. Avoid setting up unnecessary defensive climates in communication with others by making a conscious effort to *not* convey superiority, over-controlling behavior, dogmatic certainty, accusations or judgmental attitudes. Being equal, accepting, tentative and non-judgmental will assure open communication and the best possible outcome.
12. Learn to walk away from destructive, emotional situations where you can't win from losing. And don't waste your time hanging around toxic, negative people. They just drain your positive energy and rob other more deserving people of your attention.
13. Other people notice more about you when you would rather be invisible. It is during adversity or when you feel terrible that you need to act your best to leave the best impression with other people. That impression will be a lasting one.
14. Like it or not, we all judge a book by its cover. It is essential to always appear your best, regardless of the looks you were blessed or cursed with. A warm smile, stylish wardrobe, pleasant voice, proper grooming, polite manner and peaceful eye contact can put you on a level playing field with anyone.
15. Know ahead of time that people can be worse than you imagine and don't make a big deal about it. Expect the worst and you will always be pleasantly surprised.
16. Listen to others with both ears, hearing *what* is said along with *how* it is being said (or what isn't being said) to get the full meaning. Other people liked to be listened to and they like to be heard and understood even more.
17. Take a genuine interest in other people. We all have intriguing and valuable tales to tell one another.

18. We are all insecure and vulnerable enough without having to have our self-esteem attacked. Besides, belittling is probably the worst thing you can do to another human being, besides gossiping. Building up a person's self-confidence makes a friend for life.
19. If you have to criticize someone else's way of doing something, take some more time and show him or her to do it better.
20. Conflicts are the way human beings grow. Have the courage to talk honestly, apart from all the negative feelings you are having, to get through the conflict rather than run from it. The only ground rule is that both people have to be willing to do this.
21. If there is one thing people dislike unanimously it is another person with a big ego. On the other hand, a humble, quiet achiever is everyone's favorite person.
22. Don't take your stress out on others. They have enough of their own to deal with.
23. Sometimes the hardest way to be with other people is the thing that has the best impact: Being patient.
24. Don't make promises with other people, which you can't keep and always keep the promises you do make. Promise-keepers are the most popular people because anyone can be a promise-breaker.
25. When all else fails, practice the *Golden Rule* of treating others the way you want to be treated yourself.

## ACCOMMODATE PARADOXES IN HUMAN NATURE

A critical understanding of human behavior involves the realization that it is often paradoxical in nature—people are often driven in opposite directions in their thinking, motives and behavior.

Below are seventeen important paradoxes in human behavior that need to be reconciled within the leader's mind, for him or her to reconcile them with followers and achieve success.

### Creating Chaos vs. Restoring Order

This may be the underlying paradox behind all the others. We start out thinking we need to understand, control and change everything to achieve happiness and success. In the frenzy to complete the job, we make life more complex and chaotic than it needs to be. Eventually we feel a need to simplify things and restore order. However, even when we wake up to this paradoxical drive, we still continue to go back and forth between creating more chaos and trying to restore order again. The leader's job is to help others be sure they are creating the *right* chaos and restoring the *best* order, and especially knowing which is which.

### Adapting vs. Rebelling

In all our activities, we have two separate options. These are to accept things and adapt, or to rebel and try and change things the way we want them to be. Many of us choose to focus most of our energy on the second option, at least at first. When we refocus our energy on fitting in first, we get a better understanding of what actually needs changing and how we can make the best changes. An effective leader knows the importance of changing things from the inside out, starting with one's self before focusing on others.

### Following Our Heads vs. Following Our Hearts

During much of our lives a war is going on inside us. This age-old head-heart battle is not reserved just to romantic dilemmas. It pops up in ordinary choices involving careers, places to live, clothes to buy, financial matters, recreation interests and many other things. We often get the feeling that there are two stereophonic voices coming from two different locations telling us two different things. This is one paradox not even the best of leaders can help people resolve. We all have to pay a certain dues learning when to listen most to which of our two voices, until they eventually become one.

### Being Good vs. Being Bad

Most of us understand the difference between right and wrong, along with all the moral and practical reasons for not doing the wrong things. But unfortunately that understanding doesn't do much to silence the lure of temptation, especially when we lessen the degree of "badness" and "wrongness" of something we want to do, in our minds. Somehow, we each need to figure out how to take periodic, legitimate walks on the wild side, which aren't harmful to ourselves or others. By gradually taking a little of the tension away, we can become much more resolute when it comes to resisting things that can have destructive consequences.

### Being Similar vs. Being Different

We are all very much alike in many ways, but at the same time very different from one another. Strangely, we seem to have an inclination to focus more on each other's differences than on our commonalties. This unfortunate tendency usually results in much unnecessary frustration and failure. This is because we want to control other people in forcing "sameness" and that is only one side of the coin. A successful leader understands this dual reality and reaches a balance in emphasizing people's common ground, without sacrificing the importance of each individual's uniqueness.

### Demanding Freedom vs. Wanting Equality

This particular paradox in human behavior is a divergent problem that does not have a final solution. Successful leaders realize and accept that one side of this coin is not any "better" than the other and that either side, when taken to the extreme, can result in undesirable consequences. The solution is always a temporary one to restore reasonable balance when the pendulum swings too far because of some unusual crisis. The ideal solution is for all people to realize the wisdom of assertively exercising *responsible freedom.* People can only do this when they learn how to set themselves free from the many paradoxes that are holding them hostage.

### Wanting Change vs. Needing Stability

We continuously go back and forth between these two things as a part of our basic drive of creating chaos and restoring order. But unless we are stimulation addicts, we prefer to lean toward the comfort of stability and familiarity, at least until it gets too boring. We usually don't actively seek out change if we don't have enough stability to feel secure. The smart leader only introduces stabilizing change to people who are ready, in order to avoid unsettling resistance and inevitable failure.

### Being Independent vs. Being Dependent

We enjoy the sense of personal accomplishment that comes from doing things on our own, but also enjoy the sense of relief knowing we can depend on others when we get tired of carrying the burden. We also need both private introversion space and public extroversion space in which to wander around and explore. Effective leaders acknowledge the equal importance of both these basic needs. They thoughtfully arrange a team effort that joins individual complimentary roles to achieve success that provides benefits and satisfaction to both the group and the individuals.

### Being Logical vs. Being Creative

We all have right and left hemispheres in our brains and there is a built-in, natural drive to be both logical and creative. One of our biggest challenges is to reconcile this convergent-divergent split and when we do, we become doubly successful. Problems today require both logical and creative solutions. Smart leaders arrange whole brain environments to maximize opportunities and contributions for both these abilities with all people.

### Needing to be Accepted Unconditionally vs. Wanting to be Encouraged to Improve

In our drive to understand and control things, including other people, we often get too far ahead ourselves. Nobody is willing to put forth the effort to change and improve, until they first feel secure in being accepted completely as they are. No one changes until they know they don't *have* to. This feeling of unconditional acceptance is what frees us to be able to grow and improve. Becoming better is a natural thing, but it has to be freed by the certainty of acceptance first. Any leadership "demands" for change must be soft and second.

### Thinking vs. Doing

Too much thinking can paralyze us whereas too much doing without any thinking can get us in trouble. We are intellectual bystanders when we over-think, but recklessly impulsive if we act before thinking. Ironically, any thinking taken too far or not far enough can get us into trouble, but more thinking may be the only thing that can get us out of trouble. A capable leader teaches reconciliation of this paradox by making insignificant decision hastily, taking equally quick action and then saving time to deliberate carefully in more difficult situations. Simply put, there are times to act and there are times to think.

### Being Told What to Do vs. Choosing How to Do It

Smart leaders realize that there has to be a compromise with this paradoxical aspect of human nature. After all, there are leaders and there are followers. It is always the leader's responsibility to share the vision of where the rest of us are going. It is the followers' responsibility to develop a map to get there. This is good teamwork and the primary prescription for success. Whenever a would-be leader lacks followers there are two possible reasons. The first is that the destination may not be right. The second is that the choice on how to get there may not be the option it needs to be.

### Taking Things Apart vs. Putting Them Back Together Again

We enjoy reducing the big picture into smaller individual details so that we can understand and control these parts more fully. We also have fun taking things apart just so we can put them back together again. The problem is that we often forget to put things back together again. In fact, many problems we try to solve are just disassembled parts. Effective leaders help people get the right parts and put them back together in working order to see the big picture clearer.

### Being Egocentric vs. Being Altruistic

One of the most difficult opposing drives in which to reach a balance is the one between being selfish and unselfish. We are admonished if we appear to be too self-centered, always thinking and doing things for ourselves and not being considerate of others. On the other hand, if we give up too much for others we risk being judged weak and helpless and may end up empty-handed. The excellent leader helps followers apply the wisdom of a slight variation of the simple rule of *Karma*: You get most when you give most.

### Ourselves vs. Others

A spin-off of the above paradox is the question of who should we believe most—others or ourselves? Do we study ourselves in order to know everyone else, or do we study everyone else so that we know more about ourselves? Can we possibly please others and ourselves at the same time? The best leaders help people to turn inside themselves to get correct answers while demonstrating their own courage to live the answers they received by doing that. Gradually we can verify some of our most important suspicions with others we trust and respect.

### Leading vs. Following

There is no such thing as a natural born leader. We all have the ability to be both good leaders and good followers and we need opportunities to do both. That is how we learn to be good leaders. A smart leader uses people's diverse abilities to share in the leadership role so that everyone can teach and learn from each other. Smart leaders also arrange opportunities for themselves to play a follower's role to keep learning and improving.

### Assigning External Blame for Our Own Faults vs. Assuming Internal Fault for Others' Failures

Once a leader figures out this human oddity, he or she can help others reconcile this important difference. Smart leaders already know the secret of their own success. They know that it all started when they discovered the individual power inside themselves. This is the wisdom of being balanced and centered to see the power of choice that comes with each new moment of living. Sharing this secret with others is what excellent leadership is all about. It helps us all accept our differences and use our commonalties more productively in reconciling all these paradoxes of human behavior.

By understanding and reconciling these seventeen paradoxes in your own behavior, you become expert at helping others do the same. The result is widespread success.

## BECOME A PSYCHOLOGIST

You don't have to possess a Ph.D. and a license to practice psychology. You just need those things to call yourself a "Psychologist". As a leader/manager, you are required to practice psychology everyday. In addition to the information about people principles, here are some basic psychology and life principles to apply.

If you want to achieve more, get psyched! Getting psyched isn't about increasing adrenaline though. It is about applying useful psychological principles, which by the way, aren't always just common sense dressed up as fancy psycho-babble. Below are a few useful psychological principles worth exploring in your pursuit of professional excellence.

### Human Learning

One of the more influential human processes is one that isn't complicated at all. We learn everything we know by simple associations, by modeling others, through sudden insights and by getting rewarded for making desired responses. Knowing this basic process, you can manage negative behavior better and replace it with more positive, productive behavior.

To eliminate negative behaviors, you should be more cautious in avoiding simple associations that strengthen bad habits, become aware of the tendency to acquire unproductive routines just from watching others and look closer to find out what is rewarding your negative behaviors to keep them going. In developing positive behaviors to replace unproductive ones, you can start making sure you are rewarding your achievements with meaningful rewards and practicing some of these other psychological principles below. You can also increase your sensitivity and listen closer to important insights, which can give you valuable clues as to how things really work. One such useful insight is that sometimes small, but well-placed and well-timed efforts produce the best results.

### Individual Differences

People are all different when it comes to their abilities, needs, and motivations. Even the same person can be different in these things at different times. Not acknowledging these differences can be the cause of much unnecessary failure. Unfortunately, in the interest of convenience and cost we devote too much effort in identifying similarities to justify easier group prescriptions. We always want to hurry up and cure everything all at once in one easy swoop.

Sometimes you need to stop and take a little time to study the situation in order to understand it better. Things may not always be the way they appear to be. One worthwhile activity is to study and document your own thoughts, beliefs, moods and expectations just prior to a performance and then see what was connected to success and what was connected to failure after the performance is over. The performance can be a job interview, a speech, an interaction with another person, or an athletic event. This can be an eye-opening experience that questions the heart of common sense. Becoming more aware of your own individual differences gives you valuable, accurate information on which to base your goals and activities.

### Growth & Development

An important principle that has been uncovered by human growth and development studies is that such development usually occurs in a sequence of systematic stages over a period of time. Consequently, it is important to set goals and activities that follow a natural pattern of development. Missing a critical stage of development on the way toward an important goal can throw you off the right track altogether. And you don't have the swimming skills of salmon to climb waterfalls.

In personal relationships, you can't achieve genuine intimacy without first exercising patience to build rapport and then developing courage to work through difficult conflicts. To win a race you have to plan a fast start, train to maintain a strong pace and reserve something to be able to kick into high gear for a fantastic finish. When your game plan acknowledges the stages of development of something and your goals are based on getting through those stages, a positive outcome is more likely.

## Accommodation

Our eyes have to use the process of three-dimensional visual accommodation to switch back and forth between the foreground and background of something to be able to make sense of it. In a similar fashion, we must be able to switch our attention back and forth between broad focus on the external environment and narrow focus on details within that environment.

Broad focus is visualizing the bigger picture and end goal, whereas narrow focus is noticing all the particular details necessary to get where you want to go. If you over-attend to one of these at the expense of the other, you give up valuable ground in achieving your goal. You can easily forget where you are going when you get bogged down in details, and you can bump into a tree or two by looking too far into the forest.

It is the constant switching back and forth that catches subtle changes in one viewpoint that may impact the other in dramatic ways. A short-term investment of time or money may change a long-range business plan in not so small ways. And when you begin to slow yourself down enough, you begin to notice not only what you are attending to, but also how you are attending to it. You may be missing valuable information that impacts the big picture in major ways.

## Gestalt

Gestalt psychology gave us many valuable laws of perception, which can be used to understand and avoid unnecessary mistakes. One such principle is *the whole is greater than the sum of its parts*, much like the weaker individual hemp fibers making up a stronger rope. Average individual players can work well together to become an outstanding team. The synergy from something greater than our own individual efforts can provide a major boost to our achievements. On the other side of this, the whole that we create may end up developing its own identity and even have power over us. Then we become the dog being wagged by his tail. This is not the way things are supposed to be.

Other important gestalt principles are *closure*, or our tendency to finish incomplete situations and *proximity*, or our tendency to see things that are close together as similar. We may need to be aware of how we can actually be foolishly finishing something with incorrect information, just to finish it. Or, we may mistakenly think things have a connection when in fact they don't. They just appear together by chance.

### The Bell Curve

Most achievement falls within the larger average portion of the bell curve. Under this umbrella, where there is a lot of room for improvement, gains can come quickly and easily. But the closer you get to perfecting your achievements, the further out toward the end of the curve you move. Once there, the harder you have to look for new ideas or activities to keep moving forward and then the harder you have to practice them.

The last few obstacles guarding the door to being a successful expert at excellence are the most difficult ones to remove. They are either the heaviest and most bulky, or they can become invisible or difficult to see. There is no shortcut through this statistical reality but being aware of it can help you plan better.

These are just a few of the many valuable psychological principles that are available to help give you an edge in your pursuit of excellence. By practicing these and other basic psychological principles, you will be making a plan and setting goals that are more likely to be in line with the way life works. You will be getting psyched and improving your achievements.

## CREATE RIGHT PERCEPTIONS & CORRECT WRONG ONES

A person's perceptions are his or her reality. The only other thing that is more important than the perceptions other people have of you, is what you may be doing to influence those perceptions. Your general effectiveness can be greatly limited by these perceptions when they are less than favorable. Below is a useful strategy to change unfavorable perceptions people have of you.

### First, Know What the Perceptions Are

You can't change something you don't know about and it is often the unknown perceptions that others have of you that are the most damaging. I can remember once I failed to get an important top prison industries administration job that I was made for, because the Governor's interviewing committee perceived I was too practical, conservative and down-to-earth. I only discovered my failure by chance. Apparently one of my loyal references thought it would be better for me if he were to de-emphasize my creativity for such a job!

Getting to know how others see us is no easy process because we don't often get the opportunity to ask. Even if we do ask, we may not get accurate and complete information. If you don't have both formal and informal systems of getting reliable and useful feedback about the perceptions that others have of you, then that is the first thing you need to establish now. You have to know the intimate details of something you are trying to change.

### Realize the Awesome Power of Seemingly Insignificant Things

Throughout this book, I emphasize what I call *"P" points.* These psychological power points are the small, but well-timed and well-placed interventions that get the biggest results, quickly and easily. They are the teachable moments of truth. The opposite principle works in the development of perceptions sometimes—little, insignificant, one-time occurrences get in the way big time to over-flavor wrong or incomplete perceptions of us that become enduring and difficult to change.

When I was a prison warden I used to ask my managers to rate me on my management style and behavior according to their perceptions. One particular item was extremely important to me and that was to be perceived as more realistic and practical than idealistic and theoretical. Unfortunately I didn't get the direction of responses that I wanted. Much later, I came to realize it was because I used the three letters "Ph.D." next to my name. Most of the staff at the prison had the preconception that higher degrees were all ivory tower stuff and of no practical use in the real world.

### Accept and Deal with Impervious Perceptions

Certain words and actions in certain cultures mean certain things and if you say or do those things there is no way to avoid the subsequent perceptions that go along with them. These are the cases where you work with reality the way it is rather than the way you want it to be. If you are moving to a new area, take the time to learn some of the relevant cultural realities.

At one time I was working as a District Manager of a very large private security company in Miami. In the culture of my office staff, birthdays were extremely important especially for females. If I forgot a birthday, I was forgetting the person. I am not insensitive and didn't want to be perceived that way, so I had to learn how to remember several hundred birthday dates.

The actual organic perceptual processes of your brain can distort reality and you need to be fully aware of this fact when it comes to trying to change unfavorable perceptions that may have been established this way. A review of the principles of *Gestalt Psychology* can be very helpful.

For instance, your brain is always looking for short cuts because of the overwhelming amount of data that confronts you. You can't simply assume someone else will perceive you as being balanced in the areas of creativity and practicality, or playfulness and diligence, without showing those aspects of yourself in unmistakable ways.

You may also need to pay more attention to the laws of primacy and recency and proximity. Your serial position and who or what may be near you in space and time can spill over flattering or contaminating perceptions onto you. In other words who you pick for vice-president may effect how people see you.

## Use the Change Process

The process of changing perceptions people have of you has to follow the general rules of the normal change process. These are fairly simple. The benefits of change have to be sold as valuable while the disadvantages have to be minimized. Change has to be easy. People don't change unless they want to or are forced to. Willful change is usually better and change is more readily accepted when it doesn't threaten other's routine or convenience too much. Effective change has to be up close and personal and of course, to change somebody else you have to change something about yourself first.

In trying to change an unfavorable perception of yourself, you first have to embrace the above rules. Next you must identify what it is that you are doing or saying to give a particular perception. Then you have to stop doing or saying those things and substitute new highly visible behaviors that will create the desired perception. If you want to be seen as positive and optimistic, you need to frown less and smile more. If you want to be seen as hands-on, you need to quit delegating and start rolling up your sleeves.

## Rectifying Initial Character Perceptions

Most often when you start a new position of leadership, you are so caught up in all the pressing details of making an effective transition, you can forget the importance of first impressions. Unfortunately bad first impressions may never go away. It is when you first appear before an audience that you should consciously behave in such a way as to project the character traits that other people need to see *before* they will consider listening to you or following you.

Initial character traits that other people need to see are your self-confidence blended with humility, your genuine interest and respect for them, your willingness to grow and listen, your trustworthiness, your courage, your likability and your rightness. Changing an unfavorable perception that you don't have these things is so difficult, that it serves as a reminder to work three times harder in the beginning when such perceptions are formed in concrete.

### Apply the Wisdom that Actions Always Outspeak Words

You can rarely change another person's perceptions of you by words. In fact it is more likely that such words may just reinforce that unfavorable perception, making it even worse. Other people have to see and hear tangible changes in behavior before they are willing to reconsider a certain perception they presently have.

And unfortunately, people are quick to embrace a belief, even without much evidence, and very slow to give up a belief, even if they know it is probably wrong. So, your only choice is to model the type of behavior and attitudes that you want others to know you by, consistently and persistently, without going sideways for even a moment, all in silence.

I am reminded of an important insight I overheared at an earlier business workshop I attended in the late 80's. The insight was, "you can't talk your way out of a situation you behaved yourself into." So true!

When you learn how people perceive you, model the right behaviors from the beginning, pay attention to little things and certain impervious perceptions and use the change process to your advantage, you will be more certain people have the desired perception of you. When they do, you will be more successful in everything.

**Critical human nature "P" point question:** What paradoxes in your own behavior and motives have you not yet reconciled?

> **Three human nature "P" point actions:**
>
> 1. Set up a reliable system to find out how employees generally perceive you.
> 2. What particular growth cycle are you going through yourself that might be over-flavoring how you see others?
> 3. Think about how you can accommodate the three different visual, auditory and kinesthetic learning styles of employees.

"*Freedom is what most people want for themselves, and what they most want to deprive others of having*" (Thomas Szaz).

# Management "P" Point # 7: Light Their Fires

8

"*Success is not the result of spontaneous combustion. You must first set yourself on fire*" (Fred Shero).

**Management Problem # 7:** Motivation is one of the most complex human behaviors. We can only infer that it exists in the workplace if we get the work performance we desire. To make matters more complicated, each individual employee may be motivated in entirely different ways and even the same employee can be motivated differently at different times.

## DEFINITION OF MOTIVATION

Of all the human behaviors, motivation is probably the most complex. It is a complicated, intangible theoretical concept that can only be inferred or assumed from other outward behavior you can see and judge. Here is how the word *motivation* is defined in the dictionary:

Motivation: *A force, stimulus or influence that causes a person to act; an emotion or desire acting on the will and causing it to act.*

Most psychology books define motivation as the entire process of what makes a person do things. This process includes a person's internal dynamics and external circumstances and is used to explain intentions, causes and reasons for behavior.

In general, motivation has to do with the forces that maintain and change the direction, quality and intensity of behavior. We usually say a person is well motivated if he demonstrates certain behaviors, such as:

- Having a positive and enthusiastic attitude about his work.
- Consistently doing a quality, thorough job in his assigned area.
- Needing minimal instruction, direction or monitoring.
- Getting along with other employees and being a good team member.
- Showing a willingness to go the extra mile and assisting in any way possible.
- Seeking additional training, learning more about the job and making improvements.
- Following all the rules and not causing any problems.

In summary, this is a profile of an ideal top performer, of which all managers would like to have more. The challenge of management is to work with employees individually, build teamwork, create a quality work environment, remove performance barriers and apply motivational techniques to increase the number of top performers. This is not something that can happen by chance. It requires a complete, in-depth understanding of all that is involved in the concept of motivation. It also involves a certain amount of trial and error to find out what works best, with who and when.

## THINGS WORKING FOR AND AGAINST YOU

The best starting point in getting this understanding is to take a look at how things are naturally, before you try to intervene with any motivational efforts. There are some things working against you and there are some things working in your favor. Here is how things are before you even come onto the scene:

### Things Working Against You in Your Effort to Motivate Employees

Let's start with the bad news first. There are certain things that you can't do much about. These are the realities you have to accept and deal with the best you can. Here are six very real obstacles that will make your motivating efforts a real challenge:

1. People are all motivated differently and even the same person may be motivated by different things at different times. There is no one single, easy-to-apply motivator. You have to take the time to get to know your employees to understand how to best motivate them in each situation.
2. There are many factors that influence employee's motivation that are entirely out of your control. These may include influences from family and friends, restrictions of union contracts, interfering company policies, difficult geographical work locations, economic trends, and laws.
3. Many jobs are at one end of the spectrum or the other. Low paying jobs have difficulty attracting quality employees and high paying ones have a hard time keeping them.
4. Core values seem to be changing these days and we are all forced to adapt to these new changes. It isn't easy if you grew up living the values of a good work ethic and loyalty and then try to supervise employees who reject those same values.
5. People are often motivated by unconscious needs that they are not even aware of. Trying to find out what these might be is like trying to pull teeth.
6. We are a society of rebels and there will always be a certain percentage of employees who are unmotivated poor performers. Unfortunately you may spend too much time with these individuals and not get any results at all. This takes valuable time away from working with marginal employees and acknowledging the good ones.

### Things Working in Your Favor to Make Motivating Easier

Now let's look at the positive side of things. Fortunately there are several more positive things than negative ones already in place that make your motivating role as a manager much easier. Here are a few of those advantages that give you a jump-start in motivating your employees.

1. You are already well motivated yourself or you wouldn't be a manager. As a well-motivated manager you already have many of the answers inside your own head. All you have to do is stop and ask yourself the right questions.
2. Even if you only do one thing you will be highly successful. This one thing is modeling your own motivation for others to see and learn from. Others learn much of what they do from what they see.
3. Most businesses have to be competitive to survive and have cultures that encourage and enforce high performance. Many government organizations have admirable missions that employees are committed to.
4. Most people choose to work. This is good faith motivation that just needs encouragement.
5. There is usually some product that an employee can actually see as a result of his or her efforts. This is one of the strongest motivations there is.
6. Life in general is already set up to reward good performance and punish poor performance. It's called the simple law of "what goes around comes around."
7. Good performance is a very natural thing that all people want to do. Most of the time managers just need to remove barriers that keep employees from doing what they can do.
8. Selection processes these days are very scientific and unmotivated employees can easily be screened out.
9. There are plenty of helpful resources to learn more about how to be an effective motivator, in addition to the information in this section. Check them out in the *Suggested Reading List* at the end of this handbook.

As you can see, you are starting out ahead of the game without even doing anything. By reading and applying the information in this section, you will get way ahead of the curve and become an expert motivator.

## COMMON SENSE MOTIVATION

Here is a summary of all the practical principles of motivation that we know for sure.

1. Motivation is a very complex thing. There are no quick and easy techniques for motivating employees that work all the time. All employees are motivated in slightly different ways and even the same person is motivated differently at different times. You simply have to take the time to get to know employees and admittedly, a lot of success is trial and error.
2. Intrinsic motivation is superior to extrinsic motivation, because it is entirely free and is more intense and persistent. Unfortunately we spend all our time and money developing ways to motivate employees externally. When you can help an employee shift from external focus to internal focus, you have struck gold.
3. People do seem to be driven to meet general needs and they do not seem inclined to be able to focus on higher needs like teamwork and self-improvement when their more basic physical and security needs are unmet.
4. The one thing that seems to have these single biggest motivational influence on employees is the consistency with which the supervisor or manager demonstrates his or her own motivation.
5. Strong motivation and good performance is more natural than low motivation and mediocre performance. Sometimes the simple act of finding out what is preventing an employee from tapping into this natural state is all it takes to turn the situation around for the better.
6. Sometimes there are powerful informal, below-the-surface employee codes and structures that are

extremely resistive to positive motivational efforts by management. These must be found and eliminated.

7. People tend to repeat behavior for which they are receiving some kind of reward. Desired behavior needs to be rewarded appropriately. When the behavior is low motivation or poor performance, there is usually some hidden, semi-conscious reward that keeps things going, that must be eliminated and replaced.
8. Motivation for change is another complex phenomenon itself. People are not generally motivated to change unless they are totally bored, want to because they see more sure benefits than imagined fears, or feel as though they have to in order to survive. Any change efforts need to be well planned and carefully executed, after it is sold and resistance eliminated.
9. Concrete goals usually have a powerful motivating effect, especially when goal achievement is appropriately rewarded.
10. Most of the time you can only guess that there is a high degree of motivation present when an employee performs exceptionally well or a low degree of motivation when performance is poor. However, there can in fact be other explanations, especially in regards to understanding poor performance accurately.
11. The simple act of communicating clear, fair expectations to employees is a powerful motivating tool.
12. Building good teamwork can produce a collective motivation that is stronger than any of the individual member's drive and can result in better performance than any of them alone can achieve.
13. The relationship between motivation, performance and job satisfaction is complicated. The only thing we can count on is that somewhere along the line, job dissatisfaction can decrease motivation and result in poor performance. On the other hand, some job

dissatisfaction can actually motivate good performance.

14. Employees definitely need feedback about their performance. Without it they have no way of knowing how well they are doing, in case they aren't doing so well and may want to make some changes.
15. There is no doubt that a person's self-esteem has much to do with motivation and performance. Low self-esteem is most always connected with a variety of problems. Anything a supervisor can do to cultivate positive self-esteem of all employees has got to have a positive influence.
16. Simple words of recognition, acknowledgement and encouragement, when genuine and well placed, will always have a positive effect on motivation and performance.
17. Sometimes it is some critical faulty thinking or erroneous beliefs that hold motivation and performance down. Unfortunately people usually take much longer to give up mistaken thinking and wrong beliefs, than it took to acquire them.
18. Jobs that offer a reasonable degree of autonomy, require the use of varied skills, are meaningful, give a sense of responsibility and result in a finished product are more rewarding than jobs that don't offer those things.
19. Accepting the reality that success only comes after persistence through many failures can drive motivation intensely.
20. Somewhere inside each person there is a physical will that can be motivated to act one way or the other.

## LIGHT THEIR FIRES

Excellent job performance requires a raging fire of focused motivation. With all the entertaining distractions going on today, it is too easy to let a good fire go out. Below is a sure recipe for building a steady, permanent fire in your organization.

## Build the Fireplace

A good starting point is creating a fiery workplace that says, "We are on fire!" Quality workplaces hold big fires. Do whatever you can to build:

- Character that displays professional pride on the walls of your buildings.
- Organization, order, and cleanliness that results in super efficiency.
- Open communication where everyone stays informed, good ideas never get missed and all rumors are squashed.
- Organizational integrity where everyone knows and supports the mission, goals and values.
- Workforce diversity where individuals are respected for their uniqueness and also encouraged to make valuable contributions to the team effort.
- A totally positive, can-do climate with no tolerance for negativity or lack of professionalism.
- A culture of consistent sanctions that clearly reinforce good performance and effectively eliminate poor performance.

Once you build a solid fireplace, you have to make some repairs as you go. This is driven by a flaming attitude embracing continuous improvement. The key here is to set up a reliable mechanism to get accurate, useful feedback from employees so you can close the gap between how you want things to be and how they actually are.

## Open the Damper

Master motivators know an important secret. The secret is that strong motivation and good performance are both integral parts of the same natural process. This is how most employees startout—by being highly motivated to perform well. In fact, employees have to work extra hard at having no motivation and performing poorly. Managers have to work even harder to maintain such mediocrity.

The fire flows up the chimney naturally when the damper to the fireplace is open, but you do have to open it! Often, the quickest and easiest way to light employees' fires is to remove the barriers that are keeping them from raging. There can be many obstacles to a good fire. A few of these are:

- The employee doesn't understand exactly what the expected performance standard is.
- The employee is unable to do something and may feel too embarrassed to admit it.
- There may be some previous illegitimate "permissions" still lingering from previous managers.
- There may be an informal employee code interfering below the surface.
- The employee may not have the necessary tools to complete the job as expected.
- There may be some external issues going on such as family problems, financial stress or physical symptoms.

Look for real barriers keeping employees from using the natural asset of their strong motivation to perform well, *before* you automatically assume they are just being resistive, negative or uncooperative.

## Gather the Kindling

Motivational *"P" points* are what make up the kindling for the fire. These are the little things you can do to get the biggest results. There is often a tendency to want to do too much when it is a few, simple everyday things that are more effective in motivating employees. For example, one of your employees is showing a negative attitude and unwillingness to be a good team player. When you take a few minutes to explore the possible origins of these things, explain the benefits of having a positive attitude and being a good team player and maybe share a personal experience from which you learned, the fire can get started quickly.

Looking for "teachable moments" is another form of kindling. Teach problem solving skills to an employee who might be having trouble getting along with other employees, share other employee's ways of resolving conflict within a work team, and ask strategic questions to stimulate thinking in the direction you want it. Of course, the best kindling is to find out firsthand what is keeping an employee from doing his or her best.

### Use Aged, Dry Wood

The quality of the fire is often related to the quality of the wood. It is much easier to screen out green, wet wood before throwing it in and ruining a good fire. Regardless of what the wood supply looks like now, make an uncompromising pledge to get the best supply you can. The biggest clue is in a person's attitude, which reflects the degree of their motivation. Ask enough questions in the right way to get the right answers you need for a good fire. Wood that doesn't burn well should be used for other purposes, of which there are always plenty.

### Find the Matches

A basic principle of motivation that we all know but don't practice enough is this: People are all motivated in slightly different ways and even the same person is motivated differently at different times. If you have three employees, one may be driven by the possibility of getting a promotion in pay and responsibility, another by his need for public or private recognition and the third by achievement of some internal goals she has for herself.

Great motivators realize they must take the time to get to know their employees well enough to find out what brand of matches light the biggest fire. Fortunately this task is easier than we usually make it. All we have to do is ask each employee what he or she wants most in exchange for good performance.

### Stoke the Fire

The fire is likely to go out if you don't stoke it now and then. Your best stoker is good communication. Use your words to motivate. Say things with pizzazz, write upbeat memos, and learn to write headlines and speak sound bytes. Good communication is mostly good listening with both ears. Listen well enough to know what may be interfering with a particular employee's motivation and never assume there isn't a big gap between what you say and what employees hear.

Good fire-stoking communication can be greatly enhanced when you project your likability. Likability is a matter of modeling a positive attitude, being warm and friendly, and showing genuine concern and respect for others. It also involves avoiding the tendency to be judgmental, showing humility and being willing to admit mistakes and make improvements.

### Show Your Own Bonfire

There is no getting around it, the best way to motivate employees is to consistently demonstrate the enthusiasm of your own bonfire. This is especially true when you may not be feeling that confident or charged up yourself. These are the times you need to light your own fire for others to see.

No matter how motivating your words may be or what you do to encourage employees, the size of your own fire will always be what is seen, heard and remembered most. And your own positive response during adversity will be an unforgettable message with mega-impact. The best story is how your own motivation saved your life or gave you a big success.

### Enjoy the Flames

Part of having a good fire is enjoying its warmth and the dancing flames. Even when employees are intrinsically motivated to do well, occasional acknowledgment, appreciation and recognition can all serve to reinforce the fire. It is a proven principle that employees will repeat behavior for which they get reinforced. Of course the best schedule of reinforcement is the one that gambling casinos use well-varied rewards. Employees should know they will be getting rewarded, but not necessarily when or how much.

Avoid causing a draft that can put the fire out by making sure all the positive rewards are given consistently. This might not always be as obvious as it should be. There are many subtle, but insidious ways leaders and organizations can reward the wrong behaviors without even knowing it. Then they become bad habits, which are more difficult to get rid of.

Use these eight simple fire-building steps to get a raging bonfire going in your organization.

## ORCHESTRATE BENEFICIAL CHANGE

Regarding change, you have several obligations as a manager:

1. You must manage your own personal changes to keep them from spilling over into the workplace. This is another way of being a good role model.
2. You should anticipate important external social changes and trends that will affect the workplace. Today these include things such as speed, convenience, choice, cocooning, technology, shifting values, virtuality, age waves, quality and customer service.
3. You are required to manage workplace changes productively. This involves:
   - Establishing an organizational culture that is productive and supportive of change.
   - Understanding organizational readiness for change (See Appendices E and F).
   - Overcoming resistance by selling advantages, assuring success and dispelling risk.
   - Encouraging employee participation and active input in work teams.
4. You need to be able to spot unproductive, harmful and undesirable changes that violate known principles and implement more appropriate, wiser alternatives.

## ARRANGE A QUALITY WORK ENVIRONMENT

The first priority is to focus all your attention on creating a top quality work environment for all employees, which is both productive and supportive of change. Such an environment has to be in place *before* significant changes are attempted or all efforts will be in vain. Over 30 years ago, I uncovered an ideal model of a productive organization during my graduate research in organizational effectiveness. This model quality work environment has been validated over and over again through other organizational psychology research and my own management experience, so I am confident this information is solid.

Creating quality work environments involves managing both the physical and psychological realms of the workplace.

### Physical Work Environments

A quality physical workplace is characterized by the following factors:

1. **Organization and order.** Everything and everybody is in the most logical and functional place to perform most efficiently. Information, supplies and equipment is clearly identified, conveniently grouped, color-coded, and easily located for easy use and retrieval. Storage space is adequate and orderly. Things are easy to find and the odd things that are out of place or don't belong stand out. Paperwork and filing do not stack up. Things are clearly documented for easy reference. Written procedures are detailed and clear and are updated regularly. There is very little stumbling or fumbling.
2. **Cleanliness and neatness.** A regular system of daily and weekly cleaning is in place and vigorous spring-cleaning takes place twice a year. There are no obnoxious wall, ceiling or floor stains, dirty windows, damage, general clutter or over-flowing trash cans. Everyone picks up his or her own mess and there is pride about general appearance of the facility. The facility doesn't have to be ultra-modern, brand new class-A office space to look good. A little paint and cleaning go a long way.
3. **Comfort.** The work environment should be designed for the degree of comfort necessary to maximize productivity. At the minimum, space should not be

too cramped, chairs should be solid, window views and fresh air should be available and temperature needs to be controlled. Décor and color schemes can be warm or lively and pictures, rugs, lamps, curtains and plants can add a more home-like climate without jeopardizing professionalism. A coffeepot, refrigerator and microwave should be available in a lunchroom. Parking is as plentiful, convenient and safe as possible. Ergonomics are a consideration with furniture and equipment. Nothing is neither uncomfortable or too comfortable.

4. **Efficiency.** Supplies and resources are adequate and easy to obtain. All equipment is appropriate to do the job, in working order and accessible. Everyone knows where everything is and how it works. Valuable equipment and supplies are secured. Damaged equipment and furniture is replaced promptly. Work processes are streamlined and smooth. There are no visible or hidden obstacles in the way of getting this done.
5. **Motivation.** Motivational posters, inspirational sayings, employee awards and company pictures are all displayed for maximum impact. Bulletin boards have room for continuing education, career development and appropriate humor notices. The over-all physical environment lights your fire.
6. **Safety.** Lighting is good. Desks, doors and windows are lockable. Entrances and exits are marked and unobstructed and fire extinguishers and first aid kits are in working order and strategically located. There is a written emergency plan communicated to all employees. All potential safety hazards are reported and quickly corrected. Convenience does not rule over safety and security and safety are viewed as two sides of the same coin.
7. **Versatility.** Areas can serve more than one purpose, things can be moved around easily and furniture and

equipment are re-arranged periodically to create a dynamic environment. Space is available to other organizations when it is not in use.

8. **Character.** Memorabilia and other items are shown off to enhance the nature of the business and its image. Professional pride is evident in individual offices with awards, hobbies, art, etc.

## Psychological Work Environments

The quality of a psychological work environment may not be so easily noticeable as the physical one, but it is certainly just as important to cultivate. A quality psychological work environment includes these elements:

1. **Open communication.** There is a good information flow to and from all levels of the organization. Things get heard the way they were said and people listen. People feel free to talk openly, but inappropriate rumors and gossip are controlled. Important information is communicated to the right persons quickly and is always written down. People know what they need to know and where they can get the information when they don't know it. There are no surprises. Everyone is informed.
2. **Organizational integrity.** There is congruence between the organization's mission, goals, values and everyday routine. The organization's map of where it is going and how it is going to get there is clearly known and supported by all employees. There are a few high visibility key values, which are integral to the organization's mission and goals. These core values are always being enforced and reinforced. Policies and procedures are clear and detailed, but flexible. Everyone knows exactly what is expected in the way of performance. Mediocrity is not tolerated. The final result is that there is close agreement between what management says, what supervisors translate to employees, what employees actually do and what

customers and other stakeholders sense. Integrity is evident everywhere.

3. **Teamwork.** Employees are encouraged to work together in becoming an important part of the organization and contributing to outcomes. Everyone is cross-trained in other functions. Each week starts with a meeting to review progress, set goals and eliminate obstacles. There is no unfair or unnecessary division of labor and everyone shares responsibility for outcomes. People's talents are used effectively. People are not forced into static job descriptions but rather job descriptions evolve according to an employee's skills.
4. **Good support.** Resources are adequate, performance feedback is frequent, training is dynamic, supervision is active and all employees have a sense of being supported in what they are doing. People know where they can go to get help with their jobs. There is no responsibility without authority.
5. **Workforce diversity.** There is an openness, respect and tolerance for people's ethnic, gender, age, personality, intelligence, social, economic and other differences. People's differences are managed effectively for maximum contribution and minimal disruption. There is a good balance between the good of the organization and the good of individuals.
6. **Consistent sanctions.** The system of rewards and punishments is diligently, consistently and fairly directed to bring about the performance required by the organization to reach its mission and goals. There is no underground sanctioning system or ulterior power sources. People know what performance is expected and what the consequences will be for failure.
7. **Positive climate.** There is an obvious positive, upbeat atmosphere around the campus. Everyone shows high energy, enthusiasm and pride in the work. A "can-

do" attitude prevails and there is no room for negativism, complaining or cynicism. Problems are solved not created. Phones are answered and people are greeted in a positive and friendly manner, which stands out. Defensiveness and fear are non-existent. Employees feel free to be creative and take risks. Work is enjoyable.

8. **Improvement.** There is a formal system of getting organizational performance feedback and this information is used diligently to make continuous improvements. All improvements are driven and supported from the top down. There is a formal system of reporting problems and management is responsive to trying to solve these problems (Appendix E contains a practical system for measuring the quality of work environments).

## MASTER THE ART OF CHANGING PEOPLE

The ability to change people is an important skill for leaders to master before attempting significant organizational changes. Here are a few valuable people-changing guidelines:

1. The effort to change another person can be greatly enhanced when you first change something about yourself in your approach to that person. If an employee isn't showing enough enthusiasm about a work project, stop trying to talk about it to him or her. Arrange for some exceptionally dynamic training the next time the person is scheduled for training. Or if you aren't being successful reminding a person verbally to cut down on excessive socializing, try writing a note. When you change something about your approach, the other person has to change their reaction.
2. Most people today are overloaded with too much change, personally and professionally. If a change really isn't necessary, why add to the burden by introducing it? What may seem like unreasonable resistance to a reasonable change may just be a

temporary time-out from the hectic pace that has us all weary. Being sensitive to this overload and then looking for ways to lighten the load *before* adding anything more, is a "P" point that will get quick results.

3. It makes good sense to separate people's changeable things from the ones that are impervious to change. It is nice to be able to only hire people who don't need any changing, but that is not a prevalent luxury. You just have to learn to grow thicker skin with some employees you inherit and others that slip through the screening net.
4. It is too easy to mix performance problems with personality concerns. Only tangible, concrete performance problems are what need changing. With those problems you can clarify what is expected, help remove all possible obstacles and then follow-through with consequences. You just have to make certain the entire problem is poor performance.
5. People don't make significant changes unless they want to or perceive that they must. It is easy to encourage people who want to change, but there are ways to deal with those who wait until they are forced to change. You can speed that process up by power selling the advantages of the change, de-mystifying the paranoia of risk, eliminating visible chances of failure, getting their active participation and sincere commitment and building the anticipation of success.

## ACCEPT CHANGING VALUES

Our society is currently going through its third major transformation, which is having a far-reaching effect in changing, re-defining and displacing values at the workplace. The first major transformation, which totally re-arranged how we did things was the Agricultural Revolution. Another 360-degree change was later promoted by the Industrial Age. Now that age has been put in storage to make room for the Information Age. This new High Tech Age we are all getting swept into is bringing about significant changes in some of the more basic values that define the workplace. Below are a few critical areas of change for leaders to learn how to manage better:

## Organizational Structures

The present day ineffective and obsolete centralized bureaucracies, military hierarchies and corporate pyramids are quickly giving way to loosely defined virtual matrices, which in turn are prompting a multitude of other workplace value changes. Even newer flat organizations are becoming obsolete. The newer values these organizational structure changes are bringing about are spreading in the form of demands for diversity, unlimited multiple choices, chaos management, portfolio careers, job testing, egonomics, portable management, total participation and intrinsic job meaning.

At least for right now values such as loyalty, work ethic, obedience, management sovereignty, chains-of-command, financial secrecy, stability, and simplicity are being moved to the basement. It is a challenge for the leader to get to know the newer values so he or she can better manage employees driven by them.

## Motivation

Gone are the days in which employees can be controlled by external motivators such as wages, benefits, promotions, competition and threats. Productivity now has to be managed by focusing on internal motivators such as work schedule options, good communication, meaningful assignments, rewarding responsibilities, participation in decision-making, enjoyable work environments and personal growth opportunities. The difficulty is that all employees are motivated differently, and with the motivators changing, the task becomes even more complex and unsure.

## Management Role

Today "management" has evolved to the point of combining four complimentary roles:

- *Supervision*, which focuses on monitoring the efficiency and completion of tasks and asks "how" questions.

- *Management*, which focuses on building effective employee teams and asks "what" questions.
- *Leadership*, which focuses on visions and asks "why" questions.
- *Stewardship*, which focuses on facilitating employee's growth without control and asks all sorts of curious questions.

As you move into the leadership and stewardship roles you are entering uncharted waters without any maps. This expanding role requires today's manager to not only carry around a hefty toolbox, but to know where to look for new tools that haven't even been invented.

## Morality

Today even core values are being challenged. Yesterday's simple argument of absolute vs. relative morality is being redefined by different levels of okayness that seem to include more than they exclude. When the most basic values that hold the workplace together, such as decency, honesty, truth, patience and loyalty get questioned, the manager's job is like a referee trying to enforce the rules in a basketball game when there aren't any. Hopefully this present value revolution will force us all to take a harder look and find out what is really most important. Meanwhile the manager has to figure out how to deal with diversity of values while leading the organization toward productive growth. The starting point is to understand what these new values are all about.

## Speed

The number one concern of everyone today is speed. Everybody wants everything all at once, yesterday if not sooner. Technology just keeps getting faster and faster. There is no patience for having to wait for anything. This instantaneous nanosecond whirlwind pace in which the world is moving is making everything blurred, including our judgment and good sense. This speed value is one area I think needs questioning and resisting. In my opinion it is not a value that is healthy, productive or right. However, until more people start resisting such microwave mentality, managers will just have to tough it out and continue to improve their time management skills to work smarter in getting more and more done, quicker and quicker. They have my sympathy.

## MANAGE DIVERSITY

Another big challenge for managers today is to get a handle on dealing effectively with the ever-increasing diversity of the workplace. There is a dilemma for managers who have been traditionally taught to treat all people equally and consistently, with the emergence of the common sense notion that it is wrong to not be aware of and be responsive to differences that affect performance. What is needed is a careful balancing act that preserves important common rights while still taking advantage of individual differences fairly and productively. Below are five steps to help manage diversity productively:

1. In learning the art of managing diversity the first step is to increase awareness and sharpen sensitivity to the vast differences which changing organizational structures are revealing. Consider the differences that may affect the important management functions of communication, training, motivation, change and planning from this list:

   - Age groups
   - Gender
   - Cultural and ethnic groups
   - Intelligence levels
   - Personality types
   - Family structure
   - Geographical location
   - Physical abilities
   - Educational levels
   - Social and economic status
   - Religious backgrounds
   - Work experience
   - Morality
   - Abilities, needs, attitudes

   To view employees as similar would be denying literally hundreds of differences and missing the opportunity to get the most out of each person, each situation and the ability you have as a manager.

2. The second step in managing diversity involves self-reflection in focusing attention on the biases and limitations in your own thinking and approaches. You have to start asking some tough questions such as the following: How does your own education and intelligence keep you from communicating effectively with an employee of average intelligence and no formal education? How does your energetic, dominant, organized style inhibit unenergetic, inhibited and disorganized employees? Does your male, white, educated, middle-class, east-coast upbringing lead you to believe that certain values should be upheld by everybody else? When you feel exceptionally open to hearing the truth, you might even try soliciting feedback from trusted others to find out how you may be inadvertently allowing biases to flavor your communication.
3. The third step in managing diversity is to begin learning important differences between and within different groups. Are there critical language differences between different cultural groups, which affect communication? Do younger and older employees have the same attitude toward change? Are males and females motivated differently? Do creative employees need more initial supervision than more logical employees? Fortunately there are many valuable resources available to help a manager build this knowledge.
4. The fourth step in managing diversity involves taking the time to know employees well enough to be able to treat them appropriately as unique individuals with different abilities, needs, beliefs, interests, attitudes and characteristics. What is the best approach to take in talking about sick leave abuse to Mary who is a 35-year old single parent, with a Master's Degree, good work record, but a somewhat defensive attitude, as opposed to Bill, a 20-year old part-time employee with average intelligence, easy going nature, but a

questionable work ethic? How can you explain a work rule to Angie who has a nanosecond attention span and more interest in outrageous megametal, ear-busting music, M-TV visual effects and late night activities? How far will a little tolerance go in dealing with an emotional Mr. Williams who is going through a messy divorce? The only way to get the right answers to these and other questions is to get to know your employees well.

5. The last step in managing diversity is sorting out and applying basic principles and simple truths that are not affected by differences from diversity. Are there certain work needs all people have? Are there certain communication techniques, which can be effective with everyone? Are there certain "rules" humans have to follow to get to where they want to be? Do all people go through similar mental evolutions, just at different speeds? This last step is probably one in which most managers will be involved for the rest of their careers.

## LEADING FAST CHANGE

Both government and business are going through fast, dramatic organizational and operational changes which significantly impact management style. In order to manage such fast change effectively, managers need to play by a slightly different set of rules than under normal circumstances. Here are a few guidelines for managing a change-riddled organization:

### Take Charge and Stay in Charge

During turmoil employees need a strong leader and definitive direction. Be the boss in no uncertain terms, but still listen and treat people respectfully and fairly. Know exactly where you are going and show it with confidence. Lead your people to True North to the beat of a drum. This is where highly concentrated, intense "P" point skills come in handy.

## Work from a Set Agenda

During fast change important priorities get out of focus and individuals tend to invent their own. Set measurable performance goals, communicate expectations clearly, measure progress objectively and provide feedback frequently. Focus on change results, showing a strong sense of urgency and getting everyone to pay close attention. Project importance and urgency without the flavor of panic. Reduce everything to writing.

## Tighten Up Discipline

Change often leads to a preoccupation with self-preservation behaviors by employees at the expense of organizational productivity. People can give themselves loose permission to roam far from home during these times. Rules need to be demanding, clear and strictly enforced, with the main goal of productivity in focus. An explanation of why this is all happening helps greatly. Consistency and firmness without violating the principle of fundamental fairness is the ticket.

## Keep an Open Mind

A hectic pace of change can afford opportunities for doing things differently, which may prove to be more efficient or effective, *or both*. Pay attention to how things could be done to improve productivity. Look for new and creative answers to problems. Experiment with an open mind!

## Organize Work Teams

Study your employees closely to know what each can do best and arrange work tasks accordingly. Forget traditional job descriptions and focus on critical tasks, employee's particular skills and desired results. Give these work teams authority to go along with their responsibility.

## Stay Calm and be Steady

During massive change, employees need a steady anchor from which they can get a sense of stability. Avoid showing your own frazzled feelings, panic and insecurity. *Appear* to be in control, certain and confident. This is probably when your ideal role model has to be functioning at full capacity.

### Communicate, Communicate and Keep Communicating

During change, information is the main currency. Make it a priority to keep all employees informed in a timely manner. This reduces their resistance and insecurity and helps them focus better on the tasks at hand. Communication has to be a completely open, two-way process. Lacking the right information is one of the main causes of change failure. Lacking information is the main reason for resistance.

### Praise Lavishly

Organize the work environment for maximum productivity and do not hold back on acknowledgment of good results. The need for acknowledgment is greatest during such mayhem. Keep good notes so you don't forget the contributors in between all the other things that are on your mind. Rewards will assure loyalty from winners after the dust settles.

### Show Your Human Side

Sharing your personal side to employees, along with your steadiness and confidence will gain respect and build your position of leadership. It will also greatly increase your power to influence others. Figuring out "P" point self-disclosures, in knowing what to say to whom, when and where will have major impact. Employee's emotional responsiveness to these sorts of self-disclosures is greatly heightened during times of fast change.

After the mayhem passes, make sure you return to your normal management style. You will then be able to incorporate the less intense version these new skills into your repertoire.

By understanding the change process, being aware of external change influences and building a quality work environment that encourages diversity, the manager becomes a valuable change agent in the organization.

**Critical motivational "P" point question:** Have you spent enough time getting to know each individual employee to know what best motivates him or her to be productive and perform well?

**➤ Three motivational "P" point actions:**

1. Conduct an organizational assessment of the quality of your workplace (Appendix E).
2. Place posters and other inspirational messages in your office for others to see.
3. Ask for feedback as to the enthusiasm you project, especially when things might not be going as well as you would like.

"*There is real magic in enthusiasm. It spells the difference between mediocrity and accomplishment*" (Norman Vincent Peale).

# Management "P" Point # 8: Attack Difficult Things Assertively

9

*"Understand that most problems are a good sign. Problems indicate that progress is being made, wheels are turning, you are moving toward your goals. Beware when you have no problems, then you've really got a problem...problems are like landmarks of progress"* (Scott Alexander).

**Management Problem # 8:** Dealing with complex problems, complicated conflicts and costly mistakes are all part of the daily management routine. These things are all typically viewed as the heartburn of the job, whereas they should be viewed as opportunities to teach employees important problem-solving, conflict resolution and mistake recovery strategies. All difficulties should be attacked assertively to create such opportunities.

## TEACH PROBLEM-SOLVING SKILLS

Teaching effective problem-solving skills to employees is an integral part of management delegation and empowerment of those employees. However, actually teaching these skills is an extremely complex and difficult "problem" itself. It is a problem requiring the cooperative efforts of both hemispheres of the brain working together and then moving to a higher level to metacommunicate *about* this process itself. Quite a mental activity!

To teach problem-solving to employees, you have to: (a) invent and discover various problem-solving strategies through a mixture of creative, intuitive, deductive and analytical thinking, feeling and "knowing"; (b) gain experience by applying those solutions consistently and completely in getting results with real live problems; (c) avoid making common mistakes approaching problems; (d) learn to talk about all this abstract process in simple, clear, concrete and meaningful ways; and (e) demonstrate and practice those skills in the real world. Each step along the way is a real challenge.

Below are a few useful problem-solving strategies, along with examples of practical applications.

## Developing a System

The most common problem-solving approach is the medical model. This approach uses four stages of problem-solving: (a) diagnosing the problem; (b) identifying potential solutions; (c) analyzing alternatives; and (d) prescribing the best alternatives. Each step in this model becomes increasingly important. First, if the diagnosis stage misses the real cause to the problem, then the rest of the steps are in vain. Second, if one of the more valuable solutions is not uncovered, then further efforts in the next stages may not be as productive as they could be. Third, if risks, costs and benefits are not thoroughly and carefully analyzed, the wrong alternative may seem to be the best choice. Finally, if all these first three stages are not followed diligently then there will be no right prescription or any at all.

## Identifying the Real Problem

Frequently, when a difficult problem haunts us, it is because we really haven't identified the hidden "core problem" from the visible "symptoms". We spend considerable time and effort temporarily suppressing symptoms and nothing much changes. The way to apply this strategy is to keep working backwards with the "why" question until there isn't anywhere else to go.

For example, recruitment may be a serious problem for a human resources department in a large service company. The manager may identify the problem as a shrinking labor pool, low unemployment rates, poor wages, undesirable work locations, or competitors offering more benefits. But what if the real problem is the way in which the *quality* of the job itself is being perceived by potential applicants? I once analyzed the problem of younger security officers quitting at a much higher rate than other employees only to find that they felt like clowns wearing our uniform. Thinking these individuals had a poor work ethic was way off the mark.

What if you aren't looking in the *right* places for applicants? Or, what if recruitment is more of a "program," rather than a one-person job? The first stage of problem-solving is always asking the right questions to separate the more obvious symptoms from the deeper underlying causes of a problem.

### Realizing the Problem May be Unsolvable

Some problems are never going to get solved completely or go away and never come back. Wasting too much time and effort on trying to solve these type of problems is not smart management. Temporary or tentative solutions are best applied once such a problem is identified, along with the open attitude of getting ready to deal with it again when it re-occurs, as it inevitably will.

There is wisdom in the saying, "Life is not a destination, but rather a journey." Our need for certainty and closure in dealing with unsolvable problems only leads to unnecessary frustration. Bottom line type goals such as business growth, usually fit into this category. The recruitment problem above may also be such a perennial problem. Another common example is the irritating personality clashes with employees that don't actually spill over to performance, at least overtly. Eliminating the "mandate" of permanent resolution of these types of problems can reduce unnecessary frustration and free energy for more constructive problem-solving.

### Ignoring the Problem

Every *once* in awhile, when we ignore a problem, it will in fact go away. Don't count on this happening very often though, and then it is usually because we have over-focused on something to make it seem more of a problem than it really is. Temporary staff conflicts due to changing priorities may fit into this category. If the problem isn't going to hurt the company or the employees and ignoring it won't aggravate things, then this approach is worth a try. If ignoring it doesn't work, there are plenty of other strategies to apply. Time always has a funny way of diminishing the importance and urgency of problems. Whenever time can be used constructively like this, use it to your advantage.

## Brainstorming

When a certain problem may require the creating of an abundance of possible solutions, then this freewheeling technique is suitable. Brainstorming requires explicit permission to think wildly without qualification or judgment. The more different the viewpoints, the more the variety of solutions. When there is a problem with sales, brainstorming can come up with 50 or more possible solutions, ranging from a bonus program for employee leads to splurging for a box seat at the local sports stadium. The same brainstorming process can work with getting ideas to reduce employee turnover.

When implementing creative problem-solving teams it is important to establish some implicit rules. These can be requiring active participation by all, measuring the group's performance objectively against an agreed-upon standard, setting reasonable time limits, assurance of using valuable solutions and letting all participants know their individual performances will be "graded".

## Problem Break-Down

Large, complex problems can be overwhelming unless they are broken down into manageable parts. The tendency is to wander aimlessly from sub-problem to sub-problem without every finishing any resolutions. Complex problems such as employee turnover, business decline and increased expenses require a combination of strategies and consistent, systematic analysis of each part, one by one. The most difficult scenario is when two or more large, complex problems are inter-related.

Another thing to realize with a complex problem is that part of the solutions themselves may be interdependent and thus require some sort of sequencing or weighing. For example, reducing a high rate of turnover may involve raising pay rates or implementing a new training program, both of which will drive up costs. This in turn may put some business at risk and reduce revenue.

The key is to see how one solution may open the door to solving another part of the puzzle, piece by piece, as opposed to causing more problems. For instance, improving employee retention will *decrease* recruitment efforts and training investments will improve employee job satisfaction and performance, which may in turn lead to better service and justification for higher service charges. The end results may be higher client satisfaction and more business.

### Changing Languages

Sometimes the "language" in which a problem is presented is most of the problem. Remember those difficult mathematics word problems? The most effective solution in that situation was to translate the words into numbers and equations. Once you do that, the solutions are just a matter of adding, subtracting, multiplying or dividing. When you get the feeling that you can't see the forest from the trees, it is time to step back and try another "language" to help distance yourself enough from the problem to get a clearer view. When you start talking in circles that is a sure clue you need another "language."

### Making a Picture

We are very visual people, and sometimes seeing the problem as a picture wakes us up to an obvious solution, which was hidden from our mind's eye. Diagramming a flow chart on how a process actually works can quickly identify bottlenecks, unnecessary duplications or other inefficiencies. Organizational charts are also the best way to spot communication problems. Furthermore, more efficient delivery routes can be seen better on large wall maps with colored pins. I once mapped out the geographical location of supervisor's areas of responsibility and it turned out to show unfair work loads, which was the real cause for the repeated lack of follow-up with clients.

## Analogizing to other Fields

In our professionalism, we often tend to be territorial in our own area of expertise. However, our colleagues in mechanics or engineering or social work, are probably working out the solution to a similar problem we may be groping with, having a slightly different twist. Or, they may have already resolved the problem. Most great inventions such as cameras, stereos and computers looked to the human body parts for solutions. Today, government is following the business world in decentralizing, right-sizing and entrapreneuring for more efficiency, and advertising has always studied psychology for solutions. The "forest from the trees" analogy plagues effective problem-solving a lot, so this is just another way to gain access to a better vantage point and get a clearer picture. Sometimes we need new information to go past where we are stuck.

The "P" point concept I borrowed from the engineering field was highly successful in solving a variety of problems in other fields including college classes, mental health settings, prison environments and the business world. I also applied useful psychological principles to solve sport-coaching problems.

## Working Backwards, Upside Down & Inside-Out

Sometimes there is no logical flow to a problem and starting at the back end may be easier in removing the obstacles to resolving it. A good example of this is in improving the golf swing by working on the mechanics of the follow-through *before* the initial approach or back swing. Also, some core problems hide themselves well in between surface "causes" and end results. This strategy is useful in producing novel perspectives, which may be needed in dealing with "newer," unfamiliar problems from the "Information Age."

## Re-Applying Older Solutions in New and Unusual Ways

There just might be something to the saying, "Nothing is new, it is just old and retold." Present criminal justice solutions of community policing, court diversion programs and industrializing prisons are older solutions being reapplied more effectively the second time around. Sometimes, the older solution to a difficult problem was very logical, but the timing or something else just wasn't right then, but it is now. What else is employee "empowerment" but delegation of responsibility, this time with authority, direction and training? Sometimes, the renaming of an older process is all that is needed to approach it with the needed vigor to make it work.

Problem-solving cannot be taught abstractly. Strategies such as those listed above have to be demonstrated firsthand and practiced on the spot with real live problems, to be adequately transferred and learned for later use. Practice, in the case of problem-solving, does "make perfect," in the sense of building confidence in approaching problems. And of course, the larger the repertoire of strategies, the more likely the successful resolution to the problem will be.

## AVOID COMMON MISTAKES

Sometimes it helps to review some common mistakes we all make, before you try to teach others how to solve a difficult problem. The problem may pre-occupy you and keep you from remembering what you already know about effective problem-solving. Here is a list of common problem-solving mistakes:

1. Not working through an approach systematically and completely.
2. Making a critical wrong assumption about the cause of the problem.
3. Getting too much or too little information.
4. Misperceiving the size of the gap between the existing situation and the desired results.
5. Not asking dumb questions that need to be asked.
6. Over-attending to irrelevant factors of alternative solutions.
7. Avoiding the tendency to *not* discount irrelevant, useless information.
8. Over-embracing the illusion of control.
9. Spending too much time trying to solve petty, insignificant problems and not attacking the important ones.

10. Giving in to the tendency to look for disproof of unfavored alternatives.
11. Selectively imitating others' solutions without adopting the full context from where these solutions were "borrowed," e.g., *Aikido* as a non-meditative, offensive sport.
12. Letting emotion over-flavor certain solutions.
13. Stopping at intermediate causes and not digging deeper for root, core causes to the problem.
14. Not fully evaluating short and long-range costs and benefits of alternative solutions.
15. Favoring convergent strategies and solutions over more unusual, divergent ones.
16. Underestimating solvability time, costs and payoffs.
17. Not prioritizing several problems in order of importance.
18. Not anticipating other problems in solving a problem.
19. Getting into decision-making ruts once all the hard work has been done.
20. Fixating on trying to apply yesterday's solutions on today's problems.

## MAKE DECISIONS

Once all the difficult work has been completed in solving the problem, the *real* problem emerges: Making the decision to choose a certain alternative. This is a critical teachable moment when all eyes are on you as a manager. When it is time to make such a decision, that is the time to put the emotions aside and adopt a strictly rational approach.

The most productive decision-making approach is to summarize the best alternative solutions in regards to all the *negative consequences* and *positive benefits* each has for the good of the organization in the long run. A critical step is to assign a *weight* to each of these factors, because they are never equal. For instance, choosing a new vehicle may have several factors weighing in with more or less importance, such as overall cost, size, color, maintenance and mechanical requirements, etc. Once all this has been done correctly and systematically, implementing the best and wisest solution to the problem is not automatic. This is the time to carefully plan a strategy for making sure the solution gets applied correctly. Success depends upon your ability to manage change productively.

## RESOLVE CONFLICTS FOR WIN-WIN RESULTS

In Organization A, the rest of the work team is always complaining about Employee Jones not doing his share of work. This is disrupting the team's progress in implementing an important operational change. You initially specified goals and methods for the work team, but you are not sure what the assignments are now. How do you approach this situation?

In Organization B one of your supervisors, Supervisor Smith, walks onto a contract site she is inspecting and the client complains angrily that two of the contract employees were having words earlier and that they were being very disruptive and abusive in front of company visitors. He wants to cancel the contract. How should Supervisor Smith and you deal with this situation?

In Organization C, Manager Walker is in a budget meeting and upper-management wants to cut her budget by 20% in order to implement a new career development program for employees. What does Manager Smith do in response to this plan?

Conflicts similar to these happen routinely in organizations. Managers need to become experts at resolving conflicts, which occur in their own interactions. They also need to learn how to teach employees the necessary skills to deal with a variety of conflict situations that happen on the job and negatively effect productivity of the organization. Conflict management is both a science and an art. The science involves understanding the common elements of a conflict and gathering accurate data, while the art part involves the sensitivity of framing the most appropriate strategy and then applying the right technique.

A "conflict" is any situation, which tends to cause disruption to the "normal" routine. Conflicts can range from very minor, such as a change in meeting time, to very major, such as downsizing an organization. Conflicts often involve the necessity of change, and change is something we seem to have a natural tendency to resist. Because of this, we try to avoid conflicts whenever possible. However, conflicts are very much a part of the natural growth process of any relationship or organization. And, no relationship or organization can ever hope to mature productively and be successful, *without* being able to get through conflicts effectively.

Managers must learn the art and science of conflict resolution as an important part of their management skill repertoires. But, make no mistake about it, this is a difficult area to master, because most conflicts do not pose a pattern to which we can practice a set response and improve. Each new conflict brings a whole different scenario and characteristics requiring a unique solution. Most serious conflicts are very complicated and have elements that make them unsolvable in a way we might prefer them to be resolved. Actually resolved is probably not the best term here, because the conflict situation has never been solved in the first place or it wouldn't continue to be a conflict.

The art and science of learning, applying and teaching effective conflict resolution involves four stages: (1) Understanding the anatomy of a conflict in general; (2) Assessing critical aspects of the conflict; (3) Framing the most important strategy; and (4) Selecting and applying to right technique to use. Each of these stages is discussed below:

## Understand the Anatomy of a Conflict

*High*

| | |
|---|---|
| **Importance** | **Impact** |
| **Investment** | **Implementation** |

*Low*

Every conflict has four values, each ranging from low to high in relation to the issue and outcome: *Importance, Impact, Investment, and Implementation.* It is important to be aware of these four elements and how the particular conflict at hand fits into these values.

The degree of *importance* the issue has to all the stakeholders is always critical. Examples of high importance issues are random drug testing of employees, changing primary business focus from pricing to customer service or changing a company name. Examples of low important issues are re-arranging lunch hour schedules, selecting stationary vendors and a misspelled word on a routine report. Sometimes issues are important to some of the stakeholders and not important to others and this difference must be exposed and worked through.

The *impact* the issue outcome will have on all the stakeholders is another primary concern. Examples of high impact issues are downsizing, moving the organization to a different state and declaring bankruptcy. Examples of low impact issues are temporary work schedule changes, making a minor payroll error change for a single employee and adding another stop on a delivery route. Again, the issue may impact different stakeholders differently. The key is to identify all the stakeholders and what the impact will be on each.

The amount of time, effort, personal values and money already *invested* in a certain issue/outcome or all the other things that are required to make a change, will always be an important priority to review. Unfortunately, we often invest too heavily in the wrong issues and correcting those situations are usually more costly than we can afford until it isn't an option. A good example of this dilemma is spending more money to replace expensive computer systems that can't be serviced quickly. Examples of high investment issues are changing payroll programs, changing building security systems and updating computer equipment. Examples of low investment issues are making a temporary procedure permanent, following the recommended maintenance schedule for equipment and terminating an unproductive employee during probation.

The degree of effort and "cost" of *implementing* a resolution is a practical but critical consideration. The more planning that goes into high implementation issues, the better the success.

Examples of high implementation issues are organizational re-engineering, changing contract services and starting up a new satellite office. Examples of low implementation issues are changing the front door lock, removing an ineffective employee from a site or requiring biweekly activity reports instead of monthly ones.

## Access Critical Aspects

With each conflict that occurs, it is important to do an objective assessment of the value of each of the above conflict aspects. Many hard questions need to be asked. Who is the issue really most important to? How is the degree of importance determined? What actual impact will the issue outcome have on the whole organization or on the individuals who are involved? Will the potential impact spill over to external stakeholders? What kind of investment has already been made in the way of time and resources toward a particular outcome? Is more good money being thrown on top of bad money? What kind of personal values are involved in the investment? How difficult will it be to apply various resolution options?

Obviously, the strength of the conflict and the difficulty of resolution are tied to the value strength of these critical aspects. The tasks involved during this stage of conflict resolution are mostly asking the right questions and getting honest, accurate and thorough answers.

Now let us go back to the first of our opening scenarios. In Organization A, with the one employee not pulling his work load in the work team, what are the questions which a manager may want to ask to determine the values of the four critical aspects?

### *Importance*

As far as assessing *importance* goes, here a just a few questions to which the manager may need answers: How important is the operational change that the work team is trying to implement? Has this situation happened frequently in other areas of the organization? Are there major personality conflicts within the team that may be affecting other work areas? How widely is this situation known in the organization?

### *Impact*

Some questions to ask to assess impact in this case may be: What will happen to the planned change if this situation is not addressed quickly? What will the over-all effect be on the organization? Can team members be switched without disrupting other things? Is this conflict a symptom of something bigger?

### *Investment*

To assess the value of investment in this situation, these questions might be asked: How long has the team been working on implementing the change? Have their efforts involved large resource expenditures? Is this change part of something bigger where substantial money and people have already been committed? How much value will the change have for the organization? Has the team been working together on other projects? How long has the "problem" employee been around?

### *Implementation*

In assessing implementation value in this Organization A scenario, the following questions can help: Is there a simple explanation as to why the problem employee isn't doing his or her share? Is this person resisting because he or she sees the process going sideways? How much effort will be involved in holding a discussion meeting? Will it be easiest to replace this person? Are there any other alternatives to implementing this change?

## Frame a Strategy

Once the four critical aspects of the conflict are assessed then the next task becomes framing the most appropriate strategy of resolution. Table 1.0 outlines the four basic strategies with practical application examples. These four basic strategies are *Acting, Adjusting, Accommodating* and *Avoiding*. Acting is exercising an authoritative position to resolve a conflict quickly without discussion or input and is generally most appropriate to emergency situations when all issue and impact aspects are running high and a quick solution is mandatory.

Adjusting is working to get to common agreement and is most appropriate in situations when important goals are incompatible or where both sides have valuable contributions. This is compromising to get positive consequences for everyone while minimizing any important and valuable sacrifices.

Accommodating is yielding but putting self-interests aside for the good of the situation or others. It is most appropriate when one person is wrong, when temporary solutions can buy time for more complex resolutions to be worked out, or when you can give in to gain more in the long run.

Avoiding is walking away from the issue and is most appropriate when all the issue aspects are low, when time alone can resolve the issue or when you just can't win.

**Table 1.0 Management Conflict Resolution Strategies**

| Strategy | Definition | Application |
|---|---|---|
| **Act** | Exercising authority or power to declare outcome. | Emergency situations requiring quick, decisive action when issue aspects are high.<br>When the welfare of the organization is at stake, and the solution is right.<br>With important issues that involve widespread, unpopular decisions. |
| **Adjust** | Splitting differences, exchanging concessions, giving and taking to get to a middle ground. | For temporary settlements to complex issues.<br>When high impact, important goals are mutually exclusive.<br>To merge valuable insights and different perspectives. |
| **Accommodate** | Sacrificing self-concerns, yielding to the other person. | When expedient solutions are needed under time pressures.<br>For temporary settlements.<br>When you are wrong. |
| **Avoid** | Withdrawing, sidestepping or postponing the issue. | When all the issue aspects are low.<br>When the issue is just symptomatic of something bigger.<br>When time will bring about a natural outcome. |

Assessing critical aspects by asking the *right* questions and getting the *correct* answers will help assure the framing of the most appropriate conflict resolution strategy. Let us go to our second opening scenario with Organization B and the angry client. Assessment of all the four critical aspects of this conflict will show all of them as high.

The incident with the employees arguing in front of others at the client's facility was high in importance, investment, impact and implementation. The very chance of cancellation of the contract is very important to all the stakeholders. It is also high in investment for all the stakeholders, including the client, contractor, employees and supervisor, and the public. The outcome will impact all concerned in a very costly and time consuming manner, as some employees may lose their jobs, there will be lost revenue, the client may lose valuable business and the supervisor will be judged on his or her performance. Implementation of a resolution will involve such difficult actions as disciplining employees, trying to convince the client not to cancel the contract, finding suitable work for those laid off if it is canceled, making up lost revenue, and renegotiating another contract.

The primary strategy in this situation will dictate *Action.* The employees must be removed from the site and replaced and the client must be convinced that the situation is being corrected and that it will not occur again. The supervisor must be directed to investigate the situation thoroughly, write a detailed report and follow-up on any needed action. In time, this situation may involve some *adjusting* and some *accommodating,* especially if the client was working from incomplete or wrong information about what did or didn't go on with the employees.

Adjusting generally involves making compromises when the issue is high in importance and impact and the goals are exclusive. The art of adjusting is to view the concessions as the only available means of gaining the desired outcome (keeping the contract), and not giving up something (billing adjustment, replacing the employees). More than likely, this situation will also require *accommodating* the client in anyway possible to buy time to save the contract with impressive actions. What it probably won't involve is any *avoiding* (unless of course, it is a lost cost because of repeated past disasters).

## Learn Techniques for Applying Strategies

When a conflict requires the manager or employee to *act,* there are certain techniques that can help bring about effective action. For instance, it is very wise to anticipate any likely fall-out and potentially destructive consequences beforehand and to have a contingency plan ready to activate. For instance, what if one of the employees you are trying to discipline just walks away from you? Or what if he or she presents different evidence than what you have found? What if the client gave you the wrong names?

Another good technique in acting is to focus on your own state of calmness. In the majority of conflicts, emotion runs high and the uncontrolled expression of feelings makes resolution difficult if not impossible. When the other person is ranting and raving and you can remain calm, you can eventually calm the other person down long enough to get him or her to see important points about the situation that might be wrongly contributing to those feelings and *preventing* a successful resolution.

Half the battle in the majority of conflict situations is to *listen* well enough to really *understand* the other person's position. It is that *lack of understanding* that might really be the conflict itself. Furthermore, it is both imperative and fair to speak precisely what it is you are going to do and why. Finally, effective action is carried out with precision and decisiveness. In times when action is the only recourse there is no room for hesitancy or confusion.

*Adjusting* often requires mediating the conflict with an impartial, objective third party "referee". This technique involves identifying the pros and cons of all the giving and taking. For instance, in our third opening scenario, what will the organization be gaining with the new career development program and what will it be loosing in cutting the other budget by 20%? Can the target program actually save the organization enough money to implement the new program in stages? What relevance does the fact that the company has just doubled it's assets and number of employees, have on downsizing the one department? These pros and cons need to be explored and discussed in depth.

When a conflict is best resolved by adjusting, it is critical to get both parties to prioritize and buy into the exchanges and concessions. Agreement is essential on the most important compromises and less essential on the less important ones. A good way to end such mediating is to summarize common agreement, ask for recommitment on carrying out the required actions and to set a date for a follow-up meeting to check progress.

An *accommodating* strategy can be useful in several different situations. One such situation is when one of the parties is *wrong*. If the contract employees were not actually arguing in public, but rather behind closed doors, then the strategy for approaching the client will shift. The object becomes getting the other person to admit it when he or she is wrong. There are a few ways to do this including the presentation of indisputable proof in the way of facts. Other ways are by separating feelings from thoughts to allow for objectivity to set in, or the careful introduction of appropriate humor. Sometimes all we need is a good laugh at ourselves and how we over-bond to issues.

Other situations lending themselves to this strategy are when the issues are much more important to one person rather than the other or when temporary solutions can buy some time until a more permanent long-term solution can be applied through careful *adjusting*. The best techniques for applying this strategy include explaining why one person needs to yield and how it will be beneficial; interpreting the accommodation in a positive light rather than negative one; and consciously thanking the person doing the accommodating.

There are certain situations that will deserve an *avoiding* strategy. These include when all the issue aspects of the "non-conflict" are all low, when the apparent conflict is just a symptom of something bigger or deeper and when time alone will bring about the desired outcome naturally. A good question to answer is this: If I don't do anything right now, what is the worst that could happen? Or, put another way, what is the least I can do and still keep my options open? Before an avoiding strategy is chosen, it is wise to make certain all the issue aspects are in fact low.

Good techniques to apply with the avoiding strategy are to always explain why you are not dealing with the issue at the present time, to let people know you are separating them to let time and distance cool them off and to identify the superficial symptoms from the core problems to be worked on later.

It is quite feasible that very complex conflicts may require a combination of all four of these strategies and several of these techniques. When such conflicts are so complex, it is best to break them down into more manageable "mini" conflicts and attempt to resolve them part by part. Also, missing information can change resolution strategies.

Going back to the division of labor problem in Organization A, what bearing would the fact that the work group was made up of all volunteers as opposed to being assigned the task, have on the resolution strategy? In the second situation, say our two employees are new on the job. What effect would that have on framing the best strategy? Might it indicate that there are some other equally important problems that need to be resolved, such as poor training, inadequate supervision or unclear operating procedures? And, in our third scenario, how would the fact that the new program wasn't that popular with the company employees, affect the values of that issue?

In conclusion, successful conflict resolution involves a process of first assessing critical aspects of the conflict issue's importance, investment, impact and implementation, then framing the most appropriate strategy of acting, adjusting, accommodating or avoiding and finally applying the right technique. Good questions must be asked to get the best possible information. Managers who follow this process will improve their conflict management skills and help their organizations to grow productively.

## RECTIFY MISTAKES GRACEFULLY

I was once wrongly convinced that a worthy goal of personal and professional excellence was to avoid making mistakes. Mistake making was a seal of doom. Consequently, I would go out of my way to avoid doing anything risky enough to result in a mistake. Like everyone else, I would rationalize the mistakes I couldn't avoid making or deny the ones from which I couldn't dodge blame.

Fortunately a close friend kindly reminded me that a person who doesn't make any mistakes doesn't make much of anything. I also reminded myself that I usually didn't learn much from my successes; but as far as my mistakes go, now that is a different story. What I have learned from all this is that you are bound to make mistakes, but you don't have to be bound to those mistakes you make.

The pursuit of personal and professional excellence invariably involves making mistakes. What we need to learn is how to make mistakes and recover gracefully. Mistakes allow us to learn valuable lessons and make needed improvements. Mistakes also remind us of the importance of humility. Most importantly, mistakes bring out our humanness.

Long ago, I discovered a simple strategy that has kept me from drowning on more than just a few occasions. This mistake recovery strategy can be adapted to any situation. The win-win strategy has five key steps:

### Own the Mistake

When you make a mistake, take immediate ownership. Don't go looking for a place to hide. Openly confess, "I made a mistake." Denial, blaming, lying and other conniving strategies can only have unhappy endings, as at least two recent Presidents know. Honesty in admitting a mistake can often preclude any negative consequences of your mistake.

At the least, such an admission will always take the wind out of the sails of a person who may have an axe to grind with you. I remember once being forewarned about an angry client of a major account calling to cancel service. When I answered the phone with, "We really screwed up this time and we probably deserve to be canceled," there was an unexpected silence. This frank admission turned out to save the account. It also completely avoided a potentially unpleasant conversation.

### Apologize

It may seem unnecessary to say you are sorry once you accept blame for the mistake. However, a genuine apology is often the simple cue that encourages the forgiveness that is waiting to be given. A quick, sincere apology defuses hostility no matter how grievous the injury.

An apology is not only an expected social propriety, which can hurt you when not offered, but it is also a practical act that can help open the door to further communication. Sometimes an apology is as necessary as ice in lemonade on a hot summer's day. A mistake without an apology is one that often isn't forgiven or forgotten.

### Implement a Quick Fix

It doesn't impress anyone by admitting you goofed, asking for forgiveness and then not doing anything about the situation to make it better. This is lack of follow-through at its worst. It puts the credibility of your apology at risk and it wastes the energy it took to courageously own the mistake and humbly apologize.

People want mistakes rectified *now*. Even if you have to plug up a hole with your finger, you are showing a willingness to try and correct a problem you created. This step of the process will buy you some thinking time until you can figure out what to do next. And not correcting a smaller mistake while you still have the opportunity may result in one too big for you to do anything about later.

### Develop a Cure

When you are a victim of a mistake, you usually want the other person to admit fault without your having to conduct a major investigation. You also want the satisfaction of hearing an apology and getting some immediate relief from the consequences of the mistake. At some point, you also want to be reassured that the same problem isn't going to reoccur. Why not treat others the way you want to be treated?

When you take the time to think about some permanent preventative solutions, you are showing admirable behavior with which no one can find fault. While doing this, you are also learning a valuable way to stop making mistakes. I can remember being very impressed with a security guard who suggested a daily exchange of personal keys for building keys when he finally got tired of being called back to return the key to our front door. Once the new procedure was in place, the problem never happened again.

### Offer Some Penitence

This last step of the recovery strategy guarantees success. It is the ultimate follow-through, which completes the mistake correction circle on a positive note. When you make a mistake that causes loss or inconvenience to someone else, it is not only a polite gesture to offer some sort of penitence, it is the *right* thing to do to properly finish business. When you pay good money for a service that you don't get, you want at least a partial refund.

Offering victims of our mistakes a token of penitence acknowledges their worth and confirms the sincerity of our apology. When I get served a lousy meal at an expensive restaurant, I don't expect the whole meal to be free, but a complimentary dessert is a nice touch. *Something*, no matter how small, will always be remembered positively.

When you make a mistake, first openly admit that you made it. Then apologize for making the mistake. Next take immediate action to fix things on a temporary basis. Follow this up with some long range planning to prevent the same mistake from happening again. Complete the mistake recovery process by offering some penitence. This strategy will help you to recover from mistakes gracefully.

**Critical problem-solving "P" point question:** Do you dread conflicts or see them as an opportunity for growth?

> **➤ Three problem-solving "P" point actions:**
>
> 1. Apply the conflict resolution strategy outlined in this section to the next conflict that occurs in your organization.
> 2. Look for live, real-life work problems to teach others how to apply the strategies you have learned.
> 3. Discuss the most perplexing problems you have with friends outside your career field.

*"A problem clearly stated is a problem half-solved"* (Dorothea Brande).

# Management "P" Point # 9: Use a Telescope and a Microscope

10

"*The successful man is the average man, focused*" (Unknown author).

**Management Problem # 9:** There are a gazillion important things to focus on and there are even more tempting distractions ready to steal our attention. You have to first identify the most important things to focus on, such as all these ten core management activities, and then keep reminding yourself not to let them fade or get replaced by more glamorous new gimmicks. Then you have to remember to focus back and forth between the big picture out there and the details in here. This is tough mental discipline and there is nothing to make it easier.

## MAINTAIN STEADY FOCUS

If there is one action verb that can best define the most important aspect of the management process, it is the word *focusing*. To achieve excellence, a manager must stay well-focused. It is through this intense and steady focus, that he or she communicates important things to help the organization become as productive as possible in achieving it's purpose. Without such intense and steady focus, the manager is reduced to *wandering* and *reacting*, neither of which are conducive to productivity. Below are ten critical areas for managers to focus on:

### Mission

Every productive organization has a powerful and clear purpose which directs all activities. The best missions are those that are simple, admirable, practical and widely beneficial, and ones that communicate a vivid image. The manager has to hold this mission in intense focus and communicate it passionately and frequently to motivate employees to embrace it fully and carry it out enthusiastically. The mission is the big picture which always has to stay in the background of a manager's general focus. All these other focus points need to stay in the foreground.

### Values

Every good mission needs a few core working values to help make it alive and workable. The simpler the mission, the simpler the values and in some cases a single value is all it takes. The chosen values, such as "extra mile" customer service; long and disciplined work hours, or casual, spontaneous creativity, are what define the culture of the organization. When these values are not in line with the mission or not supported by all employees, then the organization starts going sideways. The few core values are what the manager has to keep in focus to enforce and reinforce consistently and persistently, in a variety of ways.

### Results

Excellent managers set goals, measure progress and get results. They are excellent time managers who set priorities right and always work on meeting deadlines. It is the results which help the organization achieve it's mission, not necessarily the activities along the way which may or may not be getting those results. There is one important caveat here. Focusing too much on the outcome doesn't always get the desired results. Sometimes you have to focus on the *change* that is needed to get results.

### Training

A manager must focus on when employees need what training and on how to make training opportunities available at the right time to have the most effect at the least cost. It is also important to know when to take advantage of critical situations to teach employees how to do something, such as applying problem-solving strategies, by working on an actual problem-solving situation at hand. Finally, it is important for the manager to focus on his or her own training needs, for the purpose of improving skills, demonstrating credibility and strengthening self-motivation.

### Employees

A great deal of a manager's time should be spent focusing on employees. This focus involves paying close attention to employees' productivity, competencies, motivations, needs, preferences and problems. The more the manager knows about employees, the better the team will function. Although a manger must always keep the big picture of the over-all company in focus, it is equally important to also keep the individual concerns of employees in focus, because those concerns are their *main* focus. Letting them know you know that, has big payoffs.

### Details

The knowledge of details of how things are done offers real power to the manager to teach others, gain credibility and win cooperation. It is the focus on such details as how to actually fix a piece of malfunctioning equipment or do a job more efficiently, which helps identify procedures which need improvement or ones which could be effective in other areas. Granted, in complex organizations, a manager can easily get lost in too many details, but getting too far removed from being "hands-on" has worse consequences.

### Feedback

With all that may be going on in an organization, it is easy for the manager to not even seek feedback or if it is given, not to listen to it too carefully or apply it. However, the importance and utility of feedback must be kept in sharp focus, because it is often the precise information which can help the manager avoid going in the wrong direction or making a destructive mistake. Solicited feedback is extremely important to keep in focus for the right application. No organization or individual can move forward without using some sort of feedback system and it is the manager's responsibility to not lose focus on this very important operational element.

### Improvement

Excellence in anything requires a dedication to always look for ways to improve. The feedback system discussed above will provide the necessary information to identify the areas which need improvement. Excellence in management involves using feedback to improve productivity mainly by focusing on the removal of obstacles to productivity and on identifying more efficient means to reach goals and get results. One special area of improvement for managers to keep in sharp focus is *self-improvement*, because improvement efforts always have to start at the top.

### Trends

We are living in a world of constant change, so management excellence requires constant focus on important trends which can effect productivity in the workplace and success of the organization. Not paying attention to important changes such as employees need for meaningful responsibility, flexible work schedules or home-based work opportunities, could leave a manager with a serious recruiting problem. Also, failing to focus on trends of the marketplace or of the competition, can leave the organization in the dust.

### Self

The smart manager realizes something very early in the game: His or her own activities are always under a microscope and consequently, actions do speak louder than words. When managers fail to keep the importance of their own role-modeling behavior in focus, core working values in the organization can easily get contaminated and start disintegrating. An important aspect of this self-focus, is accurate awareness of employees' perceptions of the manager. Another part of the self which is as equally important to keep in focus is wellness, in avoiding stress overload. The pressures of management are unique and need special relief.

By focusing on these ten areas alone, the manager will avoid wasting time doing other unproductive things. He or she will be busy leading the organization to a place where all the stakeholders will enjoy and benefit from.

## CLOSE GAPS

Leading is a continuous process of creating and closing gaps. Imaginative, gap-creating dreaming is fun, but closing the gaps is where all the hard work is. Of course the big gap to close is the one between where your organization is and where you want it to be. In order to close this big gap, there are many littler ones making it up that need closing first. A few of these critical gaps are discussed below.

### The Gap Between What You Say and What They Hear

It is never a good idea to assume communication is good; it is usually as smooth as glue. When you think about it, there is little chance that what you mean to say will be heard, interpreted and acted upon exactly the way you meant or said it, without constant examination and improvement of all the words you use and how you convey them.

Good communication also requires knowing and connecting to your audience. There are just too many possible interferences between you and your audience in the way of personal word connotations, different perceptions, various comprehension levels, unique information processing styles and many other individual characteristics and needs.

Accuracy and impact of communication is something you may never be able to perfect, but constantly striving to improve these things will yield noticeable and continuous results. Closing this gap has to start with learning how wide it has gotten without your knowing that. You find this out by openly seeking, listening to and using honest feedback from all sources.

### The Gap Between What You Know and Don't Know

The process of mental evolution involves the gradual separation of fact from fiction. The first step in closing the gap between what you know and don't know is the hardest one to take. This is admitting that which you think you know may not be necessarily so. This takes much openness and courage!

It seems we only start learning when we realize how little we know. Sooner or later you must face that much of what is in your head is from superficial thinking, inadequate judgment, erroneous beliefs and unclear creative and intuitive sensations. Then you can begin to grasp a better understanding of how things really are apart from your limited and biased perceptions.

Before you can recognize the truth of anything, you need to clean your glasses from the smears caused by all the selective assumptions you have made and not verified. With an empty and open mind, you become much more receptive to life-changing critical thoughts, creative urges and intuitive feelings that get you closer to magical moments of serendipity. With these valuable discoveries you become more successful in eliminating the real obstacles in your way. The biggest one of all may be your own thinking, especially what you think you know.

### The Gap Between Organizational Mission, Goals and Values and Everyday Behavior

Once when I was a prison administrator, I conducted an interesting exercise. I had four levels of the organization—upper management, mid-level managers, line employees and inmates, all write down what they thought the mission, goals and values of the organization were. The vast incongruences between and even within different levels were disconcerting, but at least it was a good start in improving things.

Sometimes you have to be honest about how bad things really are and become uncomfortable enough with that reality, before you are motivated enough to do anything about the situation. And you just can't assume everything is okay without checking it out. Also, some wisdom I learned in building prisons was to pour most of the sidewalk concrete where the footsteps already were, rather than where I wanted them to be.

## The Gap Between You and Your "Customers"

Whether your "customers" are employees, the public or clients, there is going to always be a gap between you and them that needs constant attention. It seems that just as you figure out something and make progress in closing this gap, the market and rules change and make the gap wider.

Obviously, the key to staying ahead of the curve is to have a good system of feedback that anticipates the market and rule changes. Another good practice is to record history and review it periodically, as history does have a way of repeating itself. If you know where you've been and where you are now, you are in an excellent position to know where you are likely to be going in the future. Asking the most difficult questions, such as those posed by Kevin Freiberg in *Nuts!* will give you useful information too.

## The Gap Between *What* You Are Trying To Do and *How* It is Being Done

Personally, I think one of the most common shortcomings of many popular self-help and business management books is the tendency to tell the reader *what* needs to be done and then leave out the specifics of *how* to actually do it. Granted, we often focus on the wrong *what* and need to be reminded of that fact in a gentle or humorous sort of way, but people can't be totally left to sink or swim in figuring out how to apply the good advice.

There has to be a delicate approach to telling someone how to do something. In the most effective organizations, leaders decide the "what" of the organization, empowering employees by leaving the "how" up to them, only guiding them subtly to the water trough when necessary. Being too aggressive in this domain can be perceived as an infringement on freedom and get quickly rejected. The book *Fish* describes the right technique of affecting good change when it becomes obvious that it is needed.

Probably the safest approach is to orchestrate situations that encourage employees to ask how you managed to do something. Making several neutral, concrete how-to suggestions when the time is right is usually a good approach too. At any rate, whatever the solution is, the person has to have some sense of discovering it by him or herself without too much assistance. A careful mixture of unconditional acceptance and a challenge to do better always seems to work best.

### The Gap Between What You Expect and What You Get

Closing this gap starts with having realistic expectations, clearly communicating these expectations to everyone who needs to know them and closing the sale by getting everyone to buy into them. Of course it can't hurt to keep open to more possible outcomes than just a certain one you may prefer. Also, expectations don't need to be set in stone, they can be changed through thoughtful negotiation.

Expectations are not something you quickly share and then never refer to again. Your expectations are the standards with which you measure organizational performance and this is an everyday activity requiring consistent and persistent enforcement and reinforcement. It is also helpful to allow a two-way street regarding expectations, as we all have them.

### The Gap Between Discovering Generalized Advice for Others and Applying It to Your Own Self-Management

All the wisdom learned from a leading experience is empty and useless unless you can resist the temptation of your ego's need for recognition and give into a quiet achiever's profound sense of humility. After all, all great ideas are open for ownership by everyone and no one in particular. An important leadership discovery is that nothing is new, it is just old and retold in newer and more unusual ways.

The ultimate priority of leadership is really self-growth in the discovery of what Stephen Covey calls "true-North principles and enduring truths." Role modeling of this self-growth knowledge is always the best method of passing it on to others. This is the subtle but powerful unspoken action that effectively closes the gap between what you know and what others need to know so that you can make progress at closing these other little gaps and eventually get to where you want to be. Again, the trick is to skillfully merge two messages simultaneously. These are communicating acceptance and recognition of what a person knows, while issuing a subtle challenge to know more.

The more little gaps you can identify and act to close, the closer you will get to where you want to be.

## SEIZE THE MOMENT

If there was one positive thing the decadent, hedonistic drug and sex culture of the sixties taught me, it was the wisdom of the omniscient fiat "Tune into the now". The only trouble was, it took me over thirty years to fully understand the real message through its psychedelic cellophane wrapper.

It is fine to analyze the past in order to understand it better and then plan for the future to better arrange desirable outcomes. That is responsible living. However, nothing ever gets done to change anything in any temporal zone other than the *now*. If there are things going on today that are not so desirable, we must seize the moment right now to act. We can't wait until we can get it perfect or be assured of flawless outcomes. We need to do what we can now, not later. Talking won't do it, only doing will get it done.

How can we seize these moments of opportunity? A good starting point is to slow down and try to understand why something is happening, especially seizing the moment to see some positive lesson in the most unpleasant circumstances. The older generation may not like the moral erosion, artificial affluence and other destructive influences that are going on today, but guess what? We all helped create this state of affairs. We invented the "Information Age" and embraced all that was to come with it. That realization may be a bit difficult to swallow.

It may be the little things we can each do to help influence positive changes that count most. Here are a few little things I find to have a big influence on producing positive change.

### Understand What is Going On

All the unhealthy things going on today can't be changed without some understanding. First we have to take the time to understand how we helped bring about these things that disturb us and understand what we are doing to perpetuate them. Then we need to learn how to stop doing that. It is through this type of understanding, that we will begin to see some opportunities to seize in acting now to play our own small, but important role in making things better.

Why did we create all this unhealthiness? Maybe so we could experience its unpleasantness firsthand in order to know this is not what life is really supposed to be like, instead of just taking someone else's word for it. When you begin to know something is "wrong" from direct experience, you are more likely to be able to stop it, in the right way and for the right reason. I hope we weren't just bored, but if that is the case, we may need to explore more productive alternatives to getting unbored. Whatever the reason, taking ownership of the consequences is always the first step in correcting the problem.

### Challenge Assumptions

The biggest assumption I have been challenging lately is the one about so many bad things needing remedies. Who's to say most things aren't really progressing the way they are suppose to? Or maybe we are just over-focusing externally on the big group picture at the expense of our own internal, smaller individual ones. I know that when I don't challenge this assumption, I get caught up in fighting symptoms and never discovering any cures. I also know that when I start challenging this assumption I begin to catch glimpses of the little things I can do myself to make it a slightly better world.

Are we assuming the youth today aren't voting because of apathy or laziness, when it may be that they are saying something we need to be listening to? Are we assuming that couples are just giving up too easily in their marriages when they have never learned the art of loving or how to select the right mate? Are we assuming that the present chaotic socioquake of values is destructive when it might be just what we need most? These and other assumptions are worth challenging.

### Ask More Questions

I used to think you had to be born with common sense, but when I started applying my own best advice of asking more questions, my own store of common sense started growing exponentially. Asking questions to increase common sense is useful in many ways. One important use is in solving problems. If we want to learn how to stop violence, sexual promiscuity and moral corruption, then we need to ask some questions, particularly, "what am I doing myself to perpetuate these things?" If you want to learn how to be a better parent or employer, then you need to ask your children and employees how to do that. If you want to find out about something you don't understand then you need to ask someone who does. You need to ask more questions.

Just asking questions may not take advantage of an opportunity fully enough. You may need to ask the right person the right question in the right way. There is an art to asking questions that get the most accurate and useful information. Asking questions to which you already have your answers is certainly not a way to do this. Nor is forcing artificial, incomplete or dishonest answers.

### Listen, Listen, Listen

You haven't begun to listen until you force yourself to shut up when you are on the edge of your seat and want to say something so badly you can't stand it. After that you can start mastering the art of "two-eared" listening, which is hearing *what* is actually being said through all the noise of *how* it is being said. This is probably the case with violence. When you start using both ears you can also hear what is *not* being said that may be more important than what *is* being said. This is probably the case with corruption and immorality.

Good listening skills also include fine tuning your sensitivity to catch moments of opportunity. One powerful moment is waiting to share what you know until someone else asks you, rather than imposing it. Another one is listening for questions because that is when your answers will actually be heard. Also, none of us should underestimate the power of being a good role model and that is an opportunity that occurs continuously. Do as I do has always been the simplest and surest way of instruction.

### Shed the Stress

The speed and demands of modern day living bring much stress. Trying to avoid this stress can be stressful in itself. We all know that we need to establish healthier routines to limit the destructive effects of distress, but what we don't know is how the stress we are feeling effects other people with whom we are interacting. According to the children, it is not good.

Shedding stress is a conscious decision to make now. The next time you are in the middle of getting stressed out and you are about to talk with another person, stop and think about how contagious stress is. Having one interaction that is not contaminated by a previous situation's stress can open the door for many more. That is an opportunity to seize right away. We need all the stress-free moments we can get.

### Focus on Now

It is ironic that we have to fight so hard to not do this. Our escape is in thinking back to better times in the past and dreaming ahead to better ones we hope for in the future. Oddly, both are actually occurring *now*. The only trouble is, we are not taking advantage of all the opportunities to act now. We are too busy trying to get it perfect or guarantee certain results. Now the trouble with that sort of thinking is that it may be based on wrong assumptions, not asking enough questions or poor listening.

Focusing on now requires that you slow down and understand why and how something unpleasant is happening. This is so that you may see how you are taking part and then learn what to do to stop that. If I am annoyed at my psychology students' lack of motivation and deficiency of critical thinking, then I have to be bold enough to ask them and myself, "How I am contributing and what I can do to change my teaching approach for the better?" If I think good motivation and good critical thinking skills can be used to change some little things that may be wrong with the world today, take the time to find out if this is really true, and then act, I have seized the moment. I will be changing things for the better.

**Critical focusing "P" point question:** Do you keep both the big picture and the details in clear focus?

> **Three focusing "P" point actions:**
>
> 1. Make a list of your top three distractions and make a pledge to do something to eliminate their lure over you.
> 2. Question the order of priorities you are currently focusing on to make sure they are the little things you can do to get the biggest results.
> 3. Catch yourself the next time you are not present in the now moment.

"*The mountains are okay I guess, but they sure do get in the way of the view*" (Canadian Flatlander).

# Management "P" Point # 10: Live a Success Formula

# 11

*"If you are going to build something in the air it is always better to build castles than houses of cards"* (George C. Lichtenberg).

**Management Problem # 10:** It is somewhat ironic, but we really need to be all grown up and self-actualized *before* we can be the most effective leaders. But, it is often the process of learning how to be a leader that helps us fulfill our potential. These two processes are obviously intermingled and have much to teach each other.

## GO FOR THE GOLD

I wrote an earlier book entitled, *You Can Have Your Cheese & Eat It Too.* Discovering the solutions to riddles like this may have more to do with being successful in life than you may first imagine. Today, everything is so fiercely competitive that success depends upon widening your vision and challenging such sacred cow injunctions as "you can't have your cheese and eat it too." The plain truth is that you can and should try with everything you've got. Why settle for anything less? Who wants to choose between a rock and a hard place? Be the canary that swallowed the cat and have a high-paying, low stress job. Go for the whole *Kahuna.* Have your cheese and eat it too!

Below is a simple and easy success formula that can result in more cheese than you will ever know what to do with.

### Dream Huge

Many people do not see the connection between their dreams and reality. Most successful people do. The simple truth is this: Anything you can dream, you can do. You can act to shape reality or you can react to what it seems to be doing to you. Fortunately, you don't have to have an IQ of 150, be drop-dead good looking, know people in high places, have an Ivy League MBA or be born with a silver spoon to be successful in life. But you do have to dream BIG and then be willing to do *whatever* it takes to make that dream come true.

Anyone can dream little dreams, but it takes boldness to dream big, and then an extremely clever approach and tons of hard work to translate those big dreams into reality. It is usually somewhere in between that process where dreams are likely to fade. Sometimes it takes hard work, undoubting belief and blind courage to keep dreams alive. It certainly takes considerable energy. One thing is for sure, you must translate your dreams into concrete goals. They can easily evaporate if you don't take them from your head to your hands.

Your beliefs are what drive dreams and keep them from fading. You have to believe in your dreams and you have to believe in your ability to make them come true. You also have to believe that you are meant to prosper beyond your wildest dreams. Abundance is a reality, not shortage. You are only limited by what you allow yourself to believe. If that notion is tough to swallow, try some water.

Unfortunately many things can happen in life that dampen your spirit and self-confidence. One such thing is the experience of failure. Some failures at the wrong time even have the power to convince you to cancel your dreams. Then you end up choosing between eating it or having it or worst of all, no cheese at all.

There are always two ways out of this dreadful failure dilemma. First, most failures can be seen as great opportunities to start over again with better information. Actually the greatest inventions and discoveries followed repeated failures. So, your reaction to failure is a choice. Secondly, if the failure is that devastating, you can always re-arrange your dreams to accommodate the situation. That is the beauty of dreaming. Dreams don't have to be that specific. They are only limited by your imagination and they can certainly be fluid and changeable.

It is the next two steps of this success formula that require the particulars.

## Be Clever

Beware of something: No matter whether you are dreaming of being a famous movie star, a wealthy dot.com entrepreneur, a gold medallist in the Olympics, a best selling author or a top college professor, the competition is much fiercer than you can ever imagine. The first step in taking a dream to success is to come up with a remarkably unique and clever approach that separates you from the crowd. This is where you have to get rid of *everything* you think you know. It is what you think you know that is too common and unclever. Most present knowledge is based on mistakes and incorrect information that encourage staying stuck in the status quo.

Being clever is a complex process that goes way beyond simple creativity. Cleverness may involve a combination of using critical thinking, listening to intuitive feelings, becoming sensitive to the importance of good timing, studying principles in nature, or developing 3-D/360-degree vision. It also requires utter mental flexibility and openness to suspend all pre-judgments and delete expectations as to certain outcomes as a result of your efforts. Moreover you must have an insatiable drive to verify basic assumptions, challenge sacred paradigms, and let go to the unknown. The only safe assumption you can make about being clever is that you can never be clever enough.

Being clever is not something you can do by chance when you feel like it. You have to embrace the attitude of continuous growth and self-improvement. You also have to loose your ego so that you can ask for, listen to, and apply valuable feedback. When you think you are onto something exceptionally clever, it may just be your pride. Or, your dream may not be directed at doing the right things for the right reasons. These are times when you need a second opinion that may contradict your own.

The most ingenious cleverness involves the application of *psychological power points,* or "P" points for short. These are the well-timed, well-placed little things you can do to get the biggest results. "P" points help you reverse the typical 80-20 rule so that you can begin to get more by doing less. This is the simple art of being smart.

Common examples of commercial "P" point applications are newspaper headlines, media sound bytes and advertising jingles. Common examples are the strategic use of silence, proactive preventative actions and competing against yourself. Personal "P" points are being an excellent role model, learning the art of power communication and maintaining a positive attitude during adversity.

## Work Hard

By the time you start getting clever, you have already experienced the value of hard work. Being clever *is* hard work. Life seems to make things most difficult once you get to the point of making some progress in translating your dream into a product. This is when you need to muster all the reserves of strength you have stored deep inside you. Even though your awareness of this strength may have faded from failures and setbacks, it is still there. You can never quit. Success is often just around the next corner you are most likely to give up getting to.

The challenge ahead requires mental, emotional and physical strength. This means maintaining a totally positive attitude in extreme adversity, voiding your mind of all negative thoughts, and conjuring up a supply of tenacity that you thought never existed. Then you must adapt a do or die mission statement and carry out specific activities persistently and consistently, one by one until they are done.

The most important "P" point to discover is the value of getting more in sync with the natural way of life. This means taking the time to understand, appreciate and learn from the things that happen in life, *before* charging ahead in a frenzied, misguided attempt to force artificial control or unnatural change. First things first is the wise admonition here.

Somewhere along the line luck may introduce your hard work to opportunity. At this point, it may require fine tuning your sensitivity to hear and see the little things you can do, which will get the biggest results. Stopping short of complete follow-through of these little things may jeopardize much effort and rob you of what you now deserve. Close but no cigar. Like being clever, you can never work too hard, especially when it comes to follow-through with critical details, close to the end.

Success is guaranteed by following three simple steps. When you dream big, become clever and work hard, there isn't any success beyond your grasp. However, don't be deceived by the simplicity of this success formula. Success won't come quickly or easily, but you will be so involved you won't even notice that. You will be having your cheese and eating it too.

## PRACTICE PERSONAL "P" POINTS

Your personal and professional development is a combined package. The dual effort of personal development excellence and professional success can be greatly accelerated once you start identifying and then managing important "P" points in your own life and career. These personal "P" points are portals that open up to vast new worlds of self-actualization and professional development. Here are ten specific personal "P" points to identify and manage better:

### Paradigms

A critical "P" point regarding paradigms, or basic viewpoints, is the realization that they are only temporary road maps pointing the way toward something we need to know now, not necessarily forever. Another important "P" point is the flash of understanding that greatest liberation and the biggest changes occur when we can let go of obsolete paradigms. We do this by understanding that the reality we hold so dearly is really more a function of the particular location from which we are looking at it rather than the "reality" itself. In the extreme, *paradigm-morphing*, or over-identifying with a particular viewpoint we have, keeps us a slave to this perspective and restricts vision of other possibilities, thus stunting growth. We must learn to separate our thinking from these paradigms, so the tail is not wagging the dog.

## Principles

The volume of information that confronts us today requires us to work smart mentally. A valuable "P" point to help out here is the process of identifying useful *principles*, which can guide us quickly and surely to where we need to be going. These principles are simple but powerful clues as to the way life really works, all the time. An example is in understanding our mutually exclusive drives of wanting to belong and be dependent on something bigger vs. wanting to be unique, autonomous and independent from everything.

Another example is the awareness of the amazing similarity between an individual's own evolution and that of an overall civilizations' same evolution. The trick is to apply these principles to get practical benefits. To accommodate our opposing drives, the wise leader provides structure for security, equality and belonging, and opportunity for individualism, freedom and unique creativity. Smart individuals anticipate personal life cycles by knowing those that have already occurred in history.

## Priorities

We can't ever begin to close the gaps between where we are and where we want to be until we get our priorities straight. A starting "P" point is to refocus back onto the basic priorities we all share, such as meaning, security, freedom, competence and growth. This process then involves ordering the activities necessary to give life to the values, which support these priorities.

For instance, if competence is our top priority, then we should be learning everything there is to learn about something from as many sources as we can. Then we need to practice these new skills until we perfect them. If growth is our top priority, then we need to start shedding familiar habits and move to a place where there is an abundance of growth opportunities.

## Perceptions

Two important "P" points about perceptions are: (a) they produce realities that are highly likely to be inaccurate due to typical perceptual distortions such as biases, incorrect information and our closure tendency of filling the gaps on incomplete information; and (b) they are what people generally act on, and without knowing exactly what these distortions are doing, we are not able to react appropriately. Slowing down to tune into important perceptions affecting us can help improve personal relationships greatly. If we are perceived as having a "bragging" personality, our helping efforts may always be resisted as being imposed and not credible, rather than welcomed and valuable.

## Paradoxes

A particularly challenging "P" point involves solving contradictory dilemmas or *bisociations*, such as, "you have to lose control before you gain control," or "you can't have your cake and eat it too." Understanding these "riddles" can open a lot of other "P" point insights as to how life really works. The key here is to slow down and listen to how such contradictions occur naturally in life and to comprehend how opposite appearing things may just be the flip side of the same thing, much like heads and tails on a quarter.

Another trick to solving paradoxes is to avoid getting caught up in the *language* that holds you "hostage." You can do this by separating what is actually being said by the content, from what is being *implied* through meaning. Take the common cake paradox as an example. Who says you can't just eat a portion and save the rest?

## Perfection Points

It is easy to develop a bad habit of overdoing things and going past the point of perfection. An important art to learn in personal development is becoming more sensitive to when imperfection goes past perfection and turns back into imperfection again. The funny part about it is that we always seem to know just when this happens, just *after* it happens.

Unfortunately, the window of opportunity for this particular "P" point is fairly narrow and we just have to work hard at sharpening our senses to "see" and "hear" this delicate point when it comes, *before* it goes. A visit to an antique car show and one glimpse of a white and turquoise classic 1958 Chevrolet Corvette will bring this point to life for anyone. And for photography lovers, a trip to Ellis Island and viewing the spectacular black and white images will do the same.

### Polarizations

Another bad habit we have which limits our growth is the one of *polarizing* life into *either-or* opposites, which we have to choose between. This *yes-no, good-bad, right-wrong, okay-not okay* habit causes us to exclude half of life from our consumption. That reduces all chances for success by 50 per cent. Rejoining these divisions is a bridge-building exercise that is contagious and can shorten the distance between here and there very quickly. The "P" point comes with the realization of the interconnectedness of opposites, such as the necessity of disorganization to appreciate order, ignorance to show the benefit of education and fasting which paves the way for feasting.

### Personalities

The most important personality "P" point is that our personalities are a reflection of our basic attitude towards life. The most useful "P" point about attitudes in general, is that *attitudes are everything*. A small change in attitude almost always produces major results. This is always the cheapest solution to any problem because it is always free. The right attitude can close gaps quickly and easily.

A critical discovery is the relationship between the things that happen to us and the resulting feelings we have from those events. The attitude "P" point is the particular thoughts we tell ourselves, which largely determine those feelings. The simple "P" point solution is that wrong thoughts produce unpleasant feelings. In the end it really isn't the things that happen to us that bother us so much as our thoughts about those things. For instance, negative feedback can be viewed as either derogatory criticism or helpful instruction. Failure is either a disaster or an opportunity to start over again.

### Prejudgments

If we don't take care we can easily give into the tendency to approach new situations with too much excess baggage. This unfortunate tendency to prejudge new ideas, people, places and things against past similar experiences or future expectations spoils a lot of excitement, fun, stimulation and growth.

Furthermore, in our efforts to quickly understand things we let this speed thing fool us into believing some of our quick judgments are actually correct. Judging a thing before all the facts are really in can set up wrong paradigms, which spread false realities. The "P" point is the practical knowledge we already have: We already know that no two situations can ever be exactly the same, and that the majority of things we expect to happen never come about in the exact way we anticipate them to. We waste a great deal of time anticipating, worrying and fearing imaginary disasters. We waste even more time rehearsing our planned responses to these unreal things.

### Problems

Problem situations are special "P" point opportunities to apply all the "P" point solutions above. Creative problem-solving strategies use small, well-placed and well-timed efforts to suspend prejudgments, solve paradoxes, change paradigms, avoid polarizations, and apply important principles to produce major results. An important "P" point about a problem is our attitude about it. A problem is really a sign that something isn't right. The problem is an opportunity to correct a situation that needs correcting.

Another important problem "P" point involves *timing*. In any action, timing *is* everything. We have all probably lost out on marvelous opportunities because we didn't "strike while the iron was hot." Usually the clues are right there in front of us, but these clues are hard to see and hear because we have an important priority mixed up: We are running and talking, instead of looking and listening. Slowing down helps us see and hear this critical "P" point.

## PAY YOUR DUES

Achieving personal excellence and professional success is a process that requires payment of substantial dues. Nothing as good as this package comes free. The following ten dues investments are required for the self-actualization you need for effective leadership.

### Discovering a Unique Mission

You are born for a unique purpose and given a special talent to accomplish that purpose. You contracted to carry out your private mission in exchange for the opportunity to live. Loitering and not paying attention to the nagging suspicions about this reality only prolongs unnecessary unhappiness and failure.

Discovering your unique purpose isn't an easy process though. Often you are already two-thirds the way to where you are going without realizing where your destination actually is. At some point you have to stop, listen and look to see clearly what you enjoy doing most and what you are best at doing. Then you have to invest everything you have into developing and using your one talent fully and frequently for the right reason.

### Inventing a Success Formula

You don't really have as much of a choice as to *what* you are supposed to be doing, as you like to think. Luckily though, the universe is a fundamentally fair place and so the *how* is left entirely up to your imagination and fancy. You have to develop your own signature style for being effective and achieving success. Most proven success formulas involve variations of five steps. These are dreaming big, being clever, working hard, staying focused and never quitting.

You are only limited by the smallness of your beliefs and dreams, the competition is always keener than you think, and you have to struggle to get to the simplicity just the other side of all the chaos to make sense out of it. In doing all this, you have to keep your mission in constant focus by resisting all distractions, while persevering with the hope that success is just around the next corner that you are inclined to give up getting to.

### Discovering Governing Principles

There doesn't seem to be enough time to learn or do everything, so you have to discover some valid shortcuts. The most valuable shortcuts are the discovery of governing principles of which people and life follow. This is the so-called natural way of life. The simplest governing principle is the *Law of Karma*. Everything you think or do has consequences. The object of success is to choose to do the thing that has the best consequences.

There is no secret in getting the right results in any situation. All you have to do is do the right thing in the right way. Unfortunately this is often more easily said than done and more often than not, success involves learning from our failures. Fortunately they also follow governing principles.

### Developing an Arsenal of "P" Points

Since you always seem to be short on time, it makes sense to work smart. Working smart requires you to find little ways to invest the least effort to get the biggest results. This strategy requires you to master the art of using *psychological power points*, or "P" points for short. These entry points involve well-placed and well-timed strategic interventions that have mega-leverage value. Commercial examples are newspaper headlines, media advertising slogans and political sound bytes. Practical examples are all these other dues investing activities.

### Becoming a Likable Salesperson

Success is partly a sales process. Most successful sales people are likable. Likability is being friendly and helpful, having a positive, can-do attitude, being humble, showing interest in others and being honest. Likability is also acting smart, looking good, demonstrating balance and having a willingness to grow and improve.

More than anything though, likability is good communication. Good communication avoids anything that can make another person defensive, such as superiority, judgment, superficiality, control, neutrality and certainty. Oddly, you have to work extra hard at being unlikable. Being likable is free and a natural way to be. So is good communication. All you have to do is listen more.

### Reconciling Opposites

Everywhere you look there are polar opposites: Good and bad, up and down, black and white, valuable and worthless, and right and wrong. Everything in the universe can be categorized as yang and yin, either this or that. Critical thinking questions whether or not this is reality or an oversimplification of our lazy dualistic minds.

Regardless of the origin of this either-orness, success requires you to get in touch with the creative process, which often involves reconciling seemingly opposite things to make something new. Reconciliation starts with suspending judgment about the okayness or not-okayness of something in your left hand so you can get to know and understand it better and see how it might work together with the other thing in your right hand.

### Getting the Two Halves Working Together

Whether we are all born with split personalities or just invented this reality, we still have to get these two different halves eventually working together in concert as a team. Much of the time we hear two stereophonic voices coming from two different places telling us to do opposite things. Our heads scream and our hearts whisper. We want to be free but we need to be equal. We need to obey but we want to rebel. We are confronted with logical problems and confused with vague creative impressions. We want both change and stability, to lead and follow and to be independent and dependent.

The main challenge you have is to achieve a workable balance between your two halves. You can start by reconciling your basic drive to create chaos and restore order, or at least knowing which is which so you can create the right chaos and restore the best order.

### Expanding Your Comfort Zone

The road to personal excellence, professional success and spiritual contentment is anything but easy, quick or comfortable. Sometimes it is like getting sucked up with everything else in a giant vacuum cleaner and then being dumped in some ragging rapids headed for a major waterfall to lead to a dry riverbed in the desert with vultures circling. Lots of tumbles, bruises, headaches, thirst and worries.

Success usually requires reaching and leaping outside your comfort zone to increase its size. You can do this best by resetting your thermostat, re-arranging furniture, doing things backward, getting out of formation, and believing in Santa Clause and the Easter Bunny. Making growth surges in expanding your comfort zone often requires you to close your eyes, let go of your sacred beliefs and paradigms and give into something unfamiliar outside yourself. This can be aggravating and frightening and definitely difficult. The giant vacuum cleaner awaits you.

### Including

Achieving the total success package is a process of *including* things rather than *excluding* them. Part of the spilt personality with which we are all afflicted involves the knowledge that we are similar in many ways with each other, but also very unique with our individual differences. Subsequently, you have an unfortunate tendency to focus of the differences of other people, with the illusion that you can control and force them into the sameness you prefer. Of course, this attempt is futile and frustrating and can only end in failure. The thing to learn is to only dismiss that which offends your soul, while exploring ways to include something from everything else. Inclusion is progress.

### Listening to Feedback

Paradoxically, success is most often born out of failure. It is from these failures which you must learn. No matter how clever you are or how hard you work to be successful, you won't get there unless you first find out what you may be doing wrong. Part of this answer may be in learning how others have typically failed. At any rate, you have to start asking more questions and really listening to the answers. The first step is verifying previous assumptions about the progress that you think you are making. Intimate friends are the best source for this information.

## BE YOUR BEST

As I already mentioned, achieving personal excellence and professional success is a big package that has big dues. Those who already know this are still amazed at the size of the payoff though. Here are twenty-five self-motivational tips to help you become your best:

1. First and most important, realize that becoming your best is a very natural, normal process. You actually have to work harder to *not* be your best. Life is designed to help you to be your best and become all that you can be.
2. Strive to achieve the ultimate motivational goal—to be *intrinsically motivated.* This is doing things simply because they are fun and enjoyable to do in and all by themselves, without an ulterior motive or external payoff. Intrinsic motivation gets the best results, because it produces the highest intensity of energy and persists the longest.
3. Always question the value of what you think you *want* and pay closer attention to what you may actually *need.* Your wants are often superficial and fleeing, whereas your needs are usually more substantial, permanent things. When your goals are based on your wants, they are *extrinsic*; when they are based on your needs, they are *intrinsic.*
4. Write your goals down on a piece of paper so they are readily and frequently visible to you. Don't trust them to the whim of your mind or memory. They have a funny way of moving to the back burner that way.

5. Focus on *intermediate goals*. These are the things you need to be doing right now, to get to the next better place, so you can get to a further better place and so on. The big goal might be to win the Super Bowl, but the intermediate goals are being in top shape to avoid injury each week and being where you are supposed to be each and every play of each game.
6. Dreams, wishes and hopes are fine, but unless they are translated into clear, concrete, specific and doable goals, they soon evaporate into thin air.
7. Be ruthless in setting and keeping your own priorities necessary to achieve your goals. Stop wasting precious time reacting to other people's perpetual "emergencies" and "non-priorities."
8. Focus all your attention and energy on your one main goal and be willing to make sacrifices and exchanges. If you want to be rich, you may have to work 16-hour days. If you want to be physically fit, you may have to give up ice cream, beer and Big Macs. And if you want to be smart you may have to quit your job and go back to college.
9. Pay very close to the connection between the choices you make and the results you get. To achieve your goals, you must make the *right* choices. Making these right choices is where all your power is. Only right choices get right results.
10. Realize the paradoxical nature of being human. You are often pulled in opposite directions and this can be an obstacle in the way of your goals. Your head shouts one thing and your heart whispers another. You want to be recognized for your uniqueness and be given the freedom to be different. Yet in the same breath, you want to be treated fairly and equally, just like everyone else. Sometimes you have to struggle to reconcile these opposing things to achieve a healthy mix and balance to get to the best position to achieve your goals.

11. Don't give in and sacrifice a half of the *Big Kahuna* when you are forced to choose between two worthy things. Get creative and figure out how you can get both. And don't get caught between a rock and hard place in having to choose between two undesirable things. Don't choose either and walk away.
12. At any given moment you can let go of the past and join the future. Positive change always starts when you allow yourself to start living more in the now moment. Pay attention to what is going on around you right now.
13. Don't try to do everything by yourself. Many people have valuable clues that can help you stay on course and make the road less bumpy or winding. All you have to do is ask and listen.
14. Study success. Read biographies of great people, watch inspirational movies, enjoy motivational posters and get psyched by outstanding speakers.
15. Learn to be brutally honest with yourself, no matter how much it hurts. We all tell lies, but any dishonesty just widens the gap between where we are and where we want to be. Practice telling the truth in every situation from here on out.
16. The first step to changing for the better is not as difficult as you think. In fact, it is thinking that makes it more difficult. The longer you think about leaping off a high dive platform, the more frozen you become.
17. Practice having a more positive attitude during neutral times when you are getting mixed results. That way you will have a positive attitude to draw upon when you face your worst adversity, which you inevitably will, sooner or later.
18. Realize you are only limited by the smallness of your dreams and beliefs. You can accomplish *anything* if you have the desire and a plan, and the discipline and determination to carry out that plan no matter what gets in your way.

19. Face your fear of failure head-on. There are no successes without plenty of failures. Failures are not permanent, they are just an opportunity to start over again with better information.
20. If you have a bad habit that is getting in the way of your goals, stop and figure out what your payoff is for continuing that bad habit. In at least one respect, we humans are very simple. We only do things that we get rewarded for doing. Unfortunately, life rewards action—positive or negative. Fortunately though, we always know what we should be doing. The little voice inside won't let up.
21. Don't worry too much about burnout. As Judge Judy says, "It's better to burn than rust."
22. Follow Lou Holtz's simple but profound advice: "Always do the right thing, always treat others the way you want to be treated, and always do your best."
23. Life is *both* a journey and a destination. Know where you are going and have a map to get there. Enjoy both aspects of the trip.
24. There really are no short cuts. You have to dream big, translate your dreams into real goals, be extremely clever, work very hard, keep focused and *never* quit.
25. When you achieve success, which you will, share it with others. We are all meant to enjoy success and we all have valuable secrets to help each other get there.

## ABANDON YOUR COMFORT ZONE

This topic is important enough to say some more things about it. We are all on a combined personal, professional and spiritual development journey and there might not be as much time to make progress, as we would like to imagine. Loitering too long in your comfort zone actually makes the journey more uncomfortable than it needs to be. Here are ten ways to step out of your comfort zone and make a major surge in your growth efforts.

### Let Go & Give In

The first step in abandoning your comfort zone is to question yourself as to why it is so difficult to let go of the illusion of control that you don't even have. You can waste half a lifetime needlessly trying to over-control uncontrollable things, completely missing the only thing that is actually under your control—making the right choice to get the best results each new moment that comes along. The image of closing your eyes and falling backwards into a swimming pool is a good one to get started on to reach the beginning boundaries of your discomfort zone. What you are doing is increasing the size of your comfort zone.

### Eat Dessert First

We can easily accept the given order of things and fail to question the logic or utility of them being that way. Personally, I think we have a lot of what I call *priority reversals.* These are situations in which we are oblivious to the fact that we have put the cart before the horse and the tail is wagging the dog. After all, if dessert is so great, why do we have to wait until the end of the meal, when we are full, to enjoy it? Or, why do we make the least amount of money in the beginning of our lives when we need it most? You can make a real surge in abandoning your discomfort zone by questioning the order of your own priorities. One good way to start with is to question why we have to fail first before succeeding.

### Re-Arrange the Furniture

Structure, order, routine, familiarity, organization and conventional thinking all reinforce comfort, but when overdone, they can limit growth severely. Sometimes you have to re-arrange the furniture in your house or office in order to forget unproductive habits that inhibit growth. Sometimes you need a new point of reference to stimulate a new idea. You may even have to get rid of some stuff to make more room. Such physical changes can set the stage for mental and emotional ones. Also, the things you look at frequently have more impact on your thinking and acting than you may want them to have. Make sure you change the view occasionally.

## Reach Out & Jump In

Personal growth requires some reaching and risk-taking. Sometimes you may be stuck and not know it and the only way to get unstuck is to step outside your own backyard. Make friends with someone who thinks and acts entirely different than you. Visit a foreign country whether by plane or in the movies. If you are a self-help reader, pick up one of Dean Koontz's new novels. Take a course at a local community college on a totally unfamiliar subject. Go somewhere sometime and do something that you are not used to doing. Find a way to take a risk that has potential payoffs.

## Get Out of Formation

Dare to be the one goose out of formation from the rest of the flock that may be off course. The formation of which you are presently part may be stepping to the beat of mediocrity and going nowhere fast. That won't do you any good. Or it may even be going in the wrong direction faster, which can be worse. The viewpoint of your present formation actually determines what you are looking at and what you see. This can limit your view needlessly. The quickest way to expand your arsenal of useful realities is to change viewpoints frequently. You see and learn much more that way and increase the size of your comfort zone by tenfold.

## Reset Your Thermostat

Self-regulation can facilitate growth spurts. It is important that you locate your internal thermostat and become its master instead of its slave. If you are out of balance, get back in balance. If you are too balanced, go out on a limb now and then. If you work too hard, take more time off. If you are too logical, talk to someone who is irrational. If you are drowning in low energy set your thermostat higher. If you are unemotional, go visit Ellis Island and feel all the emotion there. Forward movement always requires making some changes and making them voluntarily by yourself is always easier and more comfortable in the long run.

### Create

The idea that people are born with creative abilities is fictional. Creativity is a natural force in our universe that we can all tap into. It is actually more of an attitude to rediscover than a particular skill to develop. We all have right hemispheres in our brain but some of us have allowed that side to sleep for one reason or another. To be creative all you have to do is slow down and look at ordinary things with renewed, childlike awe and amazement. Half of creativity is appreciation of the hidden beauty and value of things. When you see something of natural beauty and value, all you have to do is figure out how to communicate that information with clarity and impact to others. That simple task doesn't have to be limited to creative geniuses.

### Believe in Santa Claus

We all have one basic choice in our approach to life. That is to act to make realities happen or to react to the ones that happen to us. We can be optimistic actors or pessimistic reactors; idealistic dreamers or conventional realists. Oddly, reactors are trying to build familiarity and comfort, but are they really being successful at doing this? Actors dream a lot and know that the biggest influence on producing an academy award performance is the size of their dream. Dream big, work hard, be clever and never quit and your comfort zone will be bigger than most other people around you. You can make it even bigger by sharing your success secret.

### Arrange Spontaneity

Some of the most enjoyable, memorable and life changing moments come through the magic of serendipity. These densely packed growth moments are a product of planned spontaneity. They come when you least expect it. Try to set aside some time each day that doesn't have to be accounted for and see what happens. Stop looking so hard and you will find it. In the meantime, sharpen your powers of observation and sensitivity, lest you miss it when it does come. Realize that in anything, timing is everything.

### Include

Our brains are designed for efficiency, and unfortunately this design excludes all but that which fits easily with what we already know and believe. That is a lot of exclusion. If you figure all that everyone knows can probably fit on the end of a pinhead, there is much, much more to know out there. Having the honesty to admit what you don't know can open the door to learning all sorts of new things. A major surge in personal development can occur when you start looking closer at the more subtle similarities between things and people instead of their noisy differences. The process of inclusion is the best way to assure fast forward movement.

When you have the courage to start wandering outside your comfort zone a funny thing happens. Your comfort zone starts expanding exponentially. And the bigger your comfort zone is, the more comfortable it becomes.

## ASK AND ANSWER FIVE GROWTH QUESTIONS

Personal and professional growth can be greatly stimulated when you ask yourself five critical questions and then struggle to get the right answers. This process requires you to use critical thinking, creativity, open-mindedness and above all else, brutal honesty. Here are the five questions:

### What can I Really Control?

It seems to me that the process of growing up involves the gradual realization of how we have wasted so much time trying to control uncontrollable or irrelevant things. Once we start becoming more aware of the illusion of control, we begin to see the few things we can in fact control. Then we go about learning how to best influence the most important things on this short list in more positive, productive ways.

At the top of this control list is the need for more self-management. Especially critical, is the area of controlling our own interpretations of things that happen to us and our reactions to those interpretations. Our interpretations are often wrong and reactions ineffective. The smart reversal of focusing back inwards toward ourselves to better manage these interpretations and reactions is the first real step in personal growth. Unfortunately this important shift usually isn't a smooth one or one you can hurry along, but it does start with the question.

### How do I Sabotage my Own Success?

The fear of success is insidious. Probably most of this type of fear is based on some major assumptions of what might happen when you become successful. What will you have to do to achieve it? What will you have to give up? What will it be like? What will you have to do to maintain it? What will happen to you if you lose it? Your mind can go fairly wild with anticipation, before you even become successful at what you are trying to do. In this sense you are preventing your own littler successes from happening, which could have led to bigger ones.

Facing your darker side is not pleasant or easy, but you will never get anywhere until you take ultimate responsibility for where you are or where you aren't. You can't begin to close the gap between where you are and where you want to be until you see who created that gap—yourself. Once you take ownership for all your own best self-sabotaging behaviors you are ready to try and answer the next question.

### Why don't I Apply All the Good Things I Learn and Know?

Some day I would like to download my brain to retrieve all the fabulous learning that has passed through it. For nearly forty years I have been taught, guided and motivated by the best of the best from the cliffs of Big Sur to the red rocks of the Australian outback. But why did so much of that good stuff not take? Why do we learn so many good things and then not apply them? If I had applied one tenth of the things I knew were right and good, I would have blissfully dissolved in Nirvana by now.

I suppose we all have to come to grips with the question of why we keep pushing the dessert away. My own answers seem to have most to do with my insatiable need to avoid boredom and stir up new excitement. I always need a new challenge and being able to do something well is anti-climatic. In the end, though this is a question you have to look yourself in the mirror and ask and keep asking until you get *your* answer. Some say it is later than you think, so what are you waiting for?

## For Whom (Or What) am I Doing All This?

It usually takes a very long time to understand why you need to give yourself permission to do something just for yourself and for its own intrinsic worth, without any regard for other people or reasons. It takes even longer to start doing that. Long ago I learned that you couldn't make another person happy, only unhappy. But that still didn't keep me from making a mad effort to achieve things with the main intention of trying to either please or impress someone else. This was my attempt to "prove" my worth. The sense of satisfaction and accomplishment never seems to come to you when you are really doing something for someone else or for some ulterior motive.

A major growth surge occurs when you shift focus from the outside to your inside. When you stop doing things for the wrong reasons and cease competing against others and start doing them for yourself, competing against yourself, you finally start getting a genuine sense of satisfaction. And you also start winning more. The early injunction we all get against selfishness is what keeps you from making this shift. You have to shed your guilt first.

## What is the Best I am Capable of?

Many of us dream of greatness but only a few take the first step to develop a detailed plan to get there. Even less endure the difficult voyage that is usually involved. Part of the reason for this status quo is the catch-22 position that we perceive. On the one hand we are teased into believing we can do anything we put our mind to. On the other hand there are subtle warnings everywhere that tell us not to set our goals too high so we won't doom ourselves to unnecessary disappointment and failure. So to be safe we often settle for far worse than second best. Of course the rest of the reason is we can only accomplish real greatness when we cease trying to do it all for the wrong personal reasons.

The truth is you are capable of doing anything you think you are capable of doing. But that doesn't mean it will just happen by magic. If you are not willing to be flexible with your goals and how you can achieve them, to make difficult choices, exchanges and sacrifices, take risky chances and persevere long enough to make your dreams come true, then they won't. This is competition against your own self at its best. The icing on the cake is when you start accomplishing things for no reason other than it is the natural thing to do.

Having the courage to ask these five critical questions and then making the effort to find answers will open a large door ahead to your personal growth. Real growth then occurs when you become free to de-personalize it.

**Critical self-actualizing "P" point question:** Are you working as hard as you can to be the best at what you are doing?

➤ **Three self-actualizing "P" point actions:**

1. Write down a specific goal with a concrete action plan that will help you improve your performance as a manager.
2. Develop a clear and passionate personal mission statement.
3. Do a personal assessment to determine if you are living your life around your core values.

"*The greatest achievement of a man is when he becomes what he pretends to be*" (Socrates).

# Conclusion: Practical "P" Point Applications

# 12

"*For goodness sake, if you have something important to tell me start from the end*" (Anonymous).

I discovered this extremely useful "P" Point concept during my own struggle to wade through all the chaos going on around me in order to get to the simplicity I knew was on the other side. This journey also resulted in getting to a position of valuable balance, where I could see and act in all directions. I call this place the *Prosperity Zone*. This is where I began to see unlimited applications of "P" point Management.

Time is too valuable to waste and so it makes sense to spend what time you do have smartly, by doing the little things that pay the biggest dividends. Here are twenty practical "P" Points to start applying right now to get big results.

1. **Pose intriguing questions (for which you have interesting answers).** This is a good way to wok in your knowledge and skills without imposing them, which never seems to get anywhere. Examples of such questions are: What can I do to get you to work harder? What is keeping us from solving this problem? What would you do if you were the manager of someone who was late all the time?
2. **Notice right behavior.** It is tempting to focus on problems and negativity in order to apply all the knowledge and solutions that cost so much time and effort to acquire. However, it is the recognition and rewarding of good performance that builds the self-confidence necessary for continued development and productivity of employees.

3. **Demonstrate right behavior.** Correcting wrong behavior takes too much time and is often wasted effort. It is much easier to just show what is desirable to begin with. Besides, even if you criticize behavior, you eventually have to teach the person how to do something correctly.
4. **Share unwritten expectations from the beginning.** Too often employees have to guess what is or isn't okay and what is expected of them, which wastes much time for both employees trying to find out the answers to these things and management trying to explain answers after-the-fact. Not only that, but it is fundamentally unfair *not* to tell anyone what you expect.
5. **Occasionally do and say nothing in response to somebody else's problem behavior.** Also resist the temptation to explain why you are choosing to be silent. The other person will usually know what you are thinking and the impact of the silence will be better. In the meantime you can be doing something else more productive.
6. **Communicate with clarity, economy and impact.** Do this by using powerful advertising images and irresistible sound bytes. Always think about what you want to say and how to say it best *before* your mouth opens. Good communication may be the single best little thing you can do to get the biggest results. Poor communication is behind most problems.
7. **Catch yourself in the act of assuming.** Unverified assumptions can yield much incorrect and incomplete information, which can contribute to wrong, unproductive actions. Correcting wrong actions takes too much time.
8. **Teach problem-solving skills.** Make the effort to demonstrate useful problem-solving strategies in actual problem situations rather than solving the problems yourself. The supply of problems won't ever go away,

but the more problem-solvers you have, the less of the impact that those problems will have on the organization.

9. **Maintain a positive attitude during adversity.** It is easy to have a good attitude when things are going well, but the real proof is in the pudding so to speak. It is during bad times when a good attitude speaks loudest. That is when you gain the most respect and are listened to closest.
10. **Provide frequent feedback about employees' performance.** Performance problems are usually an accumulation of lesser concerns that were not dealt with when they should have been. Doing this promptly and frequently allows you to focus more on the positive aspects of the employee's performance while it still is that way.
11. **Maximize efficiency in your work area.** One of the main tools of management is information. It pays to arrange your workspace physically to put the things you need most, such as information, right at your fingertips. Looking for anything is a big time waster. Not finding it can make you appear stupid.
12. **Make insignificant decisions hastily and deliberate on the difficult ones.** Very few decisions are life threatening and many can be made with minimal thought. The object is to always choose the door that open to more doors and avoid the dead ends. Unmade insignificant decisions and wrongly made significant ones can use up too much time that can be used in getting results by applying all these other "P" points.
13. **Follow-up and follow-through.** Make a list of a few important things you have failed to follow-up on and make a promise to do so today. There are never any results without finishing the job with proper follow-through. It is not worth it to waste hours of effort by failing to do something that might take a few minutes.

14. **Set the stage for difficult discussions.** When you are headed for a potential conflict or emotional discussion, plan ahead and ensure open, productive communication by creating an easy-going, relaxed, non-defensive climate. Remember what doesn't start out right will probably finish worse.
15. **Eliminate your own worst time wasters.** We are all guilty of doing things to waste time at work, whether it be smoking, socializing, reading, working on personal things, or shuffling paper. Being a good time manager yourself is the best way to teach others the value of that approach.
16. **Be honest.** Nothing is more disarming that the truth spoken clearly and quietly. Look carefully for such opportunities. A good one is to admit lacking confidence or fearing failure during a successful situation for which you are presently being recognized.
17. **Project a mixture of critical behaviors.** The quickest way to build rapport and trust with employees is to show balance in most behavior, such as a mixture of confidence and humility, a blending of conservatism and creativity and an easy flow of talking and listening. Extremes in any behavior can be red flags that interfere with good communication.
18. **Seek feedback.** You can be going sideways and even backwards without knowing it and then getting back to the starting point may require more than you are prepared to give. It is smart to stop what you are doing now and then to make a reality check of how well you are doing it. This requires you to establish an easy and reliable way to get frank and useful feedback as to what you are doing well and what needs re-arranging.
19. **Learn something important from *every* situation.** That way you can turn a profit from even bad situations and maybe prevent such situations from ever re-occurring. Another trick is to learn from your

successes in addition to being the wiser from your mistakes. All experience has some value and you are shortchanging yourself by not seeing that.

20. **Take assertive action to stop worrying and complaining.** Worrying and complaining about things just makes them worse than they need to be. These problems won't go away until you finally do something assertively to change the thing about which you are worrying or complaining. Worrying and complaining are draining behaviors that can often be dissolved by a few minutes worth of action.

Let me make a final pause here and offer these concluding "thoughts" from my heart. Great leaders are *not* born that way, but they *are* born with a longing to be great leaders. Sooner or later, all good managers come to the scary realization they may be in over their heads in what they are trying to do to be successful. They accept the humble reality that they are just surviving by winging it on the fly sometimes, despite the many impressive accomplishments they have to show for their efforts.

This may be where you are and it is the point where you will reach deep inside to unleash your power and propel yourself from surviving to thriving. The creator didn't put a longing in your heart to do something great without giving you the ability to learn the necessary knowledge and abilities to carry out this private mission to be a great leader. And let's face an important reality: Wherever you are in your management journey, it is just training for something bigger.

"*There will come a time when you believe everything is finished. That will be the beginning*" (Louis L'Amour).

# Suggested Reading

"*Light is good from whatever lamp it shines*" (Anonymous).


### Balance

Blakney, R.B. *The Way of Life by Lao Tzu* (translation). NY: Mentor Books, 1955.

Heider, J. *The Tao of Leadership*. NY: Bantam Books, 1985.

McGinnis, A.L. *The Balanced Life*. Minneapolis, MN: Augsburg, 1997.

Watts, A.W. *The Two Hands of God: The Myths of Polarity*. NY: Collier Books, 1963.

### Change

Baum, W. *Lightening in a Bottle*. NY: Dearborn, 2000.

Belasco, J.A. *Teaching the Elephant to Dance*. NY: Penguin Books, 1990.

Bishop, C.H. *Making Change Happen One Person at a Time*. NY: AMACOM, 2001.

Bridges, W. *Managing Transitions*. Reading, MA: Perseus Books, 1993.

Drucker, P. *Managing in a Time of Great Change*. NY: Truman Talley Books, 1995.

Hartman, T. *Color Your Future*. New York: Scibner, 1999.

Johnson, S. *Who Moved My Cheese*. NY: G. P. Putnam's Sons, 1998.

Kotter, J.P. *Leading Change*. Boston: HBR Press, 1996.

Nadler, D.A. *Champions of Change.* San Francisco: Jossey-Bass, 1998.

Tichy, N.M. and Devanna, M.A. *The Transformational Leader.* NY: John Wiley & Sons, 1990.

Tucker, R.B. *Managing the Future.* NY: Berkley Books, 1991.

Seligman, M. *What You Can Change and What You Can't.* NY: Alfred A. Knopf, 1994.

Senge, P., *et al. The Dance of Change.* NY: Currency Doubleday, 1999.

### Communication

Alexander, Ray. *Power Speech.* NY: AMACOM, 1986.

Bartolome, Fernando, *et al. The Articulate Executive: Orchestrating Effective Communication.* Boston, MA: Harvard Business School Press, 1993.

Battles, Brian. *How To Listen Powerfully.* Boulder, CO: Career Track Publications, 1988.

Bauby, Cathrina. *OK, Let's Talk About It: Dynamics of Dialogue.* NY: Van Nostrand Reinhold Co., 1972.

Burkett, David. *Very Good Management: A Guide to Managing by Communication.* Englewood Cliffs, NJ: Prentice-Hall, 1983.

Caroselli, Marlene. *The Language of Leadership.* Amherst, MA: Human Resource Development Press, 1990.

Dickson, Paul. *Words.* NY: Del Acorte Press, 1982.

Eisenson, J. *The Psychology of Communication.* NY: Appleton-Century-Crofts, 1963.

Elgin, Suzette H. *Success with the Gentle Art Of Verbal Self-defense.* Englewood Cliffs, NJ: Prentice Hall, 1989.

Epsy, W.R. *The Almanac Of Words At Play.* NY: Crown Press, 1980.

Galloway, Don. *Get To The Point, Keep To The Point.* Hollywood, CA: Cally Curtis Co., 1989.

Glathorn, Allan A. *Listening Your Way To Management Success.* Glenview, IL: Scott, Foresman, 1983.

Kilkeary, Nan. *The Good Communicator: The Eight Rules the Experts Know and Never Shared.* Evanston, IL: QuikRead, 1987.

Lindsay, Peter H. and Norman, Donald D. *Human Information Processing: An Introduction to Psychology.* (2nd Ed.) NY: Academic Press, 1977

Montgomery, Robert L. *Listening Made Easy.* NY: AMACOM, 1981.

Reed, Scott. *The Miracle of Psycho-Command Power.* West Nyak, NY: Parker Publishing Co., 1972.

Taylor, Insup. *Introduction to Psycholinguistics.* NY: Holt, Reinhart & Winston, 1976.

Watzlawick, P., Beavin, J. and Jackson, D.D. *Pragmatics of Human Communication.* NY: W.W. Norton & Co., 1967.

**Conflict Resolution**

Cloke, K. *Resolving Conflicts at Work.* San Francisco: Jossey-Bass, 2000.

Dana, D. *Conflict resolution.* NY: McGraw Hill, 2001.

Evans, S. *Hot Buttons: How to resolve Conflict and Cool Everyone Down.* NY: Cliff Street Books, 2000.

Lulofs, R.S. *Conflict: From Theory to Action.* Boston: Allyn & Bacon, 2000.

Pickering, P. *How to Manage Conflcit: Turn All Conflicts Into Win-Win Outcomes* (3rd Edition). Franklin Lakes, NJ: Career Press, 2000.

Rue, N.N. *Everything You Need to Know About Peer Mediation.* NY: Rosen Publishing Group, 1997.

Schelling, T.C. *The Strategy of Conflict.* Cambridge, MA: Harvard University Press, 1960.

Stone, F.M. *How to resolve Conflicts at Work.* Boulder, CO: NetLibrary, 1999.

Van Slyke, E.J. *Listening to Conflict.* Boulder, CO: NetLibrary, Inc., 1999.

Weeks, D. *The Eight Essential Steps of Conflict Resolution.* NY: G.P. Putnam's Sons, 1992.

## Creativity

Bennis, W. *Teach Old Dogs New Tricks.* Provo, UT: Executive Excellence Publishing, 1999.

Dudik, E.M. *Strategic Renaissance.* NY: AMACOM, 2000.

Firestein, R.L. *Leading on the Creative Edge.* Colorado Springs, CO: Pinon Press, 1996.

Hesselbeim, F., Goldsmith, M. and Somerville, I. (Eds.). *Leading Beyond the Walls.* San Francisco: Jossey-Bass, 1999.

Kepner, C.H. *Managing Beyond the Ordinary.* NY: AMACOM, 1996.

Miller, W. *Flash of Brilliance: Inspiring Creativity Where You Work.* Reading, MA: Perseus Books, 1999.

Pascale, R.T., Millemann, M. and Gioja, L. *Surfing the Edge of Chaos.* NY: Crown Business, 1994.

Peters, T. *The Pursuit of Wow.* NY: Vintage Books, 1994.

Ray, M. and Myers, R. *Creativity and Business.* NY: Doubleday, 1996.

Wheeler, J. *The Power of Innovative Thinking.* Franklin Lakes, NJ: Career Press, 1998.

Zdenek, M. *The Right Brain Experience.* NY: McGraw Hill, 1983.

## Critical Thinking

Bruner, J.S. *A Study of Thinking.* NY: Science Editions, 1962.

De Bono, E. *Six Thinking Hats.* Boston: Back Bay Books, 1999.

De Kluyver, C.A. *Strategic Thinking.* Upper Saddle River, NJ: Prentice Hall, 2000.

Farson, R. *Management of the Absurd.* NY: Simon & Schuster, 1996.

Heuer, R.J. *Psychology of Intelligence Analysis.* Washington DC: CIA's Center for the Study of Intelligence, 1999.

Levitson, R. *Brain Builders.* NY: Parker Publishing, 1995.

Loehle, C. *Thinking Strategically*. Boston: Cambridge University Press, 1996.

Restack, R.M. *The Mind.* NY: Bantam Books, 1985.

Smith, A. *Powers of Mind.* NY: Ballantine Books, 1976.

Sternberg, R. and Wagner, R.K. *Practical Intelligence.* NY: Cambridge University Press, 1986.

Stewart, T.A. *Intellectual Capital.* NY: Doubleday, 1997.

**Focus**

Canfield, J., Hansen, M.V. and Hewitt, L. *The Power of Focus.* Deerfield Beach, FL: Health Communications, Inc., 2000.

Carlson, R. *Don't Sweat the Small Stuff at Work.* NY: Hyperion, 1998.

Goldratt, E.M. *The Goal* (2nd Ed.). Great Barrington, MA: The North River Press, 1992.

Horn, S. *ConZentrate: Get Focused and Pay Attention.* NY: St. Martins Press, 2000.

Langer, E.J. *The Power of Mindful Learning.* Reading, MA: Addison-Wesley, 1997.

McGraw, P. *Life Strategies: Doing What Works & Doing What Matters.* New York: Hyperion, 1999.

Nideffer, R.M. *Attention Control Training.* NY: Wyden Books, 1978.

Pashler, H.P. *The Psychology of Attention.* Cambridge, MA: MIT Press, 1998.

Ries, A. *Focus.* NY: Harper Collins, 1996.

Warm, J.S. (Ed.) *Sustained Attention in Human Performance.* NY: Wiley, 1984.

**Intuition**

Bethards, B. *Seven Steps to Develop Your Intuitive Powers.* Rockport, MA: Element Books, 1998.

Buckminster, R. *Intuition.* Garden City, NY: Doubleday, 1972.

Dumais, J. *Trusting Your Intuition.* New Rochelle, NY: Great American Audio, 1989.

Ferguson, G. *Cracking the Intuition Code.* Lincolnwood, IL: Contemporary Books, 1999.

Franquemont, S. *You Already Know What to Do: 10 Invitations to the Intuitive Life.* NY: Putnam, 2000.

Karges, C. *Ignite Your Intuition.* Deerfield Beach, FL: Health Communications, Inc., 1999.

Nicholson, N. *Executive Instinct.* NY: Crown Business, 2000.

Schulz, M.L. *Awakening Intuition.* NY: Three Rivers Press, 1999.

Weintraub, S. *The Hidden Intelligence: Innovation Through Intuition.* Boston: Butterworth-Heinemann, 1998.

### Leadership

Blanchard, K., Hybels, B. and Hodges, P. *Leadership by the Book.* NY: William Morrow & Co., Inc., 1999.

Blanl, W. *The 108 Skills of Natural Born Leaders.* New York: AMACOM, 2001.

Covey, S.R. *Principle-centered Leadership.* NY: Simon & Schuster, 1991.

### Likability

Carnegie, Dale. *How To Win Friends And Influence People.* NY: Simon & Schuster, 1936.

Cottringer, W. *You Can Have Your Cheese & Eat It Too.* Provo, UT: Executive Excellence Publishing, 2002.

Ford, L. *Human Relations: A Game Plan for Improving Personal Adjustment.* NY: Prentice-Hall, 2001.

Lama, D. *The Art of Happiness.* NY: Penguin Putnam, Inc., 2001.

Montagu, A. *On Becoming Human.* NY: Hawthorn Books, 1966.

Vanzant, I. *In the Meantime.* NY: Simon & Schuster, 1998.

Wholey, D. *Are You Happy?* Boston: Houghton Mifflin Company, 1986.

### Mistakes

Dorner, Dietrich. *The Logic of Failure: Recognizing and Avoiding Error in Complex Situations.* Reading, MA: Addison-Wesley, 1997.

Greenspand, B. *Play It Again Bud!* NY: P.H. Wyden, 1973.

Maxwell, J.C. *Failing Forward.* Nashville: Thomas Nelson Publishers, 2000.

Reason, J.T. *Human Error.* NY: Cambridge University Press, 1990.

Tabori, P. *The Natural History of Stupidity.* NY: Barnes & Noble, 1993.

Vanderslice, Carolyn. *Oops! I Messed Up.* Pleasantville, NY: Sunburst Communications, 1995.

### Motivation

Brown, L. *Live Your Dreams.* NY: Harper, 1994.

Lundin, S.C. , Paul, H. and Christiansen, J. *Fish.* NY: Hyperion, 2000.

Tracy, B. *The Ultimate Goals Program.* NY: Nightingale-Conant, 2006.

Ziglar, Z. *See You At The Top.* NY: Pelican, 2000.

### Principles

Adams, S. *The Dilbert Principle.* NY: Harper Collins, 1996.

Buckingham, M. and Coffman, C. *First Break All the Rules.* NY: Simon & Schuster, 1999.

Clavell, James. (Ed.). *The Art of War: Sun Tzu.* NY: Dell Publishing, 1983.

Cohen, W.A. *Wisdom of the Generals.* NY: Prentice Hall, 2001.

Hoff, Benjamin. *The Tao of Pooh.* NY: Dutton, 1982.

Julian, L. *God is My CEO.* Holbrook, MA: Adams Media Corporation, 2001.

Leavitt, H.J., Pondy, L.R. and Boje, D.M. (Eds.). *Readings in Managerial Psychology* (4th Edition). Chicago: University of Chicago Press, 1989.

Krass, P. (Ed.). *The Book of Leadership Wisdom*. NY: John Wiley & Sons, 1998.

Maslow, A.H. *Maslow on Management*. NY: John Wiley & Sons, 1998.

Roberts, Wess. *Leadership Secrets of Attila the Hun*. NY: Warner Books, 1985.

Smith, P.M. *Rules & Tools for Leaders*. NY: Avery, 1998.

### Problem-Solving

Altier, W.J. *The Thinking Manger's Toolbox: Effective Processes for Problem-solving and Decision-making*. NY: Oxford University Press, 1999.

Carr, C. and Fletcher, M. *The Manager' Troubleshooter*. Englewood Cliffs, NJ: Prentice-Hall, 1990.

Curtis, D.B. *Communication for Problem-solving*. NY: Wilwy, 1979.

Harwood, C.C. *Trainer's Problem-solving Manual for Kick Down the Door of Complacency*. Boca Raton, FL: St. Lucie Press, 1998.

Klubnick, J.P. *The Team-based Problem Solver*. Burr Ridge, IL: Irwin Professional Publications, 1994.

Mitroff, I.I. *Smart Thinking for Crazy Times: The Act of Solving the Right Problems*. San Francisco: Berrett-Koehler Publishers, 1997.

Quinlivan-Hall, D. *In Search of Solutions*. San Diego: Pfeiffer, 1994.

Spitzer, Q. *Heads You Win*. NY: Simon & Schuster, 1999.

Zeitz, P. *The Art and Craft of Problem-solving*. NY: John Wiley, 1999.

### Role Modeling

The Arbinger Institute. *Leadership and Self-deception*. San Francisco: Berrett-Koehler Publishers, 2000.

Benfari, R.C. *Understanding and Changing Your Management Style*. San Francisco: Jossey-Bass, 1999.

Branden, Nathaniel. *Taking Responsibility: Self-reliance and the Accountable Life.* NY: Simon & Schuster, 1996.

Fulgham, Robert. *All I Really Need to Know I Learned in Kindergarten.* NY: Ballantine Books, 1992.

Mackoff, B. and Wenet, G. *The Inner Work of the Leader.* NY: AMACOM, 2001.

Maxwell, J.C. *Developing the Leader Within You.* Nashville: Thomas Nelson Publishers, 1993.

Murray, Jacqueline. *The Power of Dress.* Minneapolis, MN: Semiotics, 1989.

Tingley, J.C. *The Power of Indirect Influence.* NY: AMACOM, 2000.

### Stewardship

Block, P. *Stewardship.* San Francisco: Berrett-Koehler Publishers, 1996.

Canfield, J. and Miller, J. *Heart at Work.* NY: McGraw-Hill, 1996.

De Pree, M. *Leadership is an Art.* New York: Dell Publishing, 1989.

Greenleaf, R.K. *On Becoming a Servant Leader.* San Francisco: Jossey-Bass, 1996.

Hunter, J. *The Servant.* Roseville, CA: Prima Publishing, 1998.

Kushner, H.S. *Living a Life That Matters.* New York: Alfred A. Knopf, 2001.

Marriott, J.W. and Brown, K.A. *The Spirit to Serve.* NY: Harper Business, 1997.

### Time Management

Haasnoot, R. *The Complete Idiot's Guide to Five-minute Managing.* Indianapolis, IN: Alpha Books, 1999.

Januz, L.R. *Using Time Management to Get More Done.* Springfield, IL: Smith Collins, 1992.

Maxwell, J.C. *The 21 Most Powerful Minutes in a Leader's Day.* Nashville: Thomas Nelson Publishers, 2000.

Moskowitz, R. *How to Organize Your Work and Life* (2nd Edition). NY: Doubleday, 1993.

Olson, J. *The Agile Manager's Guide to Getting Organized.* Bristol, VT: Velocity Business Publications, 1997.

Sobel, M. *The 12-hour MBA Program.* Paramus, NJ: Prentice Hall, 1994.

Smith, J. *How to Be a better Time Manager.* London: Kogan Page, 1997.

Snead, G.L. and Wycoff, J. *To Do, Doing, Done.* NY: Fireside, 1997.

Winston, S. *The Organized Executive: New Ways to Manage Time, Paper, People and the Electronic Office.* NY: W.W. Norton, 1994.

Youngblood, C.H. *Executive Time Management Program.* NY: Thomas Publishing Co., 1988.

# Appendices

## APPENDIX A

### MANAGER'S "P" POINT SELF-ASSESSMENT

**Directions:** Read each behavior activity carefully and then rate the frequency that you actually practice this behavior. Do this by circling one of the numbers following the statement that best represents your estimate, according to the following key:

**Key**

| | | |
|---|---|---|
| 0 | = | Never |
| 1 | = | Occasionally |
| 2 | = | Sometimes, but not enough |
| 3 | = | Almost always |
| 4 | = | Always |

| | | |
|---|---|---|
| 1. | I ask others how they perceive me as a manager and person. | 0 1 2 3 4 |
| 2. | I practice aggressive listening and hear everything. | 0 1 2 3 4 |
| 3. | I question basic assumptions. | 0 1 2 3 4 |
| 4. | I control my bad moods. | 0 1 2 3 4 |
| 5. | I keep my priorities straight and in sharp focus. | 0 1 2 3 4 |
| 6. | I follow my hunches. | 0 1 2 3 4 |
| 7. | I ask many good questions. | 0 1 2 3 4 |
| 8. | I look for ways to make change more comfortable for others. | 0 1 2 3 4 |
| 9. | I manage my time well. | 0 1 2 3 4 |

| | | |
|---|---|---|
| 10. | I analyze all the important issues of a conflict carefully. | 0 1 2 3 4 |
| 11. | I apply useful people and life principles. | 0 1 2 3 4 |
| 12. | I am active in community groups. | 0 1 2 3 4 |
| 13. | I practice a good mistake recovery strategy. | 0 1 2 3 4 |
| 14. | I try to take a middle position on issues to see both sides. | 0 1 2 3 4 |
| 15. | I take the time to teach problem-solving skills to employees. | 0 1 2 3 4 |
| 16. | I am who I pretend to be. | 0 1 2 3 4 |
| 17. | I ask for feedback about the quality of my communication. | 0 1 2 3 4 |
| 18. | I notice inter-relationships between things below the surface. | 0 1 2 3 4 |
| 19. | I am friendly, positive and helpful. | 0 1 2 3 4 |
| 20. | I stay focused and avoid distractions. | 0 1 2 3 4 |
| 21. | I use my creative and intuitive abilities fully. | 0 1 2 3 4 |
| 22. | I take immediate ownership for the mistakes I make. | 0 1 2 3 4 |
| 23. | My life is balanced. | 0 1 2 3 4 |
| 24. | I ask the dumb questions that need to be asked. | 0 1 2 3 4 |
| 25. | I plan questions carefully to get the best information. | 0 1 2 3 4 |
| 26. | I anticipate external trends that will impact the workplace. | 0 1 2 3 4 |
| 27. | I organize my physical work space for maximum efficiency. | 0 1 2 3 4 |
| 28. | I know when and how to accommodate others in a confiict. | 0 1 2 3 4 |
| 29. | I use motivational principles advantageously. | 0 1 2 3 4 |
| 30. | I build employees' self esteem in a variety of ways. | 0 1 2 3 4 |

31. I strive hard to make personal improvements. 0 1 2 3 4
32. I take the time to get to know my "audience." 0 1 2 3 4
33. I am comfortable with tentativeness and ambiguity. 0 1 2 3 4
34. I display high energy. 0 1 2 3 4
35. I set goals, measure progress and get results. 0 1 2 3 4
36. I avoid pre-judging things. 0 1 2 3 4
37. I develop long range cures to keep mistakes from re-occurring. 0 1 2 3 4
38. I avoid extremes. 0 1 2 3 4
39. I look for disproof of favored problem-solving solutions. 0 1 2 3 4
40. I avoid asking questions to which I already have answers. 0 1 2 3 4
41. I can easily overcome others' resistance to change. 0 1 2 3 4
42. I start the day with a priority do-list. 0 1 2 3 4
43. I carefully explain the reasons when I act decisively. 0 1 2 3 4
44. I resist my tendency to want to reach premature closure. 0 1 2 3 4
45. I practice mentoring others. 0 1 2 3 4
46. I am proactive rather than reactive to people and situations. 0 1 2 3 4
47. I choose words carefully and plan how to emphasize them. 0 1 2 3 4
48. I am aware of and control my perceptual biases. 0 1 2 3 4
49. I work to improve my physical and social attractiveness. 0 1 2 3 4
50. I focus on employees' needs and concerns. 0 1 2 3 4

| | | |
|---|---|---|
| 51. | I encourage employees to express themselves creatively. | 0 1 2 3 4 |
| 52. | I make an effort to learn what others know. | 0 1 2 3 4 |
| 53. | I speak up against unwise, unproductive changes. | 0 1 2 3 4 |
| 54. | I critique my own productivity. | 0 1 2 3 4 |
| 55. | I deal with conflicts in a way to encourage growth. | 0 1 2 3 4 |
| 56. | I study things closely to learn how they work. | 0 1 2 3 4 |
| 57. | I enforce and reinforce sanctions constantly and consistently. | 0 1 2 3 4 |
| 58. | I practice hindsight lessons. | 0 1 2 3 4 |
| 59. | I am balanced between thinking and acting. | 0 1 2 3 4 |
| 60. | I am aware of the gap between how things are and need to be. | 0 1 2 3 4 |
| 61. | I project the right image. | 0 1 2 3 4 |
| 62. | I listen to understand rather than just to respond. | 0 1 2 3 4 |
| 63. | I can switch viewpoints and paradigms easily. | 0 1 2 3 4 |
| 64. | I practice fair and realistic expectations of others. | 0 1 2 3 4 |
| 65. | I take the time to learn all the details of something. | 0 1 2 3 4 |
| 66. | I say "yes" more than "no". | 0 1 2 3 4 |
| 67. | I look for ways to join together what everyone knows. | 0 1 2 3 4 |
| 68. | I work hard to assure integrity of values and actual practices. | 0 1 2 3 4 |
| 69. | I practice good stress management techniques regularly. | 0 1 2 3 4 |

| | | |
|---|---|---|
| 70. | I look for ways everyone can win in conflicts. | 0 1 2 3 4 |
| 71. | I see the inter-relatedness of things. | 0 1 2 3 4 |
| 72. | I stay up on things to be a good resource of information. | 0 1 2 3 4 |
| 73. | I spot and question important priority reversals. | 0 1 2 3 4 |
| 74. | I mix work and play. | 0 1 2 3 4 |
| 75. | I avoid being over-controlling. | 0 1 2 3 4 |
| 76. | I practice my own best advice. | 0 1 2 3 4 |
| 77. | I verify non-verbal behavior before making interpretations. | 0 1 2 3 4 |
| 78. | It is easy for me to separate my thinking from my feelings. | 0 1 2 3 4 |
| 79. | I exercise patience and tolerance with others. | 0 1 2 3 4 |
| 80. | I take good care of myself physically and emotionally. | 0 1 2 3 4 |
| 81. | I use people's individual talents rather than job descriptions. | 0 1 2 3 4 |
| 82. | I separate performance problems from personality concerns. | 0 1 2 3 4 |
| 83. | I enjoy laughing. | 0 1 2 3 4 |
| 84. | I resolve conflicts systematically and effectively. | 0 1 2 3 4 |
| 85. | I know what motivates each employee. | 0 1 2 3 4 |
| 86. | I practice virtuous behavior. | 0 1 2 3 4 |
| 87. | I exercise patience when mistakes are made. | 0 1 2 3 4 |
| 88. | I give and take equally. | 0 1 2 3 4 |
| 89. | I am both logical and creative in working through problems. | 0 1 2 3 4 |
| 90. | I avoid making assumptions. | 0 1 2 3 4 |

| | | |
|---|---|---|
| 91. | I follow-up on details of delegated assignments. | 0 1 2 3 4 |
| 92. | I set and enforce high standards of performance. | 0 1 2 3 4 |
| 93. | I am aware of the importance of people's perceptions. | 0 1 2 3 4 |
| 94. | I identify and eliminate performance barriers. | 0 1 2 3 4 |
| 95. | I plan and time my interventions carefully. | 0 1 2 3 4 |
| 96. | I take adequate time with employees. | 0 1 2 3 4 |
| 97. | I am principled but not inflexible. | 0 1 2 3 4 |
| 98. | I create a motivating, quality work environment. | 0 1 2 3 4 |
| 99. | I am aware of important gaps within the organization. | 0 1 2 3 4 |
| 100. | I know, understand and practice all these "P" points diligently. | 0 1 2 3 4 |
| | Point Total | ________ |

**Scoring:**

275-400 points = Ph.D. in "P" Point Management.

151-274 points = B.A. in "P" Point Management.

0-150 points = G.E.D. in "P" Point Management.

# APPENDIX B

## MANAGEMENT SOFTWARE UPGRADES

> *"Unless a tree has borne blossoms in the spring, you will vainly look for fruit on it in autumn"* (Hare Charles).

The fast moving "Information Age" is quickly taking us into uncharted territories, where our more traditional ways of seeing and doing things are becoming totally and utterly ineffective. Successful management in the nanosecond 2000 decade requires some major software upgrades. Below are ten such upgrades managers should give serious thought to installing:

### **Disk Management** (Thoughtfulness)

This is the most important software upgrade because it interfaces with and instructs the other nine. Thoughtfulness involves creative but disciplined thinking—Thinking ahead, backwards, inside-out, upside down, outside the box and every other which way but lose, *systematically*, to get "unstuck" in our perpetual quest to solve problems and grow. Thoughtfulness is the creative key which unlocks the other mental skills managers need to survive the chaos of today. The quality of our thinking has to catch up to the different problems we are confronted with today. Very few known prescriptions are still effective anymore. Problem-solving today requires an intense mix of intuition, convergent and divergent thinking, keen analysis, paradigm-shifting, perseverance, creative genius and intuitive insight.

The thoughtful manager knows important differences in employees. For example, he will know that John may require some understanding and a little leeway about some personal difficulties, that Jane needs some encouragement to continue improving her teamwork, and that James needs some more specific training and detailed instructions on report writing. When managers know their employee's concerns, competence levels and motivational cycles, then they are better able to apply the most appropriate action.

As a result, employees feel more understood and supported, and are more inclined to perform better. In turn, the productivity of the entire organization improves, which benefits everyone. Generally, there can never be too much thought, but there does come a time when action must be taken. This is when an employee has been given adequate training, clear instructions and enough fair chances to improve and then that improvement still doesn't occur. Obviously, emergency situations are another time for action to take the center stage.

### **Shareware** (Open-Mindedness)

Maybe this should be the number one upgrade because none of the other software programs will run without it. It is definitely a "shared," integrated program. An essential managerial survival skill today is to forget what you know, suspend pre-judgments against past experience and open the mind to entirely fresh new perspectives.

The key here is to let go completely. This may sound scary or even foolish, but thoughtfulness will tell us there really isn't any choice in the matter. Change is probably the only certainty today, so we better loosen our grip and get used to it. There is wisdom in the Greek saying, "*It is not the things in life which bother us, but rather our opinions about these things.*" Or, as Yogi Berra eloquently put it, "*If you come to a fork in the road, take it.*"

The open-minded manager takes a close look at routine organizational procedures and questions whether or not they can be done differently, to get better results and cost less. For instance, will metal detectors be more effective and less costly than manual searches in high security areas? Will video conferencing be a more cost-effective way to conduct meetings? Is all the information we are collecting really that necessary? On the other hand, sometimes the basics such as walking around the plant aren't being practiced enough or done consistently. In those situations, nothing new will ever make a positive difference and will probably only hide the real problem.

**Virtual Memory** (Sensitivity)

In the complex, fast-moving times of today, we are becoming blind and deaf to the important clues in life which are most valuable to us in our attempts to be successful. Critical *perturbation points* in life aren't very loud. If we don't force ourselves to slow down, sharpen our sensitivity and listen to the clues, we won't have *any.* One very important clue is the *interdependency* of all things. Application of this software upgrade requires understanding how things are related and how they work together.

The sensitive manager knows that Kris will respond better to private recognition, whereas Bill may like more public acknowledgment for his achievements. He also knows exactly when to disclose something personal to Fred, e.g., an earlier failure in his own career, to build enough rapport to be able to provide Fred with negative feedback about his reports not being thorough enough. More than anything though, the sensitive manager knows how employees learn from his own behavior. Remaining calm during an emergency and pitching in with the dirty work teaches a lot and earns the manager considerable respect.

**Uninstaller** (Simplification)

In our process of mental evolution, we seem to like to make things more complex than they need to be. Things have gotten so complex these days, that it is futile to try and grasp anything in its entirety. It makes more sense to grab a smaller chunk of information and start working on simplifying it for immediate practical use. One warning in applying this upgrade, though: *"Simplicity on this side of complexity is a quick fix; simplicity just on the other side of complexity is an enduring cure."*

Managers need to learn how to write one page letters and memos, keep meetings to one hour and talk in simple sentences. They need to translate abstract concepts into concrete actions for employees to see and feel. The more complex managers make something, the more the chance of misunderstanding by employees, resulting in less than expected performance.

In another area, the manager will get much more support and compliance by emphasizing and reinforcing just a few core values, expressed in terms that all employees can relate to, e.g. one hour response to all customer complaints, friendly and helpful attitude, and sharp appearance by the book. A too complex or sophisticated mission statement or too many goals will only get employees confused and going in different directions. Full-blown diversity of approaches is fine for gaining valuable input in the beginning of a new project, but there comes a time when the team needs to work together toward a common outcome with single-mindedness.

### **Enhanced Printer Driver** (Good Communication)

Fortunately, it is not possible to not communicate, but unfortunately, it is highly probable to miscommunicate. It is a fair assumption that we will be miscommunicating, unless we work very hard at assuring quality communication. This involves improving listening skills, developing better delivery methods, thinking about our audiences more, planning customized communication, and more than anything else, seeking feedback as to the understanding and impact of what we are trying to communicate.

The manager who practices good communication learns to actively listen to *everything*. Sometimes this involves what is *not* being said in a conversation, such as the absence of genuine acceptance of a new procedure by the majority of employees. Clarification of the reasons from employees may prompt changes, which result in better support and compliance with the new procedure when it goes into effect. Such a manager also learns to improve the impact of important points with flair, repetition and relevant body language, perhaps by studying outstanding speeches by famous people or looking at superior advertising techniques. His written communication also *speaks* to the audience in a *connected* and *alive* manner.

### **Object Linking & Embedding-OLE** (Balance)

We seem to have a tendency toward *either-or, this vs. that* mentality in which we polarize things and view one "opposite" of the pair as being more preferable than the other one. We line up things as being either okay or not okay, cutting winning potential in half for everyone. The wisdom of seeing two seemingly opposite things as different sides of the same coin, allows the smart manager to establish a strategically balanced position, being free to go to either side as might be most appropriate at the particular time and place.

This *win-win* approach results in mutual benefits and satisfactions for all the parties in human interaction. It also improves the chances of success by 50 per cent.

The balanced manager regulates his own and the organization's stress by maintaining a good mixture of work and play, both during and after work. It is time to buckle down and pass a stringent performance audit, but the success deserves a celebration afterwards. The balanced manager also *matures* into middle ground on issues such as formality vs. informality, creativity vs. conventionality, and individualism vs. teamwork. By being in the middle, the balanced manager is able to go to either approach, which may be more appropriate at a particular time. For example, the procedures in a financial audit may need to be very conventional, whereas the presentation format may be more open to a more divergent, or creative approach. However, this balancing act should not lure managers into being neutral on important issues such as employee dishonesty, mediocre performance, emergency procedures or inefficiency.

### **Optical Character Recognition-OCR** (Perceptual Filter)

We believe our own perceptions of things are the correct versions of reality worth getting beat-up, maimed or killed over, despite two very discordant facts: (a) we all see things differently based on our unlike experiences, private ways of interpreting things and unique needs; and (b) our brains selectively distort things for the sake of convenience and simplicity by filling in gaps, grouping things contiguously, tuning into or out of specific stimuli and other interesting "organizing" functions.

An essential managerial skill in the information age is clear vision and this will require changing perceptual filters to keep from putting too much of our own personal, and sometimes distorted spin on things. This won't be easy since it is our oldest habit, but the other software upgrades, especially 1, 2 and 3, will help a lot.

The manager who wisely installs this Optical Character Recognition (OCR) software upgrade, will be aware of how he is being perceived throughout the organization and will know when his personal bias of rationality is getting in the way in a discussion with an emotional employee. He will also understand that all employees will have their very own, slightly different perception of what the organization's goals are or what is supposed to be learned in a particular training session. This manager will also know the value of getting different perceptions of vulnerability of a planned flat organizational structure. It takes time to learn all these different perceptions, but they are the employee's realities and they will affect project outcomes. The time however, can be better managed as indicated in the next software upgrade.

**Data Compression** (Time Management)

The world is moving so fast today, we have a sense that there is not nearly enough time to get everything done and that we are falling further and further behind. Sometimes, though, we have to become real uncomfortable with the present state of affairs *before* we take any action to do anything about it.

An amazing reality is that time is one of the few resources that is equally distributed to everyone. There is always plenty of time when it is used wisely. When we shift our focus from putting out fires to learning how they start, we free up a lot of time to do everything we need to be doing. There has always been value in the saying, *"An ounce of prevention...."*

The effective manager will learn how to work *smart*. This means spending 20 per cent of the time getting 80 per cent of the results, rather than the usual visa versa. Two hours spent planning out a new access control route, can result in preventing a week's worth of investigation about backdoor thefts. Also, a good one-hour informal performance review with a marginal employee, can save hours of later documentation and corrective action. And as indicated above, time spent learning about employee's perceptions about a new work procedure can help smooth the way for support and compliance. A smart working manager will get paperwork done early in the morning, work from and complete a do-list, limit phone interruptions, use waiting time productively and not get caught up in fire-fighting activities or over-respond to other people's emergencies. She will also create free time to plan how she could be best spending other time.

**32 Bit Graphics Imager** (Proper Focus)

In getting swept into the 1000 mph whirlwind pace, the rest of the world is presently moving at, we allow our focus to get blurred. Either we change focus too frequently or we spend too much time gazing ahead at the hoped-for end result. Instead we should be zooming in on exactly what we need to be doing *right now*, to get to the first place we need to be at to get going through a sequence of actions which will *eventually* get us where we want to be in the end.

The manager who exercises proper focus does not change priorities too quickly or too frequently so as to confuse employees. If the focus is on quality training for good public relations skills, then that is what it stays on until everyone has demonstrated mastery of that particular skill. Employees need to be brought back into focus, by a very focused leader, as it is natural to drift without consistent and persistent reminders. Short Monday morning meetings can set the focus for the whole week and mini-posters can serve as friendly reminders. On the other hand, there is a proper time to widen the focus and that may be during quarterly or annual brainstorming planning sessions. It may be more important to have all the right things to focus on, rather than focusing well on the wrong things.

There is one area of focus that deserves special attention. In essence, before we can manage others we have to manage ourselves. The real power we have in closing the gap between our circle of concern and circle of influence is in choosing the response we make to each new situation. The effective manager will keep this point in focus at all times. The other software upgrades can certainly assist in this matter.

### **Anti-Virus Protection** (Humor)

We tend to take life and ourselves too seriously. We started out as playful kids and ended up as adults working hard to play. Actually, there are a just a few situations in life that don't have some laughable aspect. A quick trip to the zoo and observation of the hippopotamuses, giraffes, monkeys, wombats and lizards will reaffirm that reality.

One thing we take too seriously is failure. However, we do seem to learn more from our failures rather than our successes, and besides we better get used to more failures as speed alone is likely to increase their number. There is valuable comic relief in the saying, *Don't take life too seriously, after all, you're not going to get out of it alive!* The real value of laughing is that laughing can free the mind up to get all the other software programs working.

Managers need to take time out to laugh in order to reduce their own stress from both normal job pressures and frequent emergency situations. They can also use a humorous story to break the ice into a serious discussion about schedule changes or to get two upset employees to laugh at something as a diversion from a tense situation. When employees can take time out to laugh at themselves or a situation, they will be more open to getting on with the business of making needed improvements. Of course, the use of management humor has to be timely and appropriate. Employee misconduct and corporate downsizing are not laughing matters and an employee going through personal difficulties is not inclined to respond very well to misplaced humor.

In conclusion, you can probably see by now that these ten management software upgrades work together as a totally integrated office suite. It will be okay to load the programs in any order, but they do all need to be loaded to be most effective. The manager with all these new upgrades will be better prepared to deal with all the complexity, speed, changes and new problems being brought about by the Information Age.

> "*By the time your life is finished, you will have learned just enough to begin it well*" (Eleanor Marx).

# APPENDIX C

## NEW MILLENNIUM LEADERSHIP SKILLS

*"Ability will never catch up with the demand for it"* (Malcolm Forbes).

The Information Age is quickly taking us all to new unfamiliar territories without any maps. Speed, change and chaos are at the top of today's agenda. These times require leaders to develop tremendous cerebral dexterity. On the one hand, it is imperative for leaders to stay grounded with core truths and anchored with proven practices during this period of flux. Otherwise we may all lose out on something we can't afford to be without.

On the other hand, it is equally important for leaders to expand their repertoire by experimenting with newer abilities to respond to new unfamiliar situations, which will be confronting us more and more. Here are a few newer essential skills to help assure leaders continued executive excellence in the new millennium:

### Effecticiency Orientation

During the last few decades we have been part of an evolving continuum of administrative focus. This continuum started us focusing on efficiency, or using the least costly methods of doing something. This continuum then shifted our focus toward effectiveness, or doing the right thing to produce the right outcomes. Next came the focus on **effecticiency**, or doing the right thing right. The next stage of the supervision-management-leadership evolution will be *stewardship*. This will require expansion of "rightness" to include deeper reasons as to the why and how of what we are doing, beyond the obvious consequences. Some of these reasons have yet to be defined.

I once developed what I considered the ideal program evaluation model. The program involved providing outreach mental health and social services to a resistive population of troubled farmers and coal miners. The success measures where on three levels: (1) efficiency of inputs and outputs; (2) comparison to quality performance standards; and (3) actual outcome results. Outcome measures are the only thing that interest funding sources today. After struggling with the attempt to quantify desired outcomes, I finally came up with the *right* reason behind the program: Fundamental fairness. This group of hard working people who were jobless and stressed-out through no fault of their own, *deserved* equal access to services they would never seek on their own.

## Creatuitivity

New millennium leaders must tap into unconscious reservoirs of creativity and intuition to solve difficult, unfamiliar problems and resolve complicated, multi-level conflicts. There are no known prescriptions to some of the dilemmas resulting from our society's socioquake of values. We will have to learn to trust gut feelings, listen closer to subconscious whisperings, dream more and let go of our need to understand things from the single reference point of conventional logic.

First we need to acknowledge that we are running out of answers. Then we have to practice suspending judgement, stop anticipating outcomes and start experimenting more with a tentative "let's wait and see" or curious "what if…?" attitude. Along with that basic attitude re-arrangement, we have to start following and evaluating intuitive feelings as to where we are going, why and how we can get there. Sometimes the answers will be totally rational and other times totally illogical. We have to become fluid enough mentally to allow our convergent and divergent thinking processes to take us 3-D and beyond. This takes much trust and open-mindedness.

## "P" Point Interventions

Timing is a critical skill and wise leaders cultivate this important truth. There are critical points where small, effortless but well-placed and well-timed small interventions produce major results. These are perturbation points or just "P" points for short. Common commercial examples are media headlines, political sound bytes and advertising slogans. Practical examples are emphasizing a key point with voice tone and supporting gestures, teaching an emergency procedure firsthand during an actual emergency and working your statements into another person's questions when they are most likely listening to what you are saying.

An effective leader must increase his or her arsenal of "P" points to produce the kind and magnitude of impacts that will be needed and expected. There are plenty of valuable "P" points in everyday life and the key is to increase sensitivity to see and hear them. A good starting point is to observe more—look for important principles about life and people in general. Then tune into ideal times and places to apply this information.

Two important "P" points for leaders to tap into are: (1) the belief in whatever you can think is possible, is possible and (2) the subtle relationship between your beliefs and reality.

### Gap-Closing

One unfortunate side effect of the massive changes we are going through today is the pervasive phenomenon of *gap widening*. The gap is widening between those who have needed information and those who don't. The gaps between age groups are widening in the workplace. The gaps in knowledge and skills are widening between leaders, managers, managers and employees. The gap in alignment between mission, goals, values and actual behavior is widening in diverse organizations. Everywhere gaps are getting wider.

We've struggled with gaps all along without ever perfecting this important skill. Today these gaps are getting so wide that there is increasing danger of losing people to the void who are trying to jump across the gap on their own without a plan or assistance. It is time we figure out how to become masters of closing gaps before we lose too many good people.

Like other perplexing problems, we may be worrying too much about all the effort that is going to be required in applying any solution, as opposed to just focusing on finding the right approach. The right approach is simple. First you must make the allowable assumption that these gaps are much wider than you imagine. Then you have to visit the gap and get to know what it is all about firsthand, in the trenches. The purpose of a gap is to remind the leader what it is like to be a follower. You can't *think* that knowledge.

**Two-Eared Listening**

The effective leader has to be a superb listener. This talent requires the effort to learn how to listen aggressively to both what is being said and what isn't being said and to hear all that is intended through what is being said and how it is being said. Without intense listening, misunderstanding is highly likely and without accurate understanding our paths and destinations only get more blurred.

The smart leader learns to hear what is not being said in a conversation to determine how that may effect what is being said. Another important listening skill is to spot when non-verbal or other communication style factors may change the entire meaning of what is being said. If a salesperson emphasizes the reasonable cost of an item and doesn't comment on the quality or durability, is it wise to make the purchase without asking some other questions? Do you believe a person who tries to talk positively but slips with negative gestures? Do you miss important and valuable message content because the presentation package isn't appealing enough?

**Power Communication**

Time is our most precious commodity these days and since there is so much information for people to try and consume, the spoken and written words we use have to be short and sweet. The new millennium requires leaders to speak and write in power sound bytes. This skill involves studying linguistics, psychology, advertising, literature, famous speeches and drama. The object is to learn how to communicate the most important information clearly and simply enough to avoid any misunderstanding and have a direct hit with impact. When you say something exciting, lightening needs to strike.

Today's babble of confusion is a formidable obstacle to overcome. Leaders who practice power communication to overturn this tower of babble work hard to make a close connection with their audiences, learn about the many psychological dimensions of words, think up new words to make an important point and make an effort to speak with animation, flair and pizzazz. They also choose words wisely, understand how the person they are talking to processes information, master effective non-verbal communication to be complementary and eliminate annoying distractions. Above all else, they are aware of the extent of miscommunication today and actively seek feedback to make improvements in their own communication skills.

## Value Congruence

The leader has to formulate the right mission for his or her organization, based on core values. These core values are what translate this ideal mission into dynamic, practical action. Such values have to be integral to the mission and wholly supported by all management. Then they must be clearly communicated to managers, translated meaningfully to front line employees and accurately perceived by consumers. This is the paramount communication process within any organization but it is typically only attempted once and then forgotten or neglected altogether. The wise leader makes this activity an on-going priority.

Since a typical organization communication system will involve at least five layers, congruence can never be assumed and must be continuously and carefully orchestrated by the leader. Critical activities are communicating values in a variety of formats, setting up a reliable and accurate system of measuring incongruence, applying consistent reinforcement to the value congruence that there is and implementing corrective training to increase congruence. Ironically, the simpler the mission, the more complex the values are and the more intimate the organization becomes, the worse the communication gets. The diversity of today's workforce makes this leadership function even more difficult. Older, more traditional values are being re-defined and replaced with different ones and the leader has to be on the lookout to not allow these value changes to run counter to the organization's mission and goals.

### Visual Accommodation

An able leader has to have access to both the big picture and foreground details, often simultaneously. Leadership also involves seeing the advantage of both short-term and long-term goals. Sometimes the bigger picture and long range goals take priority while other times the details of something or the shorter range goals are more important. Either way, the right determination can't be made if both vantagepoints aren't seen together in relationship to one another. Sometimes a slight change in details changes the big picture drastically while other times many changes don't have any overall effect.

Attentional shifting is something leaders must work on constantly. In a business where training costs dig into immediate profits, the leader has to determine whether it is more important do go ahead and conduct the training, hoping that it will be a wise investment that will increase profits later. Other similar shifting must be done continuously. When is it wisest to favor a general consistent policy or respond to an important individual concern? Is there a point where even a minor sacrifice becomes more trouble than it is worth?

### Coopetition

Leaders must use both cooperation and competition as necessary driving forces. The trick is to avoid setting up situations where there has to be a choice between cooperation and competition. An alternative is to encourage these antagonistic motives to merge naturally into a form of coopetition. The art of leadership also involves the use of subtle influences to gradually shift focus from inter-competition *between* organizations and individuals to intra-competition *within* the organization and individual.

In order to solve today's global trade, economy and e-commerce dilemmas, leaders have no other choice than to explore ways to cooperate with whatever way the rules of competition are going to be. Cooperation is much easier to sell when leaders begin to promote the reality of an abundance mentality where we are not so paranoid about how much of the pie we are getting. There always has been and always will be plenty for everyone.

## Heuristic Thinking

Heuristic thinking is the leader's portal to creatuitivity. This is unstructured thinking that isn't trapped inside a well-defined system or specific frame of reference, which is shackled by constraining rules. This type of thinking doesn't start or finish at any particular point and makes things up as it goes along. It is like jumping into the middle of a river to figure out when, where and how to redirect the water flow. Heuristic thinking is actually becoming part of something to know it better from the inside-out, rather than trying to control it from the outside.

Why do leaders need to develop heuristic thinking? Because in some circumstances it may be the only way to understand and know what is really important when we find we have already become part of something we didn't anticipate or even choose. It could be that we are already into the second half of the game where most of what we know doesn't work anymore. To continue strictly thinking algorithmically to solve newer problems would fit the classic definition of mental illness-doing the same thing over and over again and expecting different results.

## Virtuality

Remote leadership is becoming a common practice today. It sets up all new standards and rules. It also poses some interesting questions. For instance, how do we monitor employee's accountability? How do we keep knowledgeable about what is going on within the organization? How do we avoid only being listened to for the moment and not heard after we leave? How can we assure a healthy sense of stability and continuity with such virtuality? How do we keep technology from taking over? These are just a few of the unanswered questions about a practice we have already embraced.

The whole information age has taken over so quickly that we haven't had adequate time to plan for the changes in leadership that are coming with it. Effective leadership will have to add much more tools to what we already know. We are indeed already deep into uncharted waters without a map. Solutions will require leaders to actively develop all these new leadership skills in attempting to re-answer the perennial questions of: What are we doing? Why? How do we get there?

> *"Big jobs go to the men who prove the ability to outgrow small ones"* (Ralph Waldo Emerson).

## APPENDIX D

## 50 NEW LEADERSHIP WORDS

*"All words are pegs to hang ideas on"* (Henry Beecher).

By inventing new words we can improve the impact of our communication. Here is some new leadership language to help stimulate you to coin your own new terms.

1. **Abundance Mentality.** The confidence that there is enough of everything to go around for everyone. This viewpoint does away with proprietary paranoia and cut-throat practices and promotes coopetition between competitors.
2. **Audible-Ready.** Instantaneous readiness to change a game plan when the situation demands it.
3. **Bullet-Train Thinking.** Breaking out of conventional thinking and performance expectations.
4. **Businessing.** Turning all employees into real business persons responsible for customers from order to delivery of the service or product.
5. **Celestial Navigation.** Clarifying "true north" guiding principles to maintain the proper course for the organization.
6. **Character Currency.** The ability to produce "oughtness" by making, keeping and managing quality relationships.
7. **Co-missioning.** Getting everyone to play an active role in creating and carrying out the company's main mission.
8. **Compression.** Shedding the low value-added components of the business.
9. **Connective Leadership.** Developing instrumental styles to integrate the centrifugal forces of diversity and interdependence.

10. **Coopetition.** The creative merging of two apparent contradictory strategies into cooperative competition.
11. **Cosmopolitan Leadership.** Leaders who have open minds, are receptive to new information outside their current framework and practice outreach to partners.
12. **Egonomics.** The trend for everyone to want to make a personal statement.
13. **Enactivity.** Activity between aggressive proactivity and passive reactivity in selecting critical problems to resolve appropriately.
14. **Fearless Environment.** Work environments that operate on positive principles of open communication, cooperation, innovation, open book management, high trust and strong future vision.
15. **Free Intraprise.** Free market choice inside the organization.
16. **Global Paradox.** Think locally, act globally.
17. **Heuristic vs. Algorithmic Thinking.** Solving problems by using incomplete guidelines that lead to learning or discovery vs. mechanical rules using tried and true solutions.
18. **Hypercompetion.** An active strategy of disrupting the status quo to create a series of unsustainable advantages.
19. **Intrapreneur.** A passionate hands-on champion who takes the conceptual to the actual.
20. **Irreducible Essence.** The incontrovertible truth that is left when everything is stripped away.
21. **Liberation Management.** The new ephemeral, bonkers, wow, zany, horizontal, beyond-hierarchy, chaotic work environment.
22. **Linch-Pin Connections.** Rock solid linkage between the realities of the marketplace, aspirations of top management and the actions of the workforce.
23. **Manager-Leader.** Moving toward a visionary role in going from asking how and when questions to what and why ones.

24. **Morphic Resonance.** What you unleash when you tune into your own internal creative force.
25. **Net Work.** Developing skills and relationships that unite individual and collective efforts.
26. **Open-Book Management.** Sharing, educating, and holding everyone accountable with company financial information, goals and results.
27. **Partnering Triad.** Forming productive partnerships between suppliers, employees and customers.
28. **Perturbation Point.** A critical point in which small, intensified well-timed and well-placed efforts produce major results.
29. **Portfolio Planning.** Balancing existing short-term and potential long-term strategies.
30. **Power Work.** Effecticiency, or combining efficiency (doing a thing right) with effectiveness (doing the right thing).
31. **Revitalization.** That which should follow downsizing, restructuring and re-engineering.
32. **Sandwich Praise.** Opening with praise, slipping in a criticism and then ending with praise.
33. **Servant-leadership.** Making goals clear and then rolling up your sleeves and doing whatever it takes to help people win.
34. **Socioquake.** The major transformation in values we are experiencing as we move further into the Information Age.
35. **Stewardship.** Being deeply accountable for outcomes without acting to control others or defining their purpose.
36. **Strategic Leadership.** Alignment of vision, goals and objectives, values, organizational structure, and workplace culture.
37. **Subsidiary.** Power should belong to the lowest possible point.

38. **Subtle Acuity.** Development of our intuition to know what is right and the practical application of this spiritual integrity.

39. **Symbiosis.** Cooperative relationship between two dissimilar groups.

40. **Synergy.** The capacity of two or more people to optimize one another and achieve mutual enhancement.

41. **The Control Paradox.** You are out of control when you think you are in control; you are in control when you feel out of control.

42. **The Game Metaphor.** Opening all the books to employees and then letting them follow the action and know the score.

43. **The Fatal Conceit Syndrome.** The presumption that one can move forward with central plans.

44. **Three Dimensional Thinking (3D IQ).** Mixing convergent, vertical and analytical thinking with divergent, lateral and creative thinking.

45. **Three-Hundred Sixty Degree Feedback.** Soliciting performance feedback from *all* stakeholders.

46. **Transformational Learning.** The process of discovery that leads to profound shifts in viewpoints, directions, values, behavior, beliefs and operating assumptions.

47. **TSS.** Total stakeholder satisfaction.

48. **Value Work.** Discovering useful knowledge and applying it to produce greater value than is currently available for more people.

49. **Virtuality.** Remote control management of a dispersed organization.

50. **Webs of Inclusion.** Grass roots structures within the organization that conceive and implement transformational changes.

"*Words today are like the shells and rope of seaweed that a child brings home glistening from the beach and which in an hour have lost their luster*" (Cyril Connolly).

# APPENDIX E

## WORK ENVIRONMENT SURVEY


9 Surfside Crescent, Pottsville, NSW 2489 Australia.

**Directions:** Tell us how you perceive general aspects of your work environment. Do this by circling the description from the following key, which best represents how you feel about each statement. Do NOT put your names on these surveys. Your frank responses are welcomed.

| | | |
|---|---|---|
| N/A | = | Not Applicable |
| SA | = | Strongly Agree |
| A | = | Agree |
| N/? | = | Neither, unsure |
| D | = | Disagree |
| SD | = | Strongly Disagree |

| | | | | | | |
|---|---|---|---|---|---|---|
| 1. There is a clear chain of command to follow. | N/A | SA | A | N/? | D | SD |
| 2. There is often an uptight atmosphere around here. | N/A | SA | A | N/? | D | SD |
| 3. Management is usually approachable. | N/A | SA | A | N/? | D | SD |
| 4. Training leaves a lot to be desired. | N/A | SA | A | N/? | D | SD |
| 5. Performance and other expectations are realistic. | N/A | SA | A | N/? | D | SD |
| 6. Things are disorganized much of the time. | N/A | SA | A | N/? | D | SD |
| 7. Communication is generally good. | N/A | SA | A | N/? | D | SD |
| 8. Job assignments, promotions, etc. are unfair. | N/A | SA | A | N/? | D | SD |
| 9. Expectations are clear. | N/A | SA | A | N/? | D | SD |

| | | | | | | |
|---|---|---|---|---|---|---|
| 10. There is too much change going on to keep up. | N/A | SA | A | N/? | D | SD |
| 11. Management staff is honest. | N/A | SA | A | N/? | D | SD |
| 12. Work is boring. | N/A | SA | A | N/? | D | SD |
| 13. Management staff treats employees with respect. | N/A | SA | A | N/? | D | SD |
| 14. Follow-up and follow-through are lacking. | N/A | SA | A | N/? | D | SD |
| 15. Things are too controlled. | N/A | SA | A | N/? | D | SD |
| 16. Management listens and acts on suggestions. | N/A | SA | A | N/? | D | SD |
| 17. Many managers and managers are too inflexible. | N/A | SA | A | N/? | D | SD |
| 18. Procedures and other things are usually consistent. | N/A | SA | A | N/? | D | SD |
| 19. Many employees are out of control. | N/A | SA | A | N/? | D | SD |
| 20. Work is usually meaningful. | N/A | SA | A | N/? | D | SD |
| 21. Employees are acknowledged and rewarded. | N/A | SA | A | N/? | D | SD |
| 22. There is little tolerance for mistakes. | N/A | SA | A | N/? | D | SD |
| 23. Most things are done efficiently. | N/A | SA | A | N/? | D | SD |
| 24. Our mission isn't clear. | N/A | SA | A | N/? | D | SD |
| 25. There is a strong practice of good customer service. | N/A | SA | A | N/? | D | SD |
| 26. Administrative support is lacking. | N/A | SA | A | N/? | D | SD |
| 27. Employees are given clear direction. | N/A | SA | A | N/? | D | SD |
| 28. There isn't much team spirit. | N/A | SA | A | N/? | D | SD |
| 29. There is a wall between management and staff. | N/A | SA | A | N/? | D | SD |

| | | | | | | |
|---|---|---|---|---|---|---|
| 30. This is an excellent company. | N/A | SA | A | N/? | D | SD |
| 31. There isn't enough professionalism around here. | N/A | SA | A | N/? | D | SD |
| 32. The workplace is physically comfortable. | N/A | SA | A | N/? | D | SD |
| 33. There is too much status quo going on. | N/A | SA | A | N/? | D | SD |
| 34. Problems usually get resolved quickly & effectively. | N/A | SA | A | N/? | D | SD |
| 35. There is much emphasis and concern for quality. | N/A | SA | A | N/? | D | SD |
| 36. There is little recognition for good work. | N/A | SA | A | N/? | D | SD |
| 37. Things are too formal around here. | N/A | SA | A | N/? | D | SD |
| 38. Employees are not busy enough. | N/A | SA | A | N/? | D | SD |
| 39. Work conditions are generally good. | N/A | SA | A | N/? | D | SD |
| 40. Managers are not that helpful. | N/A | SA | A | N/? | D | SD |
| 41. Workloads are fair and equal. | N/A | SA | A | N/? | D | SD |
| 42. There is a general lack of concern for employees. | N/A | SA | A | N/? | D | SD |
| 43. There are too many low performers around here. | N/A | SA | A | N/? | D | SD |
| 44. Management is untrustworthy. | N/A | SA | A | N/? | D | SD |
| 45. Management encourages employees. | N/A | SA | A | N/? | D | SD |
| 46. Things are often too hectic. | N/A | SA | A | N/? | D | SD |
| 47. There are many dishonest employees here. | N/A | SA | A | N/? | D | SD |
| 48. Equipment hardly ever works right. | N/A | SA | A | N/? | D | SD |
| 49. Work rules usually make sense. | N/A | SA | A | N/? | D | SD |

| | | | | | | |
|---|---|---|---|---|---|---|
| 50. Things are very unstable around here. | N/A | SA | A | N/? | D | SD |
| 51. Our company is a friendly place. | N/A | SA | A | N/? | D | SD |
| 52. There is too much gossip and petty politics. | N/A | SA | A | N/? | D | SD |
| 53. There is encouragement to be part of the company. | N/A | SA | A | N/? | D | SD |
| 54. Management sets a good example. | N/A | SA | A | N/? | D | SD |
| 55. Morale is not that good around here. | N/A | SA | A | N/? | D | SD |
| 56. Management is out of touch about what is going on. | N/A | SA | A | N/? | D | SD |
| 57. I enjoy coming to work. | N/A | SA | A | N/? | D | SD |
| 58. Employees are held accountable. | N/A | SA | A | N/? | D | SD |
| 59. Management staff is always changing their minds. | N/A | SA | A | N/? | D | SD |
| 60. Important decisions are fair and explained well. | N/A | SA | A | N/? | D | SD |
| 61. Employees are constantly encouraged to improve. | N/A | SA | A | N/? | D | SD |
| 62. Real authority isn't delegated very often. | N/A | SA | A | N/? | D | SD |
| 63. Job descriptions provide for reasonable flexibility. | N/A | SA | A | N/? | D | SD |
| 64. Employees aren't asked to help solve problems. | N/A | SA | A | N/? | D | SD |
| 65. This organization is fairly democratic. | N/A | SA | A | N/? | D | SD |
| 66. Management spends time planning things out. | N/A | SA | A | N/? | D | SD |
| 67. The company asks for feedback from customers. | N/A | SA | A | N/? | D | SD |

| | | | | | | |
|---|---|---|---|---|---|---|
| 68. Morale is generally poor around here. | N/A | SA | A | N/? | D | SD |
| 69. Different departments work well together. | N/A | SA | A | N/? | D | SD |
| 70. I know where to go to get help when I need it. | N/A | SA | A | N/? | D | SD |
| 71. Employees don't do it if it isn't in the job description. | N/A | SA | A | N/? | D | SD |
| 72. There is good cooperation in this company. | N/A | SA | A | N/? | D | SD |
| 73. Everyone knows what his or her work goals are. | N/A | SA | A | N/? | D | SD |
| 74. Some people contribute more than others. | N/A | SA | A | N/? | D | SD |
| 75. The company keeps employees informed. | N/A | SA | A | N/? | D | SD |

Scoring: The idea is for top management to complete this questionnaire the way they want the organization to be perceived by employees. Then the consensus discrepancies can serve to identify key areas needing attention and improvement.

# APPENDIX F

# CHANGE READINESS ASSESSMENT INSTRUMENT

## Pre-Diagnostic Assessment of Change Success Potential


9 Surfside Crescent, Pottsville, NSW 2489 Australia.

Company Name________________________Date______________

Address ___________________________________________________

**Directions:** Rate the overall chance of success for planned change by the above named company. Do this by circling the most accurate rating (substantiated by observations, interviews and questionnaire responses), which follows each factor. Use the following key as a guide to your ratings:

| | | |
|---|---|---|
| VH | = | Very High |
| H | = | High |
| L | = | Low |
| VL | = | Very Low |

| Factor | Rating |
|---|---|
| **1. Ability & commitment of top management.**<br>**Consider:** What do employees say about management on the WEQ? What is the degree of congruence between management and employees' assessment of the work environment? Does management perceive change as necessary for survival? How much are they willing to support and invest in the consulting and change effort? | VH H L VL |
| **2. Presence of a capable "evangelist."**<br>**Consider:** Is there someone to act as a go between top management and the consulting team to keep things going | VH H L VL |

| | |
|---|---|
| smoothly? Is the person competent, available and influential? | |
| **3. Supportive, Flexible organization.**<br>**Consider:** Review, analyze and tabulate consensus of responses by employees to the Work Environment Questionnaire. | VH H L VL |
| **4. Readiness of employees.**<br>**Consider:** Determine the level of employee satisfaction (high vs. low) with the level of perceived need for change (high vs. low), with the level of perceived personal risk (high vs. low) and level of agreement with change methods (high vs. low). | VH H L VL |
| **5. Value fit between client and consultant.**<br>**Consider:** How much agreement is there in basic values between the client and the consulting team? Is there agreement as to the most desirable/productive work environment? | VH H L VL |
| **6. Goals fit between client and consultant.**<br>**Consider:** How much agreement is there between the client and consulting team as to what the goals of the consulting and planned change efforts are? | VH H L VL |
| **7. Methods fit between client and consultant.**<br>**Consider:** How much agreement is there between the client and consulting team as to what methods are to be used in the consulting and planned change effort, e.g., questionnaires, interviews, financial reviews, talking to external stakeholders, etc.? | VH H L VL |

| | |
|---|---|
| **8. Competence fit between client and consultant.**<br>**Consider:** How close are the client and the consulting team with their abilities to understand and use the consulting information in the best way? | VH H L VL |
| **9. External stakeholders current dissatisfaction.**<br>**Consider:** How wide is the gap between external stakeholders' (customers, stockholders, Board of Directors, etc.) expectations and current organisational performance? | VH H L VL |
| **10. Level of consensus between client and consultant.**<br>**Consider:** How much agreement is there between the consulting team and top management regarding the quality of the organisation's work environment? | VH H L VL |

Relevant observations and comments:

______________________________

______________________________

______________________________

______________________________

## APPENDIX G

## MANAGEMENT FUNCTIONS FROM A TO Z

*"An overburdened, over-stretched executive is the best executive, because he or she doesn't have the time to meddle, deal with trivia or bother people"* (Jack Welch).

Anyone who doesn't think managers have anything to do should read this list!

1. **Acting.** Translating possibilities into reality by doing something.

   *"Know when to act and when not to"* (Attila the Hun).

2. **Building.** Making something according to a systematic plan by a definite process.

   *"Good propaganda must anticipate real events"* (Erich Ludendorff).

3. **Communicating.** Conveying information accurately to make sure all these other things get done.

   *"It's not what you tell them that is important. It's what they hear"* (Red Aurback).

4. **Deciding.** Looking at facts and making choices.

   *"When you throw a ball in the air, there are only three things that can happen and two of them are bad"* (ex-football coach).

5. **Explaining.** Making something plain by providing specific details and reasons for it.

   *"Never try to teach a pig to sing. It wastes your time and annoys the pig"* (Unknown Source).

6. **Fighting.** Striving to overcome by putting forth a determined effort; to resolve by struggle.

   *"Establish the site of conflict so that it is advantageous"* (Miyamoto Musashu).

7. **Growing.** Developing to maturity, expanding and increasing in size.

*"The key to growth is to learn to make promises and keep them"* (Stephen Covey).

8. **Harmonizing.** Orchestrating agreement, conformity, accord and order.

   *"Share everything, play fair, don't hit people. Clean up your own mess, put things back where you found them, say you're sorry when you hurt somebody..."* (Robert Fulghum).

9. **Influencing.** Using effortless power to change others, producing effects without apparent exertion of force.

   *"We can change our circumstances by a mere change of our attitude"* (William James).

10. **Judging.** Giving authoritative opinions after careful weighing of the evidence.

    *"It is not the things themselves which trouble us, but rather the opinions that we have about these things"* (Epictetus).

11. **Knowing.** Having experience, wisdom, or intelligence about something.

    *"The fox knows many things; the hedgehog knows one big thing"* (Aesop).

12. **Leading.** Providing direction for others; being in front.

    *"The first responsibility of a leader is to define reality. The last is to say thank you"* (Max De Pree).

13. **Motivating.** Inspiring, stimulating and exciting others onto action.

    *"Trying is just a noisy way of not doing something"* (Ken Blanchard).

14. **Negotiating.** Settling differences with positive compromises.

    *"Never interrupt an enemy while he is making a mistake"* (Napoleon Bonaparte).

15. **Organizing.** Arranging things systematically and logically in order to accomplish something easier.

    *"The more simple anything is the less liable it is to be disordered and the easier repaired when disordered"* (Thomas Paine).

16. **Problem-solving.** Finding workable solutions to perplexing, difficult situations.

    *"You can't solve a problem with the same type of thinking that created it"* (Albert Einstein).

17. **Questioning.** Asking for information, making inquiries; subjecting something for analysis.

    *"A leader who asks the wrong questions always hears the wrong answers"* (Attila the Hun).

18. **Reacting.** Responding to an influence; acting in opposition.

    *"The early bird gets the first worm, but the early worm gets eaten"* (Norman Augustine).

19. **Seeing.** Having a clear picture of or being aware of something.

    *"You can see a lot by observing"* (Yogi Berra).

20. **Timing.** Taking action at a desired instant.

    *"In anything, timing is everything"* (Lao Tzu).

21. **Understanding.** Grasping the meaning of something; comprehending truth.

    *"Those who know they know must be truly amazed"* (Alan Watts).

22. **Varying.** Changing or introducing variety; re-arranging things.

    *"When you come to a fork in the road, take it"* (Yogi Berra).

23. **Winning.** Succeeding or gaining victory; achievement of a goal.

    *"You can get more with a kind word and a gun than just a kind word alone"* (Al Capone).

24. **X-raying.** Seeing inside-out; getting past appearances.

    *"A horse that can count to ten is a remarkable horse, not a remarkable mathematician"* (Samual Johnson).

25. **Yoking.** Joining, uniting or holding together.

*"By flying in a 'V' formation, a whole flock of geese adds at least 75 per cent greater flying range than if each bird flew on its own"* (George Fleming).

26. **Zooming.** Moving attention in and out between individual details and the overall big picture.

    *"History is important. If you don't know where you've been, you are not likely to know where you're going"* (Carl Ajello).

# APPENDIX H

# TQC: TOTAL QUALITY COMMUNICATION

## INTRODUCTION

> "*Tell me quick and tell me true, or else, my friend, the heck with you. Less of how your product came to be and more of what it does for me*" (Sonny Harris).

Today's Information Age is bringing us all more and more information with less and less time to consume it. This situation is especially critical for anyone like managers, teachers, helpers or service providers, who must use communication to affect positive change, frequently with resistive and hard to reach audiences. In order to be successful at navigating through this new age we must all learn to become superb communicators. Information must be gotten and given with maximum speed, accuracy, ease and impact. Anything less leaves us further and further behind in the progress curve.

Good communication is not only a primary interpersonal tool, but it is also the most critical part of the total quality movement. Mediocre communication can jeopardize most, if not all personal relationships and organizational outcomes. The importance and urgency of this matter make it a top priority on everyone's do list.

The Total Quality Communication (TQC) Model is a useful system for helping anyone to develop superior communication skills. Below are the ten basic tenants of this model:

## TQC MODEL

> "*I am easily satisfied with the very best*" (Winston Churchill).

Total Quality Communication involves understanding, thinking about, planning and practicing ten rules of good communication. These ten rules are:

## 1. Understand the Dynamics of the Communication Process

Gaining insight into the human communication process is the first step toward TQC. A very misunderstood fact is that human beings have a unique dual system of communicating with both *digital* and *analogic*, or *report* and *command* aspects. This is similar to the computer, which uses digital numbers and analogic commands as to what to do with those numbers. Digital communication involves reporting information through the use of words which represent objects denotatively according to clear logical syntax rules. Digital communication has no real meaning in and by itself. For example, the word gun actually has nothing in common with the mechanical object that it represents.

Analogic communication is all other non-verbal information, which is conveyed along with the digital information. Essentially, it is information about the information. Analogic information helps define the relationship between communicants by providing connotative meaning to the report, but without definite syntax rules for accurate digital interpretation. Digital communication is thought of as having a permanent quality, whereas analogic is generally more ephemeral in nature.

These two systems are exclusive of one another: One can't communicate with the other because each plays by a different set of rules. Unfortunately, we think they can and try anyway, and this is a major source of miscommunication and interpersonal conflict. The effort is like an attempted exchange between a mathematician and an artist using formulas and paint.

Interestingly, human communication has evolved from analogic to digital to the present dual system. We originally communicated analogically, by showing things or referring to close likenesses of them. There was very little room for confusion or misinterpretation.

Two important axioms about communication are: (1) there is no such thing as non-communication: One cannot *not* communicate and (2) we do not *initiate* communication as in starting a cause and effect chain, but rather participate in the circularity of the communication process which is already going on.

Problems with the communication process itself can only be resolved at the next higher level, which is *meta-communication*, or communicating *about* both the *reported* information and the *relationship* aspect of how this information is to be taken. Communicating about this level is extremely difficult, but it is where all the most important breakthroughs usually occur.

### 2. Become Aware of the Extent of Miscommunication

In the beginning, we invented words to conveniently represent real objects, which we couldn't carry around to show firsthand. Today, there are more words than objects, words have taken on their own separate realities and the once clear representations have become too uncertain and abstract. Some words, such as "justice," "love" and "good" probably have as many meanings as the number of people who speak, write, hear or read them.

There are dozens of obstacles contributing to miscommunication, other than the ones discussed above. Just a few of these include differences in communication content and style between gender, age, ethnic and other groups; perceptual processing, the unique way each of our brains are programmed differently to hear, poor listening habits, environmental conditions, language differences, exclusive frames of references and many other violations of the tenants listed below.

Given the many obstacles to good communication, miscommunication today is much more likely than not. This is especially true for diverse organizations were the abilities, backgrounds, characteristics and values of people are so different. Becoming aware of the actual extent of this problem is an important second step toward TQC.

### 3. Practice Aggressive Listening

For this purpose we were given two ears and only one mouth—a fact we seem to frequently overlook. Aggressive listening, or listening to really understand rather than just to respond, can best shape the right initial response, which in turn always opens the door to good communication. We human beings have an almost insatiable need to be appreciated and understanding is always the first step toward appreciation.

In most situations there is usually more that isn't being said that should be heard, which could improve communication. The other person's body language, voice inflection and intonation, facial gestures, double-talk and shorthand, word choice, emphasis, posture or silence can all offer valuable clues about the real meaning of the intended message. "Yes" words with hesitant frowns can mean *no* and "Do you think that one will do?" can have a variety of meanings according to which word is stressed. Often, what is not said may be the most important piece of information being communicated.

We all know the importance of listening, but may need an occasional reminder of how *to* listen. Here are some basic guidelines to recall and re-practice:

- Stop what you are doing and give your undivided attention with enthusiasm and sincerity.
- Empty out your own pre-occupations and agenda so your ears, eyes and mind can go to work.
- Look at the person who is speaking and maintain a reasonable amount of eye contact.
- Consciously control any bad habits of daydreaming, judging, getting emotional, faking attention or tuning out for whatever reason.
- Be patient and do not interrupt the other person.
- Ask questions for clarification and repeat back information for understanding.
- Try to tune into the other person's reality as much as possible.
- Stay on the subject until all thoughts are finished.
- Mentally review the conversation afterwards.

Listening carefully to both *what* is being said and *how* it is being said takes considerable attention. However, it is energy saved rather than wasted later on a wrong response that needs to be corrected...that is, if the opportunity is even available. One final note about listening: Good, patient listening conveys genuine interest in the audience. This is one of the best ways to build a good relationship, which is always conducive to better communication.

### 4. Create a Non-Defensive Climate

Before any communication begins, it is wise to stop and carefully plan how to create a relaxed, non-threatening atmosphere to facilitate an open dialogue. When a special effort to begin in a non-defensive, supportive tone is not made, communication can deteriorate quickly and then it may be too late to reverse the drift. A useful technique is mental energizing, or consciously creating a strong positive state of mind to set the stage for a positive outcome.

Climates to avoid at all costs are ones which convey control, superiority, certainty, judgment, strategy and lack of empathy. Being un-controlling, equal, tentative, accepting, spontaneous and empathic will always keep the door open, even in the most difficult situations.

Other habits to keep in check are:

- Trying to impose information on somebody who hasn't asked for it.
- Being accusatory, especially without adequate proof you can cite.
- Being over-personalizing with the "you" word.
- Beating around the bush with negative information.
- Not leveling or being completely honest.
- Allowing passivity to build up and then hitting below the belt.

Of special importance here are the issues of control and judgment. Since management is part control and judgment by definition, less the overt reference to these two things in communication, the better. Also, never forget that many countries are founded by natural authority-resisters. Psychological freedom is a primal need.

### 5. Practice the Five "C's"

It is always helpful to get back to basics now and then. Basic rules of good communication include being: *Clear, Concise, Concrete, Correct* and *Complete.*

Just to make certain there is no confusion on the five C's, here is what *Webster* says:

| | |
|---|---|
| CLEAR: | Easily understood, unmistakable, free from ambiguity, capable of sharp discernment, plain, sure. |
| CONCISE: | Brevity of expression; free from all elaboration and superfluous detail; terse, succinct and pithy. |
| CONCRETE: | Specific, real, tangible; belonging to immediate experience of actual things. |
| CORRECT: | Accurate, precise, exact, right and nice; conforming to fact, logic and known truth. |
| COMPLETE: | A perfected state; having all necessary parts; thorough. |

Following these five C's assures a more accurate, economical and effective exchange of information. There simply isn't enough time or space to waste being confusing, rambling, redundant, irrelevant or abstract. Incomplete or incorrect communication requires even more time and effort to repair when there is none to spare. These five C's, when joined with the journalistic five W's of Who, What, Where, When and Why, can result in the outstanding quality of written reports necessary in today's management activities.

### 6. Know Your Audience

The more we know about to whom we are talking or writing, the better. What are their opinions? What do they already know? How can I connect best with them—by humor, emotion or logic? How much detail do they need? How can I avoid turning them off? What are the hot buttons? What comprehension level are they functioning at? What is the best time and place? Will the conversation get reinforced or extinguished by other influences? Taking time to answer questions such as these and others will always help make a better connection and improve impact.

Another important aspect about the audience is the particular mode, which is being used to process information. Research has discovered that people generally process information in one of three basic ways: *Visually, auditorially* or *kinesthetically*. In other words, people "see," "hear," or "feel" our messages. Detailed oral instructions will obviously miss the mark with visual or picture processors.

People also have predominant characteristics or psychological needs which can greatly influence what they prefer to hear or read. For example, accountants may want more detail than usual, busy managers need the short and sweet of it and new employees prefer concrete directions and frequent attention. On the other side, overly creative presentations will fall short with conservative, conventional individuals, just as highly intellectual ones will with construction folks. Common sense goes a long way here.

When time permits, a useful method to improve connection with the audience, is to build a *psychoprofile* on audience traits. Traits to identify can include dimensions such as thinking vs. feeling, demanding vs. easy-going, extroverted vs. introverted, intellectual vs. practical and conservative vs. liberal.

A few other important facts about audiences are:

- People all interpret the same information *at least slightly differently*.
- People generally seek out information that supports beliefs that they already have and tend to disregard information that contradicts those beliefs.
- People are often not very rational about their attitudes and beliefs.
- People are changing and important values are shifting.

Questions are an excellent opportunity for meaningful interactions. Questions can help you get to know the audience better and can give you another chance to present your information again, in a different way. People pay close attention to your answers to their questions. Try to anticipate and answer questions about your message beforehand and always follow-up on promises to provide more information later. That is the information that will often make the most impact.

A little time spent thinking about the receivers of our messages and then preparing customized communication, will greatly improve results, just as the prep work in painting a house does. It is all too obvious when this isn't done properly.

### 7. Explore the Psychology of Communication

We communicate both verbally and non-verbally. (see Table 1.) It is important to get the "what" and "how" of our messages to complement each other in order to make our words count most. This requires using the best words and analogical techniques *together,* to represent the information we want to convey, in the closest possible resemblance.

We can learn good communication tricks by studying outstanding samples of content/style perfection from historical literature, media, movies and advertising. These folks are experts at saying the *most* with the *least*, by using psychology for maximum effect in potent sound and sight bytes. A few historical examples that stand out include Lincoln's superbly written *Gettysburg Address*, *The U.S. Constitution* and *The Bill of Rights*. More modern examples are Dale Carnegie's classical *How to Win Friends and Influence People*, the unwavering testimonies of Oliver North, Clarence Thomas and Mark Fuhrman, Forrest Gump's humble quips, M-TV's flash and splash mega impact video clips, and winning advertising campaigns such as Nike's "Just do it!," the Army's "Be all that you can be," and Microsoft's "Where do you want to go today?"

The common sense approach here is to practice using analogic, or non-verbal techniques, to *magnify, emphasize* and *reinforce* digital conversation, so that the words and their intended meaning cannot *possibly* be lost, distracted or misinterpreted. This includes *appearance,* which needs to be congruent with the message. For example, a meticulous appearance supports a message involving attention to details.

**Table 1: Examples of Body Language and Conventional Interpretations**

| Interpretation | Body language |
|---|---|
| Cooperation | *Sitting on edge of chair, open hands, hand to face gestures.* |
| Insecurity | *Hands in pocket, fingernail biting, flesh pinching, thumb over thumb.* |
| Frustration | *Short breaths, hand-wringing, clenched hands, finger pointing.* |
| Defensiveness | *Arms crossed, legs crossed, fist-like gestures, finger pointing.* |
| Confidence | *Hands behind back or on lapels, stiffened back, steepled hands.* |
| Openness | *Open hands, unbuttoned coat, good eye contact.* |
| Evaluation | *Head titled, chin stroking, hand-to-face gestures, peering over glasses.* |
| Suspicion | *Sideways glance, nose touching, movement away from the speaker.* |
| Nervousness | *Throat clearing, perspiration, fidgeting, whistling, smoking.* |

*Note*: Heed the warning above in rule 1 (Understand the Dynamics of the Communication Process) about the difficulties involved with communication between the digital and analogical modes.

When Oliver North denied personal gain from the Iran-Contra arms affair, his words, "I never personally profited a *penny,* not a *single cent...,*" were repeated, emphasized and magnified by word choice, visualization, voice intonation, finger-pointing, genuine steady eye contact, stern eyebrow indentation and impeccable posture. This was all punctuated with his symbolic marine uniform and a sincere slight smile at the end.

It is important to carefully choose key words we use by thinking about the visual images, connotations or value flavors they may produce. (see Table 2) Correctly chosen *power words*, or ones that are *good*, *strong* and *fast*, can emphasize points, make connections and get remembered. "Enemies" can be de-emphasized, disconnected and forgotten with "slow," "bad" or "weak" words such as *sluggish*, *wicked* or *feeble*. Points can be remembered better when words producing powerful visual images are attached to them and attention can be grabbed quicker with unusual words or even usual words used unusually. Ambiguous words can be used when confusion is desired.

**Table 2: Examples of Different Value Dimensions of the Word "Unusual."**

| Value Dimension | Examples |
|---|---|
| Good | *Exceptional, rare, remarkable.* |
| Bad | *Freak, rogue, grotesque.* |
| Strong | *Prodigious, portentous, exotic.* |
| Weak | *Odd, unfamiliar, infrequent.* |
| Fast | *Extraordinary, phenomenal, outstanding.* |
| Slow | *Uncommon, occasional, curious.* |
| Relative | *Abnormal, irregular, unconventional.* |
| Visual | *Eccentric old man, monster, alien-ugly.* |
| Ambiguous | *Bizarre, quaint, peculiar.* |
| Unusual | *Kickshaw, whimsy, vagary.* |

There are a variety of figures of speech and other techniques, which can help give color, life and meaning to words. A few of these are included in Table 3.

Some parting advice: Occasional use of the dictionary and thesaurus and discriminating extra-curricular reading and viewing can greatly increase our verbal arsenals for improving clarity and impact. So can listening to children and teenagers.

**Table 3: Various Examples of Figurative Speech and Other Techniques to Improve Clarity, Meaning and Impact of Communication**

| Type | Meaning | Example |
|---|---|---|
| Metaphor | Joining words representing different objects to suggest likeness. | *Computer memory* |
| Simile | Comparing two unlike things by analogy. | *Smooth as glue* |
| Hyperbole | Extravagant exaggeration. | *Mile high ice cream cone* |
| Oxymoron | Combination of contradictory words. | *Eloquent silence* |
| Explication | Making meaning clear and plain. | *Dictionary definition* |
| Imagery | Language that produces mental images. | *Lightening bolt* |
| Alliteration | Repetition of initial consonant sounds. | *Wild and woolly* |
| Antithesis | Contrasting opposite ideas by parallel words. | *Action, not words* |
| Aphorism | Wise saying or proverb. | *Life is short* |
| Onomatopoeia | Vocal imitations. | *Buzz, bang, hiss* |
| Panache | Flamboyant, ornamental language. | *Happy Thanksgobble* |
| Epithet | Adjective which defines special quality. | *Wine dark sea* |
| Colloquialism | Relaxed, ordinary, everyday phrases. | *OK, skedaddle* |
| Concrete | Referring to things rather than ideas. | *Green frog, muddy pond, glass window* |
| Gimmick | Cute attention-getting approach. | *Amazing statistics, startling facts* |
| Neologism | Coining brand new words. | *Socioquake, rightsizing* |

| | | |
|---|---|---|
| Outré | Using strange sounding odd words or common words unusually. | *Gewgaw, foozle, monstrous party* |
| Personification | Representation of a thing by human form. | *Eye of a hurricane* |
| Foreign word | Using interesting, definitive foreign words. | *Ad hoc (L), 'dharma (B)* |
| Travesty | Grotesque, ludicrous imitation. | *Still as a corpse* |
| Vernacular | Regional speech. | *Ya'll come back now* |
| Slang | Informal, racy colloquial speech. | *Waste somebody* |
| Irony | Words to express opposite literal meaning. | *Sarcasm* |
| Paradigm | Providing exact example. | *Yang-yin of death* |
| Litoté | Understatement expressing the affirmative. | *Not a bad singer, a good loss* |
| Anaphora | Repetition of word/ phrase at the beginning/ ending of sentence/ paragraph. | *Trying times are a time to try* |
| Parable | Short story demonstrating moral lesson. | *The Good Samaritan* |
| Pathetic fallacy | Ascription of human traits to inanimate objects. | *The cruel sea, angry sky* |
| Allegory | Symbolic representation. | *The lion as courage* |
| Rhyme | Similarity of word sounds. | *A stitch in time saves nine* |
| Pun | Play on words. | *I right wrong* |
| Anecdote | Interesting story that makes a key point. | *A. Lincoln's resume* |
| Humor | Presenting the lighter side of the message. | *Jokes, poems, funny stories* |
| Epitome | Succinct summary. | *Outline, conclusion* |

## 8. Write As You Speak

The written word presents a unique challenge because you can't see any audience reaction to clue you into degrees of contact or impact. Also, there is no opportunity for questions or clarification. Furthermore, you have to take chances with the many desktop publishing variables, which may actually obscure the important points or message itself. On the other hand, graphics, colors, font size and variety, layout design and space can all do things the mouth can't. Handwriting can also offer some unique opportunities.

The simplest rule to follow is to write as you talk. The object is to give life to your words so they speak to the reader. Writing effectively requires being short and to the point and eliminating all possible sources of confusion and waste. This involves avoiding meaningless and empty phrases, unnecessary redundancy, lifeless or never-ending sentences, over-used words, jargon, abstract detail, disjointed paragraphs, irrelevant points and all sorts of other bad habits we seem to have difficulty shedding. (see Table 4)

In short, good writing requires a careful blend of simple, action-oriented language, well-organized, economical structure and slightly creative style. Reviewing English 101 writing tips is probably a good idea. When in doubt, start with an outline by clearly stating your main theme and then list the supporting points.

## 9. Avoid Pathological Communication

Obviously, the best prescription is to follow all the tenants described above, *especially* numbers one (understanding our dual digital-analogic system of communication) and four (making an effort to establish a non-defensive tone). However, an important reality to be aware of is this: You can become part of pathological communication so fast that you don't have the opportunity to stop it by punctuating a new cause and effect chain.

When this happens, the only answer is *metacommunication,* which involves communicating *about* the pathological

**Table 4: Examples of Various Communications Crimes to Avoid**

| Crime | Definition | Example |
|---|---|---|
| Clichés | Boring phrases made tedious by over-use. | *With all due respect, without further ado* |
| Embolalia | Using obnoxious filler words. | *Um, er, right, ya, I mean* |
| Jargon | Special technical language. | *Disc compression glitch* |
| Euphemisms | Over-conversion to nice-nelly language. | *Violence processing (combat)* |
| Fad words | Over-popularized buzz words. | *Down-sizing, sound byte* |
| Solecisms | Misuse of language. | *Irregardless, unthawed* |
| Diffidence | Hesitant, unassertive speech. | *I'm fairly positive* |
| Smoke rings | Unnecessary modifiers. | *Very, just, rather, really* |
| Over-talk | Prolonged wordiness. | *Duplicate, irrelevant redundancy* |
| Abstraction | Ideas that are difficult to understand. | *Ideas without concrete examples* |
| Gobbledgook | Empty, meaningless phrases. | *Objective consideration of vague phenomenon* |
| Twirks | Everything else that distracts. | *Much of the Simpson trial* |

communication indirectly by stepping *above* it. This requires mutual agreement and ability of both parties to do this, which unfortunately, *isn't* the case very often.

There are some special situations which require considerable caution or even avoiding. A few of these are circumstances where points of view are very different or impervious, where there is high ambiguity with little opportunity for clarification, where unpopular actions have to be made on important issues, where hidden agendas aren't accessible, where no-win paradoxical injunctions are given, and where emotions run high. Sometimes, verbal buffers such as silence, questions and listening are the best solution in these situations. And of course, knowing the audience certainly helps to identify these types of situations ahead of time, so the most appropriate response can be made.

Our best verbal judo tool in the worst of situations is *self-control.* When suddenly caught up in these situations, our best defense is to focus on controlling *our response.* The control we exercise over our speech, feelings, body language and time and space, can greatly shape the direction of the conversation. One further observation: Most major interpersonal disagreements involve differences in realities. The only solution is to try and bridge the reality gap.

### 10. Seek Feedback

We can never really improve in the future until we get frank and useful feedback as to how well or how badly we are doing here and now. This takes a bold willingness to hear things we may not want to hear, but it is the *only* course for improvement. All written memos and documents need to be tried out first on colleagues to measure clarity, readability and impact. One-on-one conversations should be paraphrased back and forth for understanding and group talks need to be measured on a post-session evaluation form. And, communication throughout the organization should be assessed periodically by formal means such as questionnaires which measure employee's perceptions of the social climate of their work environment.

In setting up any communication feedback system, the key is always to ask the right questions in the right way at the right time. Ease and painlessness should be arranged, too. A very powerful communication feedback measure is to ask supervisors, employees, and even clients what they each perceive to be the most important values being enforced and reinforced in the organization. The degree of incongruence can be eye-opening and it can certainly set the stage for improvement in communication.

## CONCLUSION

> *"Mend your speech a little, lest it may mar your fortunes"* (Shakespeare).

In conclusion, good communication is the single most important interpersonal tool and the central building block of the total quality movement. With the unfolding of the Information Age, superior communication skills are now needed by us all more than ever. The Total Quality Communication Model discussed above offers ten useful tenants for helping you develop Olympic level communication skills.

It is most important for us to first understand the information processing system and then become aware of the actual extent of miscommunication. The importance of these first two steps cannot be overstated. Next, skill refinement can be practiced in the areas of aggressive listening, re-focusing on the five C's, knowing the audience, exploring the psychology of communication, creating non-defensive climates, writing as we speak and avoiding pathological communication. Finally, constant improvement can be guided by reliable feedback systems, from readability checks by colleagues to formal evaluations of value congruence in the organization.

Total Quality Management starts with Total Quality Communication. There is no more time or space left to waste on mediocre communication.

